PLANET MONEY

PLA MO

ALEX MAYYASI
AND THE HOSTS OF
NPR'S PLANET MONEY

NET NEY

A GUIDE TO THE ECONOMIC FORCES THAT SHAPE YOUR LIFE

W. W. NORTON & COMPANY
Independent Publishers Since 1923

This book exists because of the many people who have collectively made *Planet Money* over more than fifteen years.

Executive Producer
Alex Goldmark

Editors
Kate Concannon
Paddy Hirsch • Jess Jiang
Marianne McCune • Molly Messick
Robert Smith
Amy Stevens • Bryant Urstadt

Co-hosts & Reporters
Amanda Aronczyk • Erika Beras
Quoctrung Bui • Zoe Chace
Ailsa Chang • Mary Childs
Lisa Chow • Laura Conaway
Karen Duffin • Nick Fountain
Cardiff Garcia • Jasmine Garsd
Sonari Glinton • Jacob Goldstein
Sarah Gonzalez • Jeff Guo
Sally Helm • Steve Henn
Alexi Horowitz-Ghazi
Chana Joffe-Walt
Caitlin Kenney • David Kestenbaum
Noel King • Adrian Ma
Kenny Malone • Keith Romer
Greg Rosalsky • Stacey Vanek Smith
Lam Thuy Vo • Wailin Wong
Darian Woods
And many others on occasion

Book Illustrators
María Jesús Contreras
Julian Frost

Book Creative Director
Mito Habe-Evans

Producers
Phia Bennin • Dave Blanchard
Corey Bridges • Angel Carreras
Brittany Cronin • Aviva DeKornfeld
Audrey Dilling • Constanza Gallardo
Frances Harlow • Jamila Huxtable
Sierra Juarez • Cooper Katz McKim
Sam Yellowhorse Kesler
Elizabeth Kulas • Emily Lang
Viet Le • Damiano Marchetti
Emma Peaslee • Darius Rafieyan
Julia Ritchey • Willa Rubin
Sean Saldana • Leena Sanzgiri
James Sneed • Nadia Wilson
Liza Yeager

Project Managers
Julia Carney • Emily Kinslow
Devin Mellor

TikTok & Video
Bronson Arcuri • Tsering Bista
Jack Corbett • Annabel Edwards
Mito Habe-Evans • Nickolai Hammar
Becky Lettenberger • Nick Michael
Ben Naddaff-Hafrey
Courtney Theophin

Our NPR Champions
Collin Campbell • Neal Carruth
Edith Chapin • Anya Grundmann
Laura Hogan • Ellen Weiss
Kinsey Wilson

Creators & Co-founders
Alex Blumberg • Adam Davidson

With a debt to Ira Glass
and *This American Life*

With gratitude for the hundreds of people who helped create and build *Planet Money* and the millions of listeners who've supported us over the years

Contents

Introduction ix
by Alex Goldmark

PART ONE:
Meet the Economy

1 The Pickle Problem 3
Discovering the elegant power of prices

2 Why Delaware? 13
How a tiny state became the referee of global business

A WORLD TOUR OF SPECTACULAR PUBLIC GOODS 26

3 The Raisin Outlaw 31
Escaping the commodity trap

4 The Phone at the End of the World 43
The promise and peril of free trade

5 How We All Get Richer, Forever 53
The historic anomaly of being alive after 1700

PART TWO:
Work & Career

6 How Desi Invented TV 63
Owning a piece of primetime

7 The Zoom Boom vs. Happy Hour 75
Should my company let me work from home?

8 A Tale of Two Gig Workers 89
The pros and cons of being your own boss

THE LAWS OF THE OFFICE — 105

9   The Hopeful Tale of the ATM and the Bank Teller — 107
Lessons from the life cycle of automation

PART THREE:
Love & Family

10   The Labor of Finding Love — 125
Every market has a designer

11   The Opportunity Atlas — 139
The American Dream exists, it's just not evenly distributed

12   The Rent Is Too Damn High — 153
The Squamish Nation's impossibly simple solution to the housing crisis

RELATIONSHIP ADVICE FROM ECONOMISTS — 166

13   The Global Conspiracy to Make Childcare More Expensive — 169
Why goods get cheaper and services don't

PART FOUR:
Saving & Investing

14   Bobby Bonilla Day — 183
The "worst contract in sports history" is a blueprint for retirement planning

15   How We All Fell for a Confidence Trick — 191
Banking in America, in three acts

A LOVE LETTER TO INSURANCE — 204

16 Weighing a Cow and Picking Stocks   207
    Why it's so hard to beat the market

17 The Biggest Bet of Your Life   219
    How index funds took over

18 Why Is My Money Worth Less Every Year?   229
    A brief history of the battle against inflation

PART FIVE:
Leisure

19 Why Weekends Are Like Subways and Uber   247
    A lesson in the power of networks

> HOW AN OIL SHOCK TURNED NORWAY   258
> INTO A TOURISM DESTINATION

20 What's the Deal with Credit Card Points?   261
    There's no such thing as a free lunch

21 Advanced Fairness at the Marathon   275
    Strategies for allocating scarce resources

Acknowledgments   285
Notes   287
Index   313

Introduction

By Alex Goldmark,
executive producer of Planet Money and The Indicator

Hello, and Welcome to *Planet Money*

The economy is the grandest collaborative project in human history. We all help create it, every one of us making choices, pursuing our values, chasing our individual goals. Everyone contributes to it. Everyone is shaped by it.

On good days, the economy is the background to our lives. The paycheck lands in your bank account, the debit card taps, and you carry groceries to your home, where the water is drinkable, the lights turn on with the flick of a switch, and if they don't, a new bulb is a click away.

On bad days, the economy is like a cage you can't escape: the demeaning job, the late fee on the rent payment, the eggs suddenly doubled in price. It's definitely flawed. It's certainly confusing, full of mysteries. But there is a logic to it.

Economics can be intimidating. We hear that all the time at *Planet Money*. We are NPR's economics reporting team known for making a pair of podcasts, a nationally broadcast public radio show, a wonky weekly newsletter, and more recently a popular (kind of surrealist) TikTok account.

The *Planet Money* podcast was founded in 2008 in the early days of the financial crisis. The mission was simple: Take the most complicated, confusing events in the economy and make them make sense. "The economy, explained" was the pithy, ambitious original tagline. Today, millions of people each week trust *Planet Money* to describe, without jargon or judgment, how the world of money works. We try to do it in the most entertaining and creative ways we can.

We also like to get our hands dirty. To investigate shell companies, we set one up ourselves. To find out how streaming services pay musicians, we became a record label. We made vodka to see if the top shelf is any different from the cheap stuff (it isn't, but fancy whiskey is). To understand the oil industry, we bought crude oil ourselves, direct from the well, and followed it from ground to gas tank. And because intellectual property is the new oil, we tried to launch the world's smallest superhero franchise around a forgotten comic-book character (Micro-Face: normal-size face, powerful microphone mask), complete with merch licensing deals and a fresh comic-book storyline. And now, our biggest project yet—connecting intellectual property, global supply chains, trade agreements, the history of ideas, prices, marketing, and more—the book you hold in your hands.

SO WHAT'S IN THE BOOK?

Economics, as a field, asks, How should we as a society allocate scarce resources? Who should make what, and where, and how much of it? Who should get the stuff that's made, through what system, at what cost to whom? At a personal level, economics asks, What should you, as an individual, buy, learn, do for work, or invest in? Because all resources are scarce, *especially* your time.

So we put everything we had into making sure reading this book is time well spent. We've written it to help you navigate a chaotic world, and filled it with useful lessons applicable to every facet of life. We want to help you see the world through the lens of economics—which is to say, with a little more clarity, insight, and confidence.

But the book is also an invitation to join us on some of our favorite adventures into the heart of the economy. The pages that follow contain origin stories, reckonings with unintended consequences, eureka moments about human behavior and natural resources, about fairness and primal human desires, about smarter career paths and savvy retirement planning.

We start from some of the most basic questions—What is a bank? What's the point of money? How should I spend my time?—unraveling them until they reveal foundational truths. We ask, What do prices do?

(They change our behavior! But as you'll see in the first chapter, they're also mini newspapers filled with information!) We ask, Why do companies get to exist in perpetuity? (The answer dates back to ancient Rome.) Why does inflation happen? What determines the price of a stock—or a piece of art? Why is housing still so expensive?

Our favorite way to answer economic questions, large or small, is through stories. Watching real people make real choices is the purest way to understand the economic forces acting on us, from the omnipresent ones like the laws of supply and demand behind food prices, down to obscure but powerful effects like the "cost disease" that explains why haircuts and health care get more expensive while TVs get cheaper.

Economic principles offer a set of tools for making society (and ourselves) better off—for getting the most wealth and happiness we can from our scarce resources. They also touch on almost every arena of our lives, so this book stretches just as widely, discussing investing, negotiating a raise, rising in your career, but also finding love, making the most of a weekend, beating inflation, mitigating poverty, and alleviating the housing crisis.

Planet Money has always been an ensemble project, with dozens of reporters contributing over the years, each bringing their own curiosity and backgrounds and expertise. This book gathers the most useful and essential wisdom from our reporting and adds many freshly reported stories chosen to illuminate the most practical and powerful lessons in economics today.

We are living through a period of economic upheaval and reimagining, in both the global economy and in the academic field of economics itself. Change is coming for us fast, from remote work, to automation and AI, to inequality and financial crises, to the unraveling of a trading system built up over a century. Conventional wisdom is suddenly in question. Old assumptions don't hold.

Meanwhile, economics is going through something of a renaissance. Researchers are deploying new approaches, natural experiments, and big data to find clearer answers to questions that had remained pure theory until recently. We bring you the latest research, applied to our changing world.

Our goal is to help make your life a little more rational, a little less overwhelming, and to share our wonder and awe at this big confusing thing we call an economy, because we're all in it together.

PART ONE

MEET

THE ECONOMY

1

The Pickle Problem

Discovering the elegant power of prices

In 2004, Susannah Morgan was running a food bank in Alaska. It was a small operation. She was the executive director, but she also regularly forklifted donations onto the shelves of their warehouse.

Morgan had followed her wife to Anchorage. She arrived with a shiny new MBA and past experience managing a homeless services agency, which had a soup kitchen. When she saw that Food Bank of Alaska was hiring, she applied, got the job, and loved it.

Morgan spent a lot of time trying to get more fruits and vegetables for the food bank. One resource was Feeding America, a nonprofit that distributes big donations from manufacturers like General Mills to food banks like hers. One day Feeding America called. They had a donation. But it wasn't fresh produce. It was five-gallon buckets of pickles.

"Can you feel grateful and frustrated at the same time?" Morgan asks, recalling the moment.

Feeding America was trying to help. They knew that Morgan and Food Bank of Alaska needed fruits and vegetables, but they thought that it would be too expensive to ship, say, oranges from California to Anchorage. So they offered her pickles. Pickles were unpopular at the food bank, and safety regulations prevented Morgan from repackaging them into family-size containers. Morgan had to decide: pickles or no? She said yes.

This problem was not unique to Morgan and Alaska. A food bank director in Idaho faced a similar dilemma: He kept getting offered potatoes. "I mean, come on. It's Idaho," Morgan says. "Of course he already had a warehouse full of potatoes that had been donated by local farmers."

Not long after that, Feeding America invited Morgan to their headquarters in Chicago to help them find a better way to distribute donations. She soon found herself in a room with eight fellow food bank directors, plus four economists from the University of Chicago. Feeding America's new CEO had invited the economists for a fresh perspective.

"We had to bring them up to speed on how food banking actually works," says Morgan. But she quickly realized the economists could be a big help.

Everyone in the whiteboard-lined conference room agreed the system could function better. Food banks like Morgan's felt pressured to accept unhelpful donations. But Feeding America's staff also felt trapped. Companies often donated because it was a cheap way to clear out inventory. If Feeding America didn't take the pickles or potatoes, they might lose out on valuable donations next time.

Pickles weren't the only problem. The system missed opportunities to help. Morgan had set up a way to affordably ship fruits and vegetables to Alaska, but since Feeding America didn't know about it, they didn't offer her donations like oranges.

"Very early in the conversation, one of the main problems was, 'Who were the deciders and where did the information lie?'" Morgan told us.

The staff at Feeding America were the deciders, but they had limited information. Their only criterion for allocating donations was a crude measure of each food bank's need, based on each city's size and poverty rate. (They offered LA more food than Anchorage.) Food bankers like Morgan, meanwhile, knew their current stock, how much available refrigerator space they had, and which foods local families preferred, but didn't know what donations Feeding America had. "To have a central office trying to make those decisions far away from those sources of knowledge led to all sorts of mismatches."

Morgan recalls one of the economists, Canice Prendergast, getting excited. "Once we were able to lay it out in those clear terms, then Canice, from the University of Chicago, was able to say, well, sounds like an economic problem to me . . . like Economics 101."

How many economists does it take to give away peanut butter?

WHAT IS AN ECONOMIC PROBLEM? What challenges, exactly, do you recruit an economist to solve? There's no consensus answer—some economists joke that "economics is what economists do." But one way textbooks and encyclopedias (and CliffsNotes!) define economics is the study of how societies allocate scarce resources and goods. And the food bankers were running an economy, one with a surplus of pickles and potatoes but also a limited supply of peanut butter, cereal, and pasta that each food banker wanted. Peanut butter and cereal are shelf-stable foods that turn into meals that kids will eat, notes Morgan, making them valuable.

To the economists, Feeding America's situation sounded like the challenge faced by centrally planned economies such as the Soviet Union, where bureaucrats in Moscow made decisions without knowing which canteens more urgently needed a resupply of tea and sugar. Economists call this the **local knowledge problem**. During monthly meetings in Chicago, Prendergast and his colleagues suggested that Feeding America, too, should transition from a centrally planned economy to a market-based system of buying and selling. Then the food bankers, who understood their local needs, could buy exactly what they needed.

Morgan enjoyed the insight, but not every food banker felt that way. Prendergast fondly recalls the head of West Michigan's food bank, a man named John Arnold, approaching him during a coffee break. "He said, 'I'm a socialist, okay? I do not believe in markets. The only reason I'm on this committee is to stop you from doing what I think you're about to do.'"

It wasn't just Arnold. The food banks and Feeding America existed because the real market economy often hurt their constituents. Its farms, factories, and supermarkets filled the fridges of wealthier families, but roughly 9 percent of American households with children suffer from chronic hunger. Morgan regularly met parents at the food bank who were there because they'd been laid off suddenly or bankrupted by a medical emergency. Many food bankers felt it was their job to protect their constituents from markets.

"There is such an ingrained notion . . . that markets benefit the strong and harm the weak," says Prendergast. "Their great fear is that whatever we came up with would do the same."

And making the food banks buy Feeding America's peanut butter and cereal *would* hurt the weak. Boston's and LA's food banks could buy the best food, while Morgan and Anchorage, which had a smaller budget, would be stuck with pickles and potatoes. (Selling donations also felt weird.) So the economists suggested that instead of handing out food, Feeding America could hand out fake money, which the food banks could use to buy food.

John Arnold wasn't sold. But the idea started looking appealing when the economists suggested giving needier food banks more fake money. "Maybe that was one of the early breakthrough moments," says Prendergast, ". . . the idea that the poor can actually be wealthier than the rich."

But how should Feeding America set the prices? And how should the food banks shop for donated food? There were more meetings, more flights to Chicago. And then Prendergast said, "Well, how about eBay?" Feeding America could auction off each truckload of oranges and cereal on a website just for the food banks.

"The clouds opened, and the angels sang," says Morgan. "We just went, 'We've had a breakthrough.'"

As they spent more months figuring out details, Arnold remained a thorn in Prendergast's side—in the best possible way, pointing out flaws to fix. Like when Prendergast suggested they run an open auction, where any food bank could see the top bid. Arnold pointed out that a large food bank, like the Los Angeles Regional Food Bank, could have a staff member watch the auction and outbid everyone just before it ended. But Alaska's or Idaho's tiny staff couldn't do that. So the task force switched to a sealed-bid auction, where no one could see the top bid until the auction ended.

The food bankers also pointed out that small food banks might never have enough fake money to afford a full truckload of popular food. So they made it possible for banks to team up on bids or buy on credit. They also created a committee to hear any complaints about the system and a mechanism to give food banks more faux money after natural disasters. With each tweak, the market felt more fair.

Once they'd figured out a new system, the hard part of their job began. The food banks were independent organizations that had chosen to partner with Feeding America, and the task force felt they'd be more likely to adopt the new system if they opted into it. Feeding America decided to hold a vote.

Morgan and her peers had spent more than half a year getting comfortable with the idea of a free-market economy for donated food. Outside the room, though, it sounded a bit nuts. They had to pitch a group of professionals—whose job was giving away food for free—on a system of prices and competitive auctions. So Morgan found herself "in politician mode," phoning directors and addressing concerns at conferences.

"There were a lot of little food banks who were worried that they would end up worse off . . . because they wouldn't have Feeding America looking out for them," says Morgan. She spent more time explaining the idea and advocating for it than they had coming up with the new system.

Before the vote, it was Arnold who made the final case for auctions. To hear the avowed socialist praising the free-market solution was persuasive. The food bankers approved the new system.

A tiny newspaper in every price

AFTER THREE MONTHS OF SIMULATED AUCTIONS, the new system went live. The launch was drama-free, and the effects dramatic.

"What I remember was the control of our destiny," says Morgan. They no longer had to accept pickles, but they could save up to bid on nutritious, shelf-stable foods like canned peaches.

In Grand Rapids, Michigan, Arnold, who has since passed away, became a superuser of Feeding America's free market. Prendergast recalls that Arnold liked to bid on foods that had recently sold for cheap. This was one way the market benefited smaller food banks. Since big-city food banks, which often had the essentials stocked, got into bidding wars over popular items, smaller banks like Arnold's got affordable staples. (Morgan says Prendergast also liked to stock up on cheap fruit roll-ups.) In a research paper, Prendergast calculated that food banks like Arnold's got twice as much food via the auctions, while bigger, better-stocked banks chose to receive half as much. (The task force also created a way for food banks to sell surplus food, but directors mostly opted to donate to each other.)

Ultimately, the appeals process that the task force spent two months designing—out of worries that their free market would be unfair—never received a single complaint.

The new system also improved Feeding America's relationship with donors like General Mills. Since the auctions swept donations out of their warehouses more quickly, the manufacturers donated more than one hundred million more pounds of excess food.

Why were auctions such an improvement? Because prices do not just tell customers how much they need to pay. Instead, prices are like tiny newspapers. They summarize a huge amount of distributed information into a single number. When Morgan placed a bid, she considered variables like what foods she had stocked, how much fridge space she had available, and the cost of transportation. So did every other food banker.

In other words, the price fluctuated based on supply and demand. If many bankers badly wanted (demanded) an item, they bid high, upping the price. But when bankers like Arnold saw that popcorn was plentiful, they put in stingy offers, which kept the price low.

In a mysterious, almost spooky way, the auctions revealed information unknown even to long-tenured food bankers. "All of them knew that people would prefer to have peanut butter over pickles," says Prendergast. But "everyone was astonished at the extent to which that was true." Even for popular items like cereal, the different bids showed that the variance between each food bank's preferences and situations "was just astronomical." (Pickles were so unpopular that the price went negative. Feeding America paid food banks, in fake money, to take them.) Compared to the brute force of distributing donations to the next food bank in line, the auctions were an everchanging, instantly updating duet of supply and demand, each representing unique needs and preferences.

But prices don't just reveal information and distribute goods efficiently. The economists Tyler Cowen and Alex Tabarrok describe a price as "a signal wrapped up in an incentive." In a market economy, prices push people and companies to act in ways that usually reduce scarcity and lower prices. Within the food bank economy, Feeding America saw the high price of peanut butter and asked donors for more of it. And they saw the negative price for pickles and begged for less.

LOCAL KNOWLEDGE

SIGNAL
"Puppets are getting scarce"

INCENTIVE
"Buy less or make more"

The Pickle Problem

The Grocery Store That Ended the Cold War

In September 1989, Paul Yirga, the manager on duty at Randall's grocery store in Houston, received a phone call. A Soviet official named Boris Yeltsin was visiting NASA, and he wanted to see a grocery store, too. Could Yirga show him around? Twenty minutes later, Yeltsin was poking his nose into frozen-food displays and asking about pudding pops through an interpreter.

The average supermarket in America had anywhere from 7,000 to 13,000 items to choose from in the late 1980s. Each cereal variety or TV dinner or *Star Wars* toothbrush arrived on those shelves because of decentralized decisions made by companies, farmers, or even movie studios, each responding to price signals in the market that reveal some need or want and then taking small individual risks to try to profit by meeting those needs and wants.

Yeltsin's visit came four decades into the Cold War. Capitalist and Communist countries had raced to build advanced weapons and put the first human in space, but they also bragged about their citizens' quality of life. The USSR's Joseph Stalin built massive champagne factories, and Cuba's Fidel Castro built a palatial ice cream parlor.

A *Houston Chronicle* reporter described Yeltsin "roam[ing] the aisles of Randall's nodding his head in amazement." Yeltsin expressed disbelief when Yirga said Randall's sold thousands of items. Not even Soviet leaders had this many choices, he said.

Within two years, Yeltsin had become president and dissolved the Soviet Union, in part to transition Russia toward a market economy. According to an aide, Yeltsin had reflected in 1989 on the full shelves and plentiful choices of American grocery stores and said, "I think we have committed a crime against our people by making their standard of living so incomparably lower than that of the Americans." At that moment, another aide added, Yeltsin's "last vestige of Bolshevism [Communist thinking] collapsed."

In the global economy, prices push and pull people even more strongly. If the price of peanut butter triples in grocery stores—perhaps because horrible weather killed peanut crops in Nigeria, or maybe because peanut butter and fluff sandwiches are trending on TikTok—Smucker's will have an incentive to ramp up production, and farmers in India may plant more peanuts. That's the supply side. On the demand side, people who don't love peanut butter that much will opt to buy Nutella instead or to try tahini.

This is Adam Smith's famous **invisible hand** at work: The global economy is coordinated not by a central actor, but by people responding to the incentives and information of high or low prices.

It is this power of prices—to synthesize complex information from around the world and then incentivize people to alleviate shortages and reduce surpluses—that allows market economies to delegate the stocking of grocery shelves in farmless Manhattan, the distribution of sweaters to stores across snowy Canada, and the supplying of table fans to hardware stores across Jamaica to an amorphous, decentralized force that no one fully controls or understands. It's just a wild state of affairs.

> News reports about looming shortages sometimes end up being overblown because higher prices change people's behavior and prevent a shortage.

Feeding America's auctions, which are still running today, albeit with tweaks and updates, are a case study in the effectiveness of markets. But they're also a glimpse of what markets can look like when they're designed with fairness (and making sure children get enough to eat) as explicit goals. Markets and prices are powerful tools: They can produce exploitation or justice, inequality or equity. It's the market's rules that push it in one direction or the other. So let's meet someone who sets the rules of the global economy.

This chapter includes reporting from Jacob Goldstein for the *Planet Money* episode "The Pickle Problem," November 25, 2015.

The Pickle Problem   **11**

Why Delaware?

How a tiny state became the referee of global business

O f all things, it was a court case about professional tennis that posed the biggest threat to the legal rule book that Lawrence Hamermesh tended for nearly three decades. He remembers the exact date the Supreme Court made its ruling: May 8, 2014.

Hamermesh is a corporate lawyer who oversaw a set of laws that govern how companies around the world operate. The threat came from the Association of Tennis Professionals, which is similar to the NFL or WNBA. Some of ATP's members had sued the organization over irksome changes to its tour schedule. The ATP won the court battle, but the legal fees cost it nearly $18 million. So its executives pointed to their bylaws, which said the members who sued had to cover the costs. That led to another court battle. On May 8, 2014, the Supreme Court ruled that the tennis professionals did indeed have to pay the association $18 million.

"Forgive the sort of indelicacy, but [I remember] thinking, 'The shit's really hit the fan now,'" Hamermesh says, while seated amicably in his living room in front of a painting of several ducks.

How did a tennis squabble upend a linchpin of corporate law? Answering *that* question requires asking another one, a question so basic it seems almost ridiculous: What is a company?

At the smallest level, like a mom-and-pop shop, the company is, basically, Mom and Pop. They are the owners and also the managers who run it. They invest their own money to run the shop. They decide who to hire and what to sell. If there are profits, they can keep them.

But at big companies like Apple and Chevron, the owners and the managers are different people. The owners are investors who own Apple or Chevron stock: big banks, hedge funds, and maybe even you via your retirement account. The managers who run the business work for the benefit of the stockholders.

This creates a conundrum: What keeps CEOs and executives from being irresponsible with a company's money? Why not increase their salaries ever higher, throw themselves extravagant parties, and dole out expensive perks? (Many do!)

Lawyers like Hamermesh long ago developed a solution: The executives agree to spend that money in the company's and investors' best interest, and corporate law ensures that shareholders can sue executives who fail in their "fiduciary duties."

After the tennis case, executives started adopting similar bylaws that said any investor or shareholder who sued them would have to pay the company's legal fees—unless the investor was 100 percent successful in the lawsuit. "To say that it would chill litigation is like talking about the way liquid nitrogen would chill something," says Hamermesh.

Hamermesh feared that if investors couldn't challenge misbehaving executives in court—and lost their leverage and control over companies they funded—they might no longer give companies the money they need to grow, expand, and hire employees.

Solving this was Hamermesh's responsibility. From 1995 to 2022, he was part of one of the most important groups you've never heard of: the Corporation Law Council. The functionally boring name belies the fact that the council is the closest thing corporate law has to the Avengers. Six times per year, its twenty-seven members assemble to write and revise some of the most important rules of business. Specifically, they define what a corporation is: how a corporation is born, what happens when companies try to merge, what rights the investors have, and so on. It's like modifying corporations' DNA, or tweaking their source code. And the council saw these fee-shifting bylaws as an emergency. "An existential threat," says Hamermesh. As the controversy intensified, he worked on a new proposal. It was simple: "The rule was that [corporations] can't put fee-shifting provisions in their bylaws or charter. Can't do it."

Passing this simple rule change, however, was contentious and had high stakes. The U.S. Chamber of Commerce lobbied against the idea. Powerful executives argued that companies should be free to design their own rules. The normally cordial group of lawyers held long debates. But the council ultimately agreed on the new rule and sent it to lawmakers, who voted it into the legal rule book. Hamermesh felt they'd preserved the balance of power between owners and managers. The corporate Avengers had triumphed.

But there's something you should know: The Corporation Law Council is not part of the World Trade Organization or World Bank. Its headquarters aren't in Washington, D.C., Beijing, or Brussels. Its members are not appointed by senators or prime ministers. Hamermesh lives in Delaware, the second smallest state in America, and the council is part of the Delaware State Bar Association. The court that decided the tennis case was Delaware's Supreme Court, and it was the Delaware legislature that voted to make Hamermesh's proposal corporate law around the world.

Corporations grow our food and build our homes. They entertain us with blockbusters and diagnose and treat our kidney disease. Laws and regulations, as well as corporate culture, dictate whether corporations produce economic growth or economic malaise, and whether they're aligned with our values—treating humans and the planet well—or go full Terminator.

This unusual state of affairs, of Delaware writing corporate law and resolving corporate disputes, works remarkably well, with technocrats like Hamermesh diligently maintaining this crucial piece of economic infrastructure.

But what about the costs that corporations inflict on us: The cruel layoffs and mass pollution? The political influence and harmful products? The greenhouse gas emissions and constant tax evasion? I asked Hamermesh about public-minded policies the council could have passed during his tenure, like mandating that companies allow employees to appoint a member of the board of directors.

"Yeah, absolutely," he replied. "I could do that." And then he explained why he wouldn't.

When corporations were rare

IN BIOLOGY, scientists have observed that some traits and abilities are so advantageous that they evolved independently in entirely different places and eras. In the Triassic, pterosaurs evolved the ability to fly. Some 200 million years earlier, tiny insects grew wings. And just tens of millions of years ago, tree-crawling mammals evolved into bats.

The same is true in economic history: From ancient Rome to Qing-dynasty China, societies created corporate organizations to solve a pressing problem: coordinating human activity on a massive scale.

One of these moments came in 200 BC, when the expanding Roman Republic faced the armies of Carthage, led by Hannibal. Rome's legions were losing battles, the treasury was empty, and generals were begging for supplies. So how did Rome triumph?

The Forever Corporation

Ancient Rome's *societates publicanorum* were not exactly modern corporations—they only formed to complete government contracts. But you can see in the *societates* a move toward the key characteristics that define modern corporations:

TRANSFERABLE SHARES

At the Temple of Castor and Pollux, three of whose columns still stand today, Romans assembled to pool capital. Some economic historians believe Romans swapped shares of *societates publicanorum*, like in a modern stock market. Others believe they simply recruited additional partners and financial backers. Either way, it allowed the *societates* to tap the wallets of a larger pool of people and start separating ownership from management.

IMMORTALITY

Today, it seems normal that a company like Apple can perform an action like "release an iPhone." But the idea that an abstract entity can exist, own property, and do stuff was an imaginative leap. Prior to that, businesses had been embodied by the person, family, or group of partners who started them; they disappeared when those people died. The *societates* survived the death of their partners, and each leader made decisions for the organization and could be regularly replaced. These innovations allowed businesses to potentially live forever.

LIMITED LIABILITY

A Roman merchant whose ship sunk at sea might find himself sunk financially. But the funders and partners in *societates publicanorum* seem to have enjoyed some limited liability—to an extent greatly debated by academics—so that they were not personally responsible for all the unpaid debts or damages of their *societates*. Which made participating less risky.

In *For Profit: A History of Corporations*, William Magnuson notes the usual explanations, such as a change in military tactics. "Less well known in this affair is the role of capitalists in allowing Rome to keep the war effort alive," he writes. The senate gave contracts to three *societates publicanorum*—very loosely, partnerships—to deliver food and equipment to their legions in exchange for future payments. "The government, teetering on the edge of collapse, [was] bailed out by a group of powerful Roman companies."

Imagine you are a Roman senator directing the construction of a massive aqueduct. During the Republic era, the Roman state itself was small, lacking the workforce and bureaucracy for the job. You could give the project to one of Rome's great families. But what if the aging patriarch dies? In contrast, *societates publicanorum* survive the death of any one manager or owner, and their ability to fundraise large sums from many Romans (who were not personally liable for the entire enterprise, so more willing to invest or join) allowed *societates* to tackle big, ambitious projects.

This was a powerful combination. As Rome expanded its empire, its politicians relied on *societates publicanorum* to build temples, collect foreign taxes, and extinguish fires. (And to feed the geese at Capitoline Hill. That was a prestigious one!) Across history, other early corporate forms powered wealth-building projects and transformations:

- **Precolonial Mexico:** In wealthy Aztec cities, corporate units called *calpulli* provided tribute (similar to paying taxes) by collectively farming, providing labor, or plying trades such as metalworking or sculpting.

- **Renaissance Italy:** This famous period in European history was fueled by contracts called *commendas*, which allowed wealthy residents to partner with investors and split the profits of trading voyages. The powerful Medici family also created corporate structures that resemble a modern bank holding company.

- **Seventeenth-century Holland:** The Dutch created the first modern stock market to fund corporations, transforming the tiny country into an empire and global-trade powerhouse.

Corporations were a powerful technology, but it took centuries before they'd take over economic life. For three main reasons:

- **Replaced by the state:** In many societies, corporate personhood was seen as a great privilege—a power only granted to companies performing state business. Rome's private businesses did not enjoy these privileges. After Julius Caesar became consul in 59 BC, and later, under the reign of the emperor Augustus (27 BC–AD 14), the bureaucracy was enlarged and the *societates publicanorum* were mostly sidelined.

- **Less efficient?** Developing and improving the technology of corporations took centuries. As late as 1776, Adam Smith, England's patron saint of markets and economics, criticized joint-stock corporations in *The Wealth of Nations* because he believed their managers would inevitably be more wasteful than business partners spending their own money and making their own profits.

- **Abuses of power:** In Rome, some *societates publicanorum* operating in conquered territories enslaved locals to work in mines. Similarly, Britain's East India Company, which is considered one of the first modern corporations and controlled much of South Asia until 1858, responded to the Great Bengal Famine of 1770 by continuing to export grain and maintain high taxes.

For all these reasons, rulers, politicians, and everyday people (who were often shocked by news of the *societates'* and the East India Company's sins) were wary of immortal entities endowed with personhood, fundraising superpowers, and limited consequences. English monarchs required merchants to ask the British Crown for a corporate charter, and Americans inherited this skepticism.

From 1776 through the Civil War, American entrepreneurs had to beg their state legislature for the privilege of forming a corporation. When the rare permission was granted, it was usually for things like forming a bank or building a canal, and the grant often came with constraints on how much money and property the corporation could own, or how long it could exist. Like *societates publicanorum*, groups could only get corporate powers by justifying their business as being for the public good.

But then the Industrial Revolution changed politicians' calculus—and opened an opportunity for Delaware.

A small state takes on a big job

IN 1976, Larry Hamermesh arrived at the Delaware law firm Morris, Nichols, Arsht & Tunnell. Many of his fellow Yale Law School graduates had moved to D.C. or New York. But he preferred the smaller pond, and he had a sense he'd work on business law, which he found engaging. The office was a nice, cozy twenty-five lawyers.

The pond didn't feel quite as small, though, when New York lawyers arrived to coordinate on one of his first cases. "I remember . . . marveling at how lavish the dinner was," he says. There were white tablecloths, bottles of wine, crab cakes. "I know [it] sounds kind of plebeian now . . . but it was just a whole new world for me."

It was his first experience of what a law professor once described as Delaware's "lucrative Wall Street practice in a comparatively pastoral setting."

Hamermesh began to notice more signs of Delaware's importance. Senior lawyers at his firm weighed in on proposals at the Securities and Exchange Commission (SEC), whose purpose is to prevent fraud and manipulation in financial markets.

Another time, he watched a clash over hostile takeovers, when so-called corporate raiders bought controlling shares of public companies, fired the executives, laid off employees, and, according to critics, sacrificed companies' long-term health in order to earn immediate profits. Executives wanted to be able to reject hostile takeovers. But a group of influential economists howled that executives had a fiduciary responsibility, so if someone was offering to make the shareholders rich, then the executives had to accept the offer, even if it went against their best judgment.

After eighteen years at his firm, Hamermesh left to become a law professor. In class, he stressed to students the transformative change—for the country, and for Delaware—of the rise of general incorporation. He had students read legislation from the Before period, when creating a corporation required the legislature to pass a law and the business owners to justify their enterprise's public benefits. "The recitation of the legislation was, 'This is going to help everybody, it's going to improve commerce, and [we can't do it] without a corporation,'" he explains.

During the Industrial Revolution, though, demand for corporations shot up. Building transcontinental railroads; drilling, refining, and selling oil; constructing factories—it all required the powers of corporations. Soon elites with political connections were working the system to form corporations while everyone else, like Delaware's local clam canners, were locked out.

New Jersey was one of the first to change the status quo. They invited companies to incorporate using their quick and easy process rather than incorporate in the company's home state. All you had to do was file paperwork with the secretary of state. After that, according to Hamermesh, "I think any semblance of requiring, mandating, any particular public good basically disappeared."

New Jersey also wooed businesses by removing constraints like caps on companies' size. Despite its origins in Ohio, John D. Rockefeller's Standard Oil was one of many companies that reincorporated in New Jersey. The fees paid by companies to incorporate in New Jersey soon made the state lots of money.

New Jersey would still dominate corporate law today—and host the bigshot lawyers for crab cakes—if not for Woodrow Wilson. In 1912, Woodrow Wilson was governor of New Jersey and running for president. Criticized by rivals for being too friendly to corporations, he signed a series of trustbusting laws in New Jersey. Businesses fled across the river to Delaware, which had copied New Jersey's former laws and policies and was conveniently close to New York, D.C., and Boston.

For more than 100 years, other states have tried to steal Delaware's incorporation business. Despite a few high-profile defections, Delaware has kept its crown. Almost every big-name business, from Apple to subsidiaries of Zillow, was incorporated in Delaware and follows Delaware corporate law—even if they're headquartered in another state, or even another country. And with few exceptions, every state defers to this arrangement and allows corporations to follow Delaware's corporate law and resolve disputes in Delaware.

In addition to the Corporation Law Council, another key appeal of Delaware to businesses and investors is its Court of Chancery, which unlike any other state court, exists just for business cases and has no juries. Law professor Lynn LoPucki calls it "the courts that the American people dreamed of having for themselves." The judges have a deep understanding of topics like intellectual property law, and they resolve cases quickly. (They "work like dogs," Hamermesh says.) When Elon Musk signed a contract to buy Twitter and then tried to wriggle out of it, a no-nonsense Court of Chancery judge forced him to follow through.

Since the Court of Chancery has decided just about all major corporate disputes for a century, it has built up decades of legal precedents and rulemaking. This body of case law has made Delaware something like a universal operating system—a global standard that everyone knows. With everyone choosing Delaware, corporate life is more predictable, more efficient. Lawyers for Google, Etsy, and other companies can often predict how the court will rule. Which means companies often avoid disputes and lawsuits in the first place.

Another state could copy the Court of Chancery and the council's code. But Delaware has strong incentives to fight for its position. The state earns roughly $2 billion each year from incorporation fees. That's chump change to New York, but for Delaware, it's existential: roughly 30 percent of the state budget. Like the fairy tale of the princess who can't sleep because of a pea placed under her mattress, Hamermesh and Delaware know they must serve the corporate system well and are exquisitely sensitive to businesses' needs.

For example: When COVID-19 shut down the economy in the spring of 2020, Hamermesh and his colleagues realized companies might not be able to hold annual shareholder meetings. (Companies couldn't simply switch to conference calls—the rules of corporate governance are, like presidential elections, intentionally rigid.) So on April 6, less than a month after the World Health Organization declared COVID-19 a pandemic, the governor amended Delaware's state of emergency to allow corporations to hold virtual shareholder meetings. Hamermesh says the council drafted the language.

Delaware's chancery court and other institutions, including the Corporation Law Council, helped America's economy transition from one dominated by small family businesses to one powered by dynamic international corporations, creating enormous wealth. The state makes incorporation accessible to anyone, not just elites. And it expertly runs a key piece of the global economy.

Huzzah!

Externality machines

CORPORATIONS ARE OFTEN DESCRIBED AS "GREEDY." One example of many: Some oil and gas companies covered up their own research findings that greenhouse-gas emissions cause climate change. That behavior was facilitated, and arguably even required, by the powers and laws enshrined in Delaware corporate law.

Remember the debate Hamermesh witnessed as a young lawyer about hostile takeovers and whether executives need to **maximize shareholder value**? There's a big, nerdy debate among economists, corporate lawyers, and others about whether maximizing profits for owners *should* be the one true goal of corporations and executives—rather than caring about employees, customers, and society as well.

Delaware law largely upholds maximizing shareholder value. If a civic-minded CEO of Chevron or ExxonMobil had read their climate-change research and responded by publicizing it, shutting down drilling projects, and funneling more of the firm's funds into solar-panel research, they could have been sued by shareholders.

In practice, it's hard for shareholders to successfully sue executives for not maximizing shareholder returns. Shareholders can and occasionally do tell executives they want them to value sustainability over profits, and Delaware's "business judgment" policy largely defers to managers on what's best for the company. But the shareholder-value maxim certainly helps CEOs, whose compensation is often more in stock than salary, justify profit-maximizing moves that harm people. Similarly, executives risk repercussions for considering the public good—if doing so hurts profits enough.

"As long as you're providing these benefits to everybody else in order to maximize shareholder wealth, you're okay," says LoPucki. "But if you say ... I'm not trying to maximize shareholder wealth, I'm trying to do something else, then they'll get you."

Delaware's enshrinement of limited liability also contributes to corporate misbehavior. Like tobacco companies and other corporations that have hidden their products' dangers, Chevron, ExxonMobil, and other oil companies face lawsuits over knowingly contributing to climate change and might have to pay huge fines. But the executives who made the decisions to hide the research and continue drilling projects are unlikely to suffer consequences—most are on to new jobs or retired, and it's the company that's liable, not them.

Economists have a term for things like climate change or noise pollution: **negative externalities**. The price people pay for gasoline, and the cost to oil companies to produce oil, doesn't include the costs of pollution and climate change imposed on everyone else. Corporations can choose to factor in those costs, but the system does not require it. As it is, profit-chasing, limited-liability corporations are built to largely ignore their costs to society. It is in their DNA. It's in corporate law.

If a corporation like Chevron did account for their negative externalities, the goods and services it offered would likely need to cost more and would be consumed less as a result. Without incentives from the government or consumers, a corporation just isn't designed to optimize social well-being. This is a **market failure**, a situation where the market on its own fails to deliver the efficient allocation of resources.

Hamermesh spent more time contemplating and tweaking the corporate rule book during his council tenure than perhaps anyone else. He is no corporate shill. He's an academic whose council position was prestigious but unpaid. He's sympathetic to concerns that corporate law doesn't do enough to prevent externalities such as pollution.

He and his colleagues amended Delaware law to allow for a type of entity called a B Corp, as in a public benefit corporation, whose charter includes duties to care about local communities, the environment, and staff, along with shareholder value. Of the more than 9,000 B Corps worldwide, most are small and medium-size companies, and relatively few corporations opt for the status.

Aside from providing this option, though, Hamermesh does not see it as Delaware's role to address corporations' tendency to cause negative externalities.

"You know, if you'd asked me fifty years ago, I would have been pretty comfortable saying, 'Yeah, not to worry. That's what legislatures are for. . . . If you're worried about corporations dumping all their physical externalities in the rivers and lakes and oceans, put some teeth in environmental laws.'

"I don't believe that anymore," he adds. "The political system has degraded; you can't really rely on Congress to regulate [all that]. . . . I think there's definitely a case to be made that something is missing from our system."

When the twenty-seven corporate Avengers meet, their agenda flows from a document affectionately called "the matrix," which contains all the potential changes to corporate law under consideration. These proposed rules, says Hamermesh, generally come from lawyers within Delaware. When asked how the public is represented, Hamermesh seemed surprised by the question.

One might imagine that the council receives suggestions and seeks out ideas and feedback. How do they balance trade-offs like economic growth versus pollution or inequality? Hamermesh said he could think of cases where an outside lawyer suggested a change, but very rarely a member of the public or someone outside corporate law.

In part, that's because the council's changes are mostly technical fine-tuning and clarifications. They're intentionally biased toward predictability and not fixing things that aren't broken. The council could act like philosopher-kings, remaking corporate law to force corporations to consider externalities and improve their environmental and labor policies. But "who's going to put up with that?" Hamermesh asks.

He's right, of course. Delawareans control powerful levers that could improve corporate incentives and behavior. They could, for example, revoke the charters of companies that misbehave egregiously. They could even reinstate the requirement that corporations explicitly serve the public good. But every company knows they won't, because then businesses would reincorporate in another pro-business state.

The nature and behavior of corporations is not immutable and unchanging. Societies have changed their DNA and redefined the rules that govern them. They could be changed again. For now, though, the incentives are set toward enabling corporations and prioritizing profits.

Why Delaware?

A World Tour of
SPECTACULAR PUBLIC GOODS

Markets are powerful but also often flawed. Notably, markets undersupply **public goods**, such as streetlights, clean air, and public safety.

Public goods have two main features. They are nonexcludable: If you put up streetlights or operate an air-pollution undoer, you can't force people to close their eyes or hold their breath until they pay you. And they are nonrivalrous: If I breathe clean air, there's not less of it for you.

This leads to a free-rider problem: Why bother paying for streetlights or the military if you can enjoy safe, well-lit streets without paying? Because of free riders, markets have less incentive to provide public goods, even when they're essential to our lives and prosperity. (Put another way, they have **positive externalities**.) So governments often step in.

Much like the foundation of a house, public goods are visible when they fail but demure when working well. We tend to take them for granted, even though many of them—from an underground re-creation of the Big Bang to a manmade, transcontinental forest—are awe-inspiring. So let's visit some of them.

A century ago, screwworms regularly ate American cattle alive from the inside out. No individual rancher could best the pests. So government scientists bred sterile male screwworms to prevent females, which breed just once before dying, from producing any young.  They eradicated the parasites in North America, then used the tactic farther south until they reached the Colombia-Panama border, where they hold the line by dumping millions of adult screwworm flies from propeller planes. This "worm wall" exemplifies our collective fight against nightmarish parasites—and viruses that once made the deaths of toddlers commonplace. But we have to be vigilant: Screwworm flies have broken containment several times, and in 2024, they spread north into Mexico.

Only elite physicists get time at particle accelerators, whose magnetic rings smash particles together in scientifically revealing ways. But like the billions of dollars of research funded each year by governments, its findings are a public good. Experiments conducted here don't have immediate economic benefits—many seek to reveal the origins of the cosmos. But scientists often make practical discoveries unexpectedly, and the Large Hadron Collider has created economic value far exceeding its price tag through discoveries in magnets, refrigeration, and more.

In America, weather forecasts are built on data gathered by the government from airport sensors, hot-air balloons, ocean buoys—and three planes nicknamed *Kermit*, *Gonzo*, and *Miss Piggy*. When tropical storms are brewing over the Atlantic, pilots fly the Muppet planes through them to measure their path and ferocity. Information may want to be free, but collecting this kind of information is expensive. Also worth it, even if the benefits are distributed so widely it's hard to quantify. Taxpayers fund the agencies that gather and distribute atmospheric, population, and other data. (Although the Trump Administration curtailed that funding.) Farmers and their insurers rely on weather reports. Marketers rely on census rolls. And if space tourism and travel become an everyday reality, we might rely on a similar system to track space debris.

Launching satellites so people can check which city block they're standing on is such a crazy, expensive idea you'd need a war to justify it. Which is how GPS happened. The first GPS satellite went up in 1978, during the Cold War, primarily to direct troops and American missiles. By 1983, the U.S. government had made it available for public use. Today GPS powers apps like Google Maps and Instagram, allows trains to avoid collisions, and guides automated tractors around farms.

A few weeks every year, inside the Colorado campus of the National Institute of Standards and Technology, a very special clock turns on. It measures the length of a second not by a ticking hand or swinging pendulum, but by the resonant

frequencies of atomic radiation. As the world's most accurate type of clock—off by just a second every 300 million years—it's one of several hundred around the world used to coordinate literally everyone's clocks. Without such accurate, shared time, GPS locations would be off, internet errors would proliferate, and power grids could fail. Similar intergovernmental partnerships create universal standards—like electric voltages—that underpin entire industries by coordinating everyone involved.

STRAIT OF GIBRALTAR — "PIRATE-FREE FOR 200 YEARS"

For centuries, North African pirates captured trading ships as they sailed the narrow strait that connects the Atlantic Ocean to the Mediterranean Sea. The crossing was perilous until the 1800s, when the United States sent a naval squadron to intimidate the Barbary states of Tripoli and Algier, while France conquered Algeria in 1830. Today, agreement among powerful countries to police the seas—and not seize rivals' ships—has created a complete historical anomaly: the assumption that unprotected cargo ships are unlikely to be captured by pirates. Without this Freedom of the Seas policy, prices at Walmart might include the cost of antipirate convoys or pirates stealing a share of all imported products.

A MAN-MADE FOREST THAT WILL BE VISIBLE FROM SPACE

Much of the Sahel, just south of the Sahara, looks like desert. But before widespread deforestation and overgrazing, it supported the rise of large empires and trading cities. Which is why eleven African countries and various international organizations partnered to plant millions of trees and seedlings and restore land east-to-west across the entire continent. The goal is to increase the region's arable land and sequester carbon. If they succeed, the band of greenery will be visible from space. It's an epic scale-up of public goods like tree-planting initiatives (which can cool cities several degrees), environmental governance, and parks (which generate unknown amounts of joy rather than profits).

3

The Raisin Outlaw

Escaping the commodity trap

he agents were not being subtle. Marvin and Laura Horne could see them parked on the road that ran past their farm, where they'd take photos of the large metal building the couple had built a few years earlier. Once an agent chased down a truck leaving the Hornes' facility and accused the driver of transporting illegal goods. Which the Hornes thought was nonsense. The driver told the agent that his goods were legal and he had his paperwork. Then he drove off.

"They pulled some really funny things," says Laura.

The agents worked for Rocky Pipkin, a private eye based in nearby Fresno, California. He'd been hired to surveil farmers suspected of an illegal scheme. And the Hornes' facility was at the heart of it.

The agents' stakeout produced grainy videotape of trucks entering and exiting the Hornes' building. The footage showed truck beds full of illicit goods: raisins. The raisins themselves weren't illegal. They were illicit because they were packed in containers, ready for sale. Rocky's client was a cartel, the Raisin Administrative Committee (RAC). And they had hired him to document an alleged crime—the crime of selling raisins.

Laura Horne's family has farmed grapes in Kerman, California, for four generations, picking them off the vines each summer and drying them in the Central Valley's strong sun until they wrinkle into raisins. Marvin grew up in Kerman too. "He always wanted to farm," says Laura. "He kind of married into it."

Packing and selling raisins may not sound like a criminal enterprise. But the Hornes' farm existed in an economic bizarro world: Federal law forced them to be part of the RAC cartel. Instead of selling their raisins on the open market, they had to sell them to an RAC-approved raisin packer.

Normally cartels are illegal, even if they sell legal goods, not drugs. Instead of competing to sell their products in an open market, members of a cartel collude to set a price. Usually that means a higher price and higher profits. Which undermines a bedrock of a market economy: the competition for customers that forces companies to constantly seek ways to lower their prices or improve their products.

But the RAC is one of a small number of legal cartels overseen by the Department of Agriculture. Backed by the full force of the U.S. government, it outlawed the free market for raisins, drove up raisin prices, and insulated farmers from both the competition that drives down costs for customers and the signals and incentives conveyed by raisins' market price.

For more than a decade, the Hornes packed and sold their own raisins. In the upside-down world of California raisins, this made them outlaws—they were surveilled and faced escalating fines. All for the crime of selling raisins to someone willing to pay for them.

What's so unusual about Marvin and Laura Horne is that the government gave their industry an out from fierce, profit-destroying competition. And they rebelled against it.

The commodity trap

THE ROAD TO THE HORNES' LEGAL JEOPARDY was paved with good intentions. The U.S. government was trying to help struggling farmers escape a gravitational force of economics: the **commodity trap**.

Imagine that you're the head engineer for your company's line of desktop monitors. You and your team bust your butts to create a monitor whose screen quality is so sharp it catches customers' eyes from across the aisles of Best Buy. It's such a revelation that the business team raises the price and increases the profit margin of each sale. And it sells well! You high-five and clink champagne flutes.

But within a few years, competitors have reverse-engineered your methods to produce similar monitors. Some are copycat firms that don't spend much on research and development, so they can afford to undercut your price. The VP of sales explains that you have to match their price. Now your monitors sell for barely more than the cost of making them.

You once had a differentiated product and, therefore, market power, or the power to set your own price. Now your monitor is basically a commodity—indistinguishable from all the other monitors, treated by customers and the market as interchangeable. You can't set your own price, because customers can just buy your competitors' monitors. This is the commodity trap.

It's a paradox at the heart of our economy: Markets foster competition that benefits customers and drives innovation and economic growth. But competition erodes profits, so companies constantly seek an escape from competition.

Companies can escape the commodity trap by creating new products, applying for patents, or cultivating a coveted brand, like Apple or Gucci. But many farmers and agriculturalists can't escape. To most customers, an orange is an orange is an orange.

For commodities such as raisins and oranges, says Joe Balagtas, a Purdue professor of agricultural economics, the market price tends to be the cost of growing each orange or raisin. And that's not the cost for each farmer, but the cost for the lowest-cost farm. Profits are slim, negative, or nonexistent.

> I'm vaguely aware that navel oranges are a type of orange. Are they better than other kinds of oranges? What are the other varieties? And which farms grow the best ones? I have no idea!

This is a major reason why the U.S. government, in 1922, gave agriculture some exemptions from antitrust laws, allowing cartels or cooperatives that would be considered a criminal conspiracy in other industries.

Balagtas says there are dozens. "Florida oranges, Walla Walla onions..." Economists call them cartels, but not pejoratively. That's simply what they are.

The world's most famous legal cartel is OPEC, the Organization of the Petroleum Exporting Countries, which dials oil exports up or down to influence the price of oil. OPEC's market manipulation doesn't violate any country's laws, because the organization is composed of countries. Otherwise, though, legal cartels are rare outside agriculture.

The low profits of commoditized crops are not the only justification for cartels. Agriculture has other unique characteristics:

- Historically, the United States had lots of small farmers in a hurry to sell products with short shelf lives to a few big buyers, like fruit-packing companies or dairy processors. So cooperatives helped balance the power in those negotiations—much like how the government gives workers the right to unionize.

- When good weather blesses farmers with bumper crops, their "reward" is a lower price because of the higher supply. But if a drought brings higher prices next year, farms won't benefit, because they won't have much to sell. Cartels can smooth out this volatility by coordinating the storing of surpluses to sell during down years.

- Cooperatives allow farmers to maintain helpful quality and hygiene standards that give customers confidence in the entire industry, benefiting everyone. And they allow them to collaborate on marketing, as with the California Milk Processor Board's famous "Got Milk?" advertising campaign. Fun fact: A young Michael Bay, future director of *Armageddon*, *The Rock*, and five Transformers films, directed the first "Got Milk?" commercial.

The Hornes' nemesis, the Raisin Administrative Committee, was formed in 1949, just after World War II ended. During the war, the U.S. military had bought enormous quantities of raisins for its soldiers. With the troops back home, prices dropped, and grape farmers were struggling. The RAC upheld collective standards by checking that packed raisins were not full of sand or mold. But its raison d'être was to raise the price of raisins through annual "diversions"—withholding part of a harvest to create artificial scarcity. If RAC's leaders decided on a diversion of 10 percent, then their raisin packers would set 10 percent of the crop aside for the raisin reserve storage warehouses.

This wasn't a true escape from the commodity trap—customers could buy raisins grown and dried elsewhere. But California produced so many raisins that diversion increased the market price.

In the 1980s, the RAC pulled off a coup: They hired an ad agency that created the California Raisins, a group of Claymation raisins. In ads, dressed as an R&B group, the raisins sang "I Heard It Through the Grapevine." People loved the California Raisins. They were invited to the White House, and Michael Jackson asked to join the group. Raisin sales surged.

But in the 1990s and early 2000s, the California Raisins disappeared. Turkey became the world's leading exporter of raisins, and dried grapes were unwelcome at Halloween. Each year, more of the Hornes' neighbors ripped out their venerable grapevines to plant cash crops, especially almonds, which they sold into a booming, almond-milk-fueled market.

Switching to almond groves required expensive equipment and several years of waiting for trees to bear nuts. But it was arguably the superior, free-market solution for reducing raisin supplies. In 2002, the RAC announced a big diversion: 47 percent. Almost half of every farm's crop was trucked to storage. "A lot of us, we all jumped up and yelled and said, 'No, that's crazy,'" Marvin Horne recalled years later. To no avail.

The RAC's leaders were local raisin farmers and packers, but Laura Horne says that they did not ask for input. Their decisions felt "handed down." And once approved by the Department of Agriculture, the diversions were federal law.

The premise was that farmers would be paid later, when the RAC sold the surplus during a down year. But farmers rarely received much for their diverted raisins, since the RAC deducted the costs of their staff, warehouses, and publicity programs.

Marvin and Laura decided, "No, we're not going to deliver [our grapes]. We're going to figure out what we can do."

Marvin read and reread the legislation that created the RAC. "He was a reader and loved to look things up," says Laura. At night, they read passages together. Marvin's interpretation was that if they sold and marketed their own raisins—if they weren't raisin packers but farmers who packed and sold their own raisins—they didn't have to follow the diversion program. So they built the packing plant and found a raisin broker who wanted to buy their raisins. They didn't believe they were doing anything wrong, but they knew they were taking a risk.

Raisins get spicy

THE RAISIN ADMINISTRATIVE COMMITTEE did not agree with Marvin and Laura Horne's interpretation of the law. They hired Rocky to stake out their farm and took their grainy video footage of packed raisins to court, where a judge ruled against the Hornes and ordered them to pay a fine of almost half a million dollars and another $200,000 in penalties. But the Hornes appealed the ruling, all the way to the Supreme Court.

Court proceedings dragged on for a full decade, and the amount they'd owe if they lost kept increasing. Laura says she slept poorly many nights due to stress, but Marvin would read his Bible, turn everything over to the Lord, and sleep like a baby. "I almost wanted to poke him," she says.

Some farmers considered the Hornes crooks. They were all diverting raisins and missing out on personal revenue in order to prop up prices for everyone. So when the Hornes sold their whole crop, they did so at a higher price thanks to other farmers' sacrifices. But many farmers were equally frustrated. Some had to mortgage their farms or get second jobs after the 47 percent diversion. Several joined the Hornes by using their packing plant to sell their raisins themselves.

Misadventures in Price Controls

Governments do all kinds of things to help farmers. They buy and warehouse products, pay farmers not to plant, and straight up write checks, such as the $90 billion the USDA spent from 2011 through 2021 to subsidize crop insurance. This leads to huge bills for taxpayers and some epic economic misadventures:

THE CHEESE CAVES OF AMERICA

To help dairy farmers in the late 1970s, the U.S. government bought literally tons of cheese (millions of pounds) to increase the price of milk. To store all these blocks of processed American cheese, the government rented underground storage facilities, some in old limestone mines. Ubiquitous at food banks, "government cheese" became a cultural phenomenon, associated with hard times and handouts.

EUROPE'S WINE LAKES

Who doesn't love French or German wine? Enough people that the continent suffers from a huge surplus, which is stored in cellars collectively known as "wine lakes." Over the years, the European Union has partially drained the lakes by distilling wine into industrial alcohol or paying winemakers not to produce. And yet they endure, a warning about the perils of price controls. *In vino veritas*.

SALMON SUSHI

Many of Japan's older sushi chefs have never eaten salmon sashimi, because Japanese salmon tend to have parasites. Then Norway, which had been subsidizing their fishing industry, began marketing their ample salmon surplus. They negotiated salmon sushi into grocery stores and worked their way up the food chain to izakayas and finally chef's tables.

The Raisin Outlaw

In 2015, Marvin and Laura got a phone call from their lawyer: The Supreme Court had ruled in their favor, 8–1. The judges decided that the RAC's diversion program violated the Takings Clause of the Fifth Amendment, which does not allow the government to take private property (like dried grapes) without offering fair compensation. The Hornes would not have to pay anything, and raisin farmers would be paid by the RAC for the fruit they'd diverted over the years.

"And then we had a big party," says Laura. She and Marvin met their local attorneys and other farmers in town for a toast. "We said, 'Hey, we won. You know, after all of this, we finally won.'"

Because it had taken so long to arrive, the decision did not have a dramatic effect on the industry. There had not been any diversions in the previous four years, in part because so many farmers had switched to crops like almonds and peaches.

When I ask Balagtas how he, as an economist, feels about these cartels, he says that he weighs the costs and benefits. The programs can support farmers in a tough industry, but "anybody that ate raisins over the life of the raisin program paid slightly higher prices." He points to inflation, to the rising price of eggs in 2025. "We can't take relatively cheap food for granted." Many agricultural cartels are still operating, since they don't involve the government "taking" farmers' harvests as the RAC did.

The RAC still exists, just without the diversion program. It maintains standards, markets their beloved fruit, and negotiates orders from the U.S. government, which buys their raisins for schools and food pantries. (A legal way of aiding the industry.) But farmers now face market prices, and they can decide, based on those prices, whether to stick with raisins or uproot them in favor of something else.

"All the other farmers have put almonds in," says Laura, who used to see nothing but grapevines around her farm. "I'd much rather see the grapevines . . . I just think they look better."

This is, effectively, the market-based alternative to a diversion program: Farmers voluntarily reducing the raisin supply.

Marvin had other plans. Once the court battle ended, he turned to a project he'd been thinking about for a long time: creating raisin products. He put spicy chile limón on raisins. He dipped raisins in chocolate. He paired raisins with blueberry, cinnamon, and strawberry nougats.

"He mixed a lot of concoctions in my kitchen," says Laura, who preferred the nougat mix.

Marvin even mocked up mascots for his snack packs. In a way, his battle against the RAC was about having the freedom to invent his own way out of the commodity trap. But in August 2020, after a trip the Hornes took to the coast, Marvin died unexpectedly. During what turned out to be their last drive home, Laura says, he had spoken about wanting to get his raisin concoctions into stores and customers' hands.

Since Marvin's passing, managing the farm has been challenging. Laura started working with a potential partner to sell the snack packs, but had to give it up. "I'm getting older," she says. "I just couldn't do it anymore." But if Marvin were still alive, she adds, they'd be selling them. "That was always Marvin's dream," says Laura. "He wanted to be proud of that raisin."

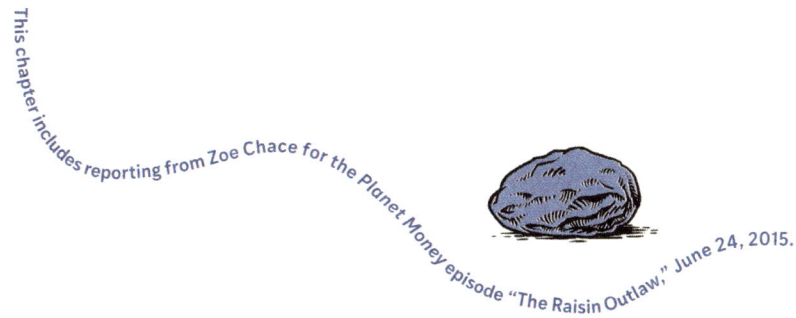

This chapter includes reporting from Zoe Chace for the Planet Money episode "The Raisin Outlaw," June 24, 2015.

Escaping the COMMODITY TRAP

PLANET MONEY

THE COMMODITY TRAP is not inevitable, even for crops that have been around for thousands of years. Farmers now have clever ways of differentiating their offerings, earning themselves more control and pricing power.

Fancy Words, Premium Prices!

Fixed-Price Cola
One shiny nickel. We're not making any money but we said this back in 1886 so we're screwed.
5¢

Peruvian Blueberries
Less tasty, more consistent, thanks to the war on drugs.
4²⁸ PINT

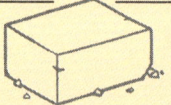

Government Cheese
Free if you qualify

Emmental and Gruyere
"Make Fondue instead!" —Swiss Cheese Union

NEIN!

Pashman's Podcast Pasta
Sauceable. Forkable. Fun.
7⁹⁸ BOX

17⁹⁸
Shrinkflation Shrimp Bag
CONTAINS 3 SHRIMP

BRANDING

CUTIES

Consider Cuties, the tasty and easy-to-peel mandarin oranges that sell in distinctive bags bearing the Cuties' trademarked name and mascot. This ensures Cuties are a brand that people recognize and trust. But Cuties are not always the same fruit; there are slightly different varieties—Clementines, W. Murcotts, Tangos—depending on what's in season throughout the year.

FREE
Pickles
Please, somebody just take these
0¢

Hot Dogs
NO TEETH
4²⁵ FOR 2

$87000⁰⁰
Black Lotus
Helps digestion, fixes MTG asset bubbles

+3 MANA

Onions*
Ready for throwing! (Into the Chicago River)
*Supply limited due to past bulk purchases & cornered markets

CHAMPAGNE

PROTECTED DESIGNATIONS OF ORIGIN

If you strip the romance out of wine, it's just fermented grape juice. If you add bubbles, it's sparkling wine. But it's not champagne! Thanks to a series of international agreements that enforce a trademark-like system called protected designations of origin, Tequila can only come from specific regions of Mexico, and sparkling wine is only champagne if it's from Champagne, France. Like with Darjeeling tea (grown only in Darjeeling, India) and Kona coffee (from a volcanic area in Hawaii), PDOs transform products from specific regions into recognized brands.

American Potatoes*
Finally available for sale across the continent

90¢ LB

*Inspected for Columbia root-knot nematode

FREX!

Hipster Pop
So cool their shelf space is free

2⁵⁰ CAN

Spicy Raisins
Prototype Pending

1⁹⁸ LB  Banananas MMM...

2⁰⁵ EA 
Lettuce
You won't find these at a Dollar Store

STILL FREE More Pickles Oh boy **0¢** Thanks for shopping!

APPLES

TRADEMARKED CULTIVARS

Not so long ago, many American grocers stocked just the Red Delicious apple. It looked like the platonic ideal of an apple, but it was not actually delicious. Then an apple breeder at the University of Minnesota, David Bedford, created the delicious Honeycrisp. It unlocked a desire for more tasty varieties. Next, Bedford created the SweeTango apple, trademarked the name, and only allowed 45 farmers to grow it.

4

The Phone at the End of the World

The promise and peril of free trade

Not so long ago, a politician became president by promising to bring manufacturing jobs back from Asia and Mexico. We aren't making things, the politician said. We need to make things! The president started taxing imported goods: If you imported shoes, you paid a 35 percent tax. If you imported cars, you paid up to 35 percent too. And importing some products, like cell phones, was effectively banned. Make those phones here, the president said. Open factories here!

The president's new laws micromanaged the economy. When one company agreed to make their hugely popular smartphone locally, the law nudged them to open a factory in a specific region.

That politician was Cristina Fernández de Kirchner, whom Argentines had elected president in 2007. The smartphone was the BlackBerry, which was one of Argentina's most popular phones and, at that time, still used by VIPs from Britney Spears to Barack Obama. Through a mix of pressure and financial incentives, the government pushed BlackBerry to open a factory in Tierra del Fuego, an archipelago at the southern tip of South America that Argentines call the end of the world.

Apple decided not to open a factory in Argentina. So when the law passed, iPhones disappeared from Argentine stores. But Argentina was an important market for BlackBerry. So BlackBerry, whose parts were largely made in Asia and assembled in Mexico and Hungary, decided to try assembling phones in Tierra del Fuego.

Economists almost universally praise the benefits of free trade, arguing that it makes everyone richer overall. Their research has inspired decades of free-trade agreements. But skepticism of globalization is common, and periodically countries elect populists like Kirchner who promise to bring back manufacturing, boss around international corporations, and bend markets to their will.

When Kirchner strongarmed BlackBerry into making phones at the end of the world, it was the ultimate test of this seductive strategy, of picking and choosing which parts of globalization to keep. And for a time, it went well.

Shall we trade?

PRESIDENT KIRCHNER'S LAW TRANSFORMED Hugo Bonifacini's world. Bonifacini was a systems engineer in Tierra del Fuego, or the Land of Fire, named for the many coastal campfires visible to European sailors in the 1500s. It's one of the most remote places on earth, closer to Antarctica than to its own country's capital, with whipping winds, rough roads, and few flights. But when BlackBerry contracted Bonifacini's employer, they started receiving giant shipping containers of parts and machinery.

"We don't have warehouse to storage," says Bonifacini, who was one of sixty employees. "They arrived and arrived, and some people said, 'Hey, in your house, you have space?'"

Bonifacini and his company were rowing against one of the strongest currents in economics: **comparative advantage**.

For centuries, countries traded for things they couldn't grow or didn't make themselves: Japan exchanged their silver for Portuguese rifles; Europeans traded with China for tea and with Turkey for coffee. But what about smartphones? They can be assembled anywhere. Should you trade for them, or make them yourself?

This is where comparative advantage comes in, which economist Emily Oster entertainingly explains through her marriage to another economist. "At the time, I was better at, more or less, everything that we do in the house," she says. She was better at cooking *and* at doing dishes. But she was only a bit better at dishwashing, and "much, much better" at cooking. So she had a comparative advantage at cooking, and he had a comparative advantage at washing dishes. She cooked; he cleaned.

The lesson is that countries can always benefit from trade by specializing in their comparative advantage. Countries like the United States and Argentina *could* manufacture smartphones. But they are better off importing smartphones from countries that have the comparative advantage—thanks to cheaper labor, perhaps, or more electronics experience—and focusing on software development, wine, biofuels, and other sectors they excel at.

Since the end of World War II, the logic of comparative advantage has increased the volume of global trade almost without interruption. This growth is driven by decreasing transportation costs and by countries reducing or removing tariffs and other barriers to trade. As barriers come down,

> ## How Some Seventh Graders Increased Their Wealth 64 Percent in 60 Seconds
>
> When *Planet Money* reporter David Kestenbaum walked into Lyons Community School in Brooklyn with ten candies and snacks, he had a point to prove. With a teacher's blessing, he randomly handed one to each of ten students. Some got Nerds. Others Sour Patch Kids, Fig Newtons, Twix, or Swedish Fish. One poor kid got raisins. Then Kestenbaum asked the children to rate their happiness with the candy from one to ten. The raisins kid said zero. The owner of a Three Musketeers bar said five. The total across all ten students was fifty. Out of a possible one hundred.
>
> The children had an idea to improve the outcome: trade. Kestenbaum gave them one minute, and after 60 furious seconds ("Want to trade?" . . . "I got Nerds, I got Nerds"), he asked again about their levels of candy satisfaction. The total had increased to 82—a 64 percent increase.
>
> This is one example of what economists mean when they use the term **efficiency**: wringing more happiness out of the same fixed resources. The schoolchildren had made the distribution of candy more efficient—even without the aid of money. Some kids were still less happy than others. But overall, the group was much happier with their treats than before. Trade can make everyone better off.

companies seeking out every competitive advantage sell in newly opened markets and move production to wherever the comparative advantage lies.

While free(r) trade is usually win-win for countries, it can create winners and losers *within* countries. When China entered the global economy in the 1990s and early aughts by reducing tariffs and trade barriers and joining the World Trade Organization, the effect came to be called the China shock. From 1991 to 2013, China's manufacturing exports went from 2.3 percent of the world's total to a whopping 18.8 percent. As factories moved to China, countries like the United States specialized more in services, and executives, lawyers, and professors got to buy cheap imported goods. The number of American factory jobs was already in decline, but economists estimate that competition from China led to a nearly 1 million decrease in manufacturing employment, and many manufacturing hubs experienced the equivalent of miniature Great Depressions.

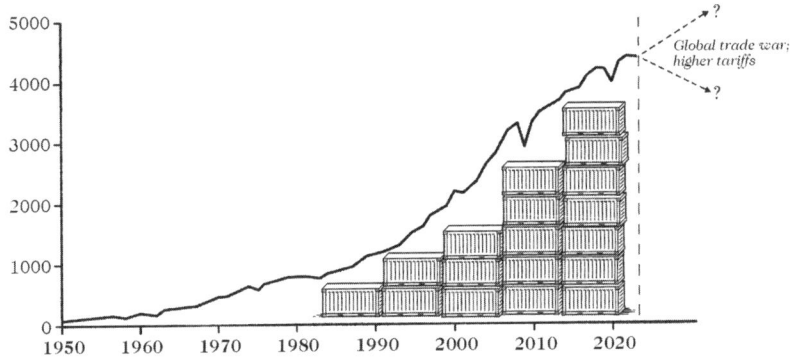

Volume of World Trade, 1950–Present

This is why politicians in Kirchner's mold are tempted to bring back manufacturing. A corporation can quickly close a plant and open one abroad, but workers can't effortlessly retrain for a new career or leave friends and family for a new city with better jobs (and higher housing costs). Politicians see constituents in pain and ask: Why not undo the mistake?

According to Wes Nicol, who ran part of BlackBerry's South America operations, there was a logic to making BlackBerry phones in Tierra del Fuego. But it wasn't economic logic. It was political logic. The region had backed Kirchner, so "she wanted to pay back those constituents and provide jobs for them." That's how BlackBerry ended up hiring Bonifacini's company.

Bonifacini says that BlackBerry's operations requirements were exacting. The new factory needed state-of-the-art machinery and a clean room full of monitors to track tiny dust particles. Nothing like that had ever been built in Tierra del Fuego. They had to order everything.

The problem wasn't just parts, but getting enough skilled workers. If they had built the factory in a place with a robust labor market—like a manufacturing hub or city with an engineering college—hiring would have been easier. But they had to recruit workers to the end of the world. "You know, the weather conditions here are very, very hard," says Bonifacini. There were few homes for new arrivals, and no worker's dormitory. Bonifacini says they had to lure people with high salaries: three times what the job would pay elsewhere in Argentina, plus great benefits.

Against all odds, they succeeded. Bonifacini was there when the first Argentine BlackBerry came off the assembly line. "Everybody was watching the line," he says. Senators and other politicians came to gawk and take photos with the workers. "Everybody wanted to catch this picture to use in political campaigns."

Soon after, President Kirchner gave a speech and declared that Argentina was becoming a manufacturing center with great new jobs. She held up the BlackBerry from the end of the world, and the crowd cheered and waved Argentine flags and jumped up and down. During the press tour, Bonifacini proudly told a reporter that if they could find any difference between their phone and a BlackBerry made abroad, he'd give them the phone as a gift. "My boss said, 'Hugo, I'll kill you.'" But no one ever pointed out a deficiency.

For a time, it seemed that Kirchner had succeeded in demanding a better deal from international trade. Foreign newspapers published articles about Argentina's economic growth, and in Tierra del Fuego, which was now home to factories making laptops, flat-screen TVs, and air conditioners, people were opening stores and driving Range Rovers.

BlackBerry had a problem though: Its Argentinian phones weren't selling. Because of all the extra time it took to set up the factory in Tierra del Fuego, the model was two years out of date compared to BlackBerry phones in other countries. And manufacturing at the end of the world made the phone twice as expensive as newer models sold elsewhere.

Argentinians didn't want to buy an outdated, overpriced phone. But they were willing to buy black-market phones. Enterprising Argentinians bought BlackBerry phones abroad. One smuggler would walk through airport customs with them hidden in shoes in their luggage or stuffed in their socks. Less than two years after Kirchner held up a BlackBerry to an adoring crowd, the company closed the plant. Bonifacini describes it as a tough time. His company shrank, and he eventually got called into the boss's office and was told his job was going away. It left "a bitter taste."

Across Argentina, companies closed factories that Kirchner had coerced them into opening. Since manufacturing in Argentina was generally more expensive—and imports were highly taxed—the price of just about everything went up.

Argentina and the smartphone at the end of the world are a case study in **protectionism**. The problem with protectionism, says Argentine economist Eduardo Levy Yeyati, is that instead of money and talent flowing to sectors like beef, wine, and biofuels (where Argentina excelled and exported globally), it went to a BlackBerry factory in Tierra del Fuego. Kirchner wanted these new factories to export their goods globally. But many of them, like

The Chicken Tax

When governments intervene in markets with tariffs and trade barriers, their goal is often to shelter a single politically prized industry from foreign competition.

This is what happened in postwar Germany, when cheap, frozen chicken from the United States flooded into the rebuilding country. When small farmers complained, Germany imposed taxes on imported American chicken of up to 50 percent. The price of chicken went up for Germans, but German farmers stayed in business.

Of course, the U.S. government wasn't pleased. So in 1963, President Lyndon Johnson responded in kind with a 25 percent tariff on "automobile trucks."

At the time, Volkswagen Beetles and buses were sweeping the United States, and the German car company was planning to sell a pickup truck next. (Basically a VW bus with a flatbed.) But when Johnson imposed the "chicken tax," as his administration called it, Volkswagen shelved its plans to export the truck. With the tariffs, it would be too expensive to appeal to American customers.

The chicken tax has shaped auto manufacturing ever since. Protected from foreign competition, American car companies got better and better at trucks and worse and worse at passenger vehicles. Today Ford does not manufacture sedans in North America.

This is why it's hard to cheat *just a little bit* on your trading partners. They usually respond, tit for tat, and protecting chicken farmers eats into truck sales.

BlackBerry's, could only produce subpar products at elevated prices. So the best they could do was sell to Argentines—who preferred the black market.

"Sooner or later, we'll need to leave the protection," Yeyati said at the time. "But by the time we do that, we have lost 10 years in which we could have developed alternative sectors where we have a chance."

Politicians can try to force their own residents to buy domestic products. But a tariff can't recreate the world in which they once had a comparative advantage. Bonifacini and his coworkers managed to build smartphones at the end of the world. But the global economy doesn't reward effort; it rewards the best products and lowest prices.

Picking winners

TRYING TO TURN BACK THE CLOCK with trade barriers tends to be self-defeating. But in some cases, future-focused countries have successfully protected, nurtured, and championed strategic industries:

- **Early America:** When the United States became independent, its manufactured goods came from Great Britain. So Alexander Hamilton devised a plan: increased tariffs on some commodities, reduced tariffs on certain raw materials, and subsidies for domestic producers of coal, raw wool and raw cotton, sailcloth, and glass until those sectors caught up with Europe. (He also offered bounties to Europeans who brought trade secrets to the U.S.) This infant-industries policy led to successes like Massachusetts' textile mills, which exported globally and spurred industrialization.

- **South Korea:** After the Korean War ended, South Korea similarly used tariffs, import quotas, and joint-venture requirements to support key industries, including automakers. This allowed companies like Hyundai and Kia to grow and learn by selling to Koreans, and then sell abroad once they were competitive with foreign auto manufacturers.

- **China:** When China joined the World Trade Organization, the government didn't embrace unfettered trade. For years, it kept the value of its currency low to make it cheaper for foreigners to buy

Chinese goods, and used very Hamiltonian policies (tariffs, economic espionage, and so on) to champion local industries. Among other examples, China's ban on Facebook and Instagram enabled the rise of WeChat and ByteDance, creator of TikTok.

Successful trade interventions are usually temporary: They give domestic companies water wings until they can swim in the deep end by competing globally. And they're often a tool of poorer countries, who might otherwise stay stuck with comparative advantages only in lower-margin industries like basic manufacturing.

In other cases, though, countries accept the costs of protectionism and the inefficiencies of picking winners for national security reasons. In 2024, for example, the United States awarded up to $6.6 billion to Taiwan Semiconductor Manufacturing Company to build a factory in Arizona, and gave Intel (an American company) billions in subsidies and incentives to manufacture semiconductors (and later demanded and received an ownership stake in the company). In 2025, the United States began imposing tariffs on all manner of imports, switching from carrot to stick to encourage a shift to domestic manufacturing.

Economic logic suggests that both of these tactics are expensive and wasteful: American companies design advanced semiconductors, but Taiwan makes around 90 percent of all advanced chips. Each country has their comparative advantage. The political logic, though, is that a Chinese invasion or blockade of Taiwan would cut off Americans' access to semiconductors, and for noneconomic reasons it's important to have independent production capabilities.

This is called reshoring. Due to countries' experiences during COVID—when supply chains shut down and countries hoarded supplies like medical masks—and the continued competition between China and the United States, it's a global trend. One that could end or slow the trajectory of ever more international trade.

Hugo Bonifacini's experience making smartphones at the end of the world shows the difficulty of defying the logic of globalization. But in a world of war and conflict, of distrust rather than open markets, more countries will prioritize politics and self-sufficiency over comparative advantage. It could bring more stability to some supply chains, but the world's goods might also get more expensive as a result.

This chapter includes reporting from Stacey Vanek Smith for the *Planet Money* episode "The Phone at the End of the World," February 17, 2017.

How We All Get Richer, Forever

The historic anomaly of being alive after 1700

ne hundred short years ago, if you'd asked anyone how the economy was doing, they would not have known what you meant. No one thought of "the economy" as an entity.

Today, we answer the question, roughly, by citing a statistic that can indicate growth and contraction. We can say something like, "In 2020, the global economy shrank 3 percent, while in 2023, it grew about 3 percent."

We have this number because of a problem during the Great Depression. At the time, the United States had many problems: unemployment reached 25 percent, breadlines stretched for city blocks, and dust storms blocked the sun over farms from Kansas to Oklahoma. But the problem that created the concept of "the economy" was that no one, not even the president and his advisers, knew exactly how bad the whole situation was, nor if it was getting worse or better.

The U.S. Senate put this problem to the new National Bureau of Economic Research, whose founder directed it to Simon Kuznets, an émigré from Ukraine and Russia and later a professor of economics at the University of Pennsylvania. Sober, scholarly, and data driven, he set about counting every single thing made in the United States each year down to the last two-penny nail or nail clipper. Whenever a New Yorker bought a Hershey's bar or a Minnesotan ordered a hot chocolate, Kuznets added that to what he called the national income—but only after subtracting the cost of the cocoa, since that was produced in Brazil and was part of Brazil's national income.

The idea wasn't totally new. In 1665, for example, Sir William Petty reviewed tax, treasury, and census records to measure England's resources and output, with the goal of determining whether the country could, say, best France in a war. But Kuznets literally counted every single thing produced, every year, so you could track *changes* to the economy's productive prowess.

The project was absurdly time intensive, like building a pyramid with tweezers. But Kuznets and his colleagues did it, and the concept of "national income" quickly proved its worth. The prose in his first report, *National Income, 1929–1932*, was yawn inducing, but the statistics and findings were so valuable to politicians and executives that it sold 4,500 copies within eight months. President Roosevelt started citing national income in speeches to say the country was recovering and to measure the impact of public works and New Deal programs.

During World War II, economists, armed with Kuznets's data, could confidently tell the U.S. government how many resources they could devote to building tanks and fighting the war without facing crippling shortages at home. A number of economics-minded scholars believe national income won the war for the Allies. We now call it **GDP**, or **Gross Domestic Product**, and most every country calculates GDP to track whether their economy is growing or stagnating.

GDP data initially tracked tough times: the Great Depression, the devastation of World War II. Then it showed rebounding growth. Then more growth and more growth. In countries such as the United States, the UK, much of Western Europe, and Japan, downturns and recessions were blips in an otherwise steady ascent. On GDP charts, the line marches up and to the right. The same has been true for China since 1978 or so.

Humans alive today—of the variety who regularly check GDP charts, anyway—are used to GDP going up. In the United States, the prospect of Millennials or Gen Z growing up to be less wealthy than their parents, rather than richer, is a scandal.

But perpetual growth, with each generation living better than the last, is a recent phenomenon. Economists and researchers have estimated coun-

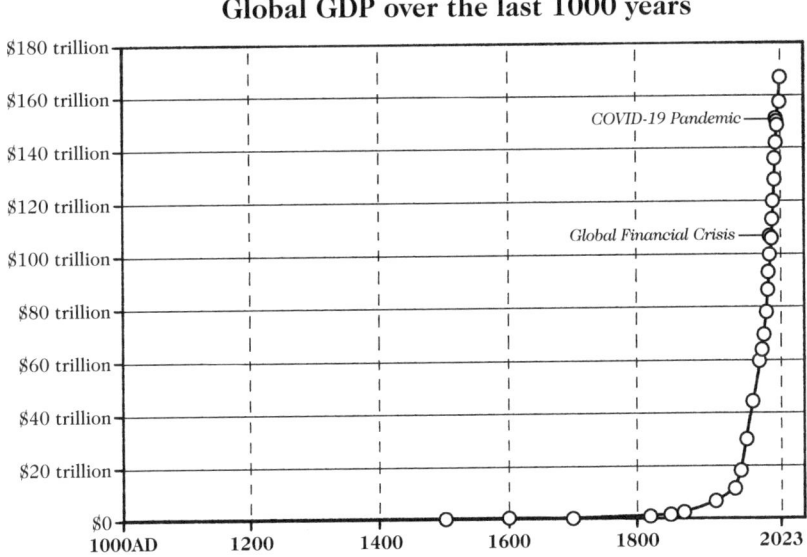

Global GDP over the last 1000 years

tries' GDP going back centuries and millennia through approaches such as calculating the likely output of farming-dominated economies via urbanization rates and accounts of prices and wages. Their big finding? For most of human history, there was little to no growth at all, until a dramatic, sustained takeoff of riches around 1700.

Explaining this sustained growth rate, this world of ever-growing riches, became a defining project for Kuznets and other economists. Why was it happening? What factors made it possible? Would it keep happening? Could it keep happening? Forever? For everyone?

Economists and historians have written entire libraries exploring and explaining this new period of growth. The short version, though, is that it's all about innovation and technology.

In the late 1950s, economist Robert Solow suggested a simple formula: GDP is a product of the labor force and of capital. If you add more workers, you get more output and economic growth. And if you add more capital—more of the machines and tools that increase workers' productivity, like automated assembly lines or factory-powering dams—that also increases GDP. More labor or more capital equals more GDP. Then Solow did some math and showed that increased capital expenditures only explained 12.5 percent of America's economic growth from 1909 to 1949.

Solow's research revealed a delightfully subtle insight about workers and machines: Increasing the labor force or stock of capital can't power forever growth, because each of them face what economists call **diminishing returns**. When China built high-speed rail between Beijing and Shanghai, it made lots of people more productive. The economy grew. But adding lines to medium-size cities had a smaller impact, and adding more lines to smaller cities had an even smaller impact. China's train network, factories, and other capital will eventually be developed enough that—without technological breakthroughs—the country would spend all of its savings just to maintain the existing infrastructure.

The same is true of a larger workforce. Say a country gets larger, whether from immigration or a growing population. Initially companies can hire more workers to pick food faster, unload more cargo at a port, keep a factory open a third shift, and so on. Eventually, though, the factory and port will have all the workers they can put to use. More workers won't produce more than they cost. Yes, from a country's perspective, a growing population and workforce means a larger economy, because there will be more ports, more factories, and more workers producing stuff. But the workers won't be more productive: GDP per capita (or per person) will be the same or not significantly improved, and the average person won't live any better or be any wealthier.

Solow attributed the rest of America's economic growth, that other 87.5 percent, to what he called "technical change," a catchall, later dubbed the Solow residual, for innovation, technological progress, and any idea that makes the economy more productive.

It seems intuitive that innovation leads to progress. The initial transition from zero-ish growth to perpetual growth varied by country, but generally happened around the time of the Industrial Revolution. But Solow described technology and innovation like fairy dust sprinkled over the economy. How do we find or produce more fairy dust? Can we get more of it? Economists debated this for decades.

In the 1990s, a new theory of growth gained popularity among economists. Led by Paul Romer, this group said you *can* make innovation happen. In his model of economic growth, technology and innovation are neither magical nor accidental; they are something countries can build. Just like a country might build a dam to create electricity, it could manufacture innovation by doing things like establishing universities and investing in education.

This insight won Paul Romer the Nobel Prize in 2018. Many Nobel Prizes in Economics go to ideas that seem obvious in hindsight. But Romer was the first to take this hunch about the centrality of innovation and create a working model that showed it in action. His model and theory also made two important points about technology and growth.

The first is that incentives and market forces are key to increasing innovation. If a country crafts and enforces smart patent laws and intellectual property rights, then people and companies will have stronger incentives to invent new products and invest in research and development. If a country promotes market competition and enforces antitrust laws, their economy will have innovative start-ups—rather than a few bloated monopolies hoarding all the resources. If a country signs free-trade deals, it will increase companies' incentives to innovate by giving them access to additional customers and overseas markets.

Romer's second point was that everyone can use new knowledge and technology. Like other public goods, they are "nonrivalrous." If a company adds labor or capital by hiring a new worker or building a new factory, they will produce more stuff. But other companies can't also employ that worker or use that factory. In contrast, new ideas and technology can benefit individuals and companies around the world, at little additional cost. One example: Ever since researchers developed the mRNA (messenger RNA) vaccine technology that allowed the rapid development of COVID-19 vaccines, every drug company has been able to use this understanding of mRNA to treat cancer, HIV, and other diseases. One company using mRNA technology doesn't keep another from using it.

Notably, this is the opposite of the diminishing returns Solow described for capital and labor. New ideas can increase productivity around the world, with people building on one another's innovations, leading to more improvements in productivity that will spread across the entire economy. The Solow residual, the fairy dust that has made the world so much richer since the 1700s, is the sum total of everyone's eureka moments. This is the source of forever growth.

The perpetual growth of the past few centuries is a story of triumph: of more and more people getting indoor plumbing and vaccines and an education, of extreme poverty decreasing, of more and more people having the means to travel across oceans and live to their eightieth birthday.

But even as Kuznets was developing the concept of GDP, he warned against treating it as the sole measure of our economy and society. GDP ignores all kinds of important work—volunteers restacking library books, parents cooking family meals—simply because that labor is hard to measure. GDP ignores whether wealth is widely shared or hoarded by billionaires, and whether that wealth is coming at the cost of 80-hour workweeks or the destruction of the environment.

As Robert F. Kennedy Sr. memorably put it during the 1968 presidential campaign:

> Gross National Product counts air pollution and cigarette advertising, and ambulances to clear our highways of carnage. It counts special locks for our doors and the jails for the people who break them. It counts the destruction of the redwood and the loss of our natural wonder in chaotic sprawl. It counts napalm and counts nuclear warheads and . . . the television programs which glorify violence in order to sell toys to our children. Yet the gross national

product does not allow for the health of our children, the quality of their education or the joy of their play. It does not include the beauty of our poetry or the strength of our marriages. . . . It measures neither our wit nor our courage, neither our wisdom nor our learning. . . . It measures everything in short, except that which makes life worthwhile.

In this first section of the book, we've learned some of the most fundamental ideas economists have for keeping perpetual growth humming: the power of prices; the enabling technology of corporations; market competition; the benefits of comparative advantage and trade.

The rest of this book is a guided tour of additional economic ideas and forces—some of them crucial to perpetual growth, some important to the part of our lives not measured by indicators like GDP, and most of them helpful for navigating your career and money matters but also your free time and love life.

Let's get started.

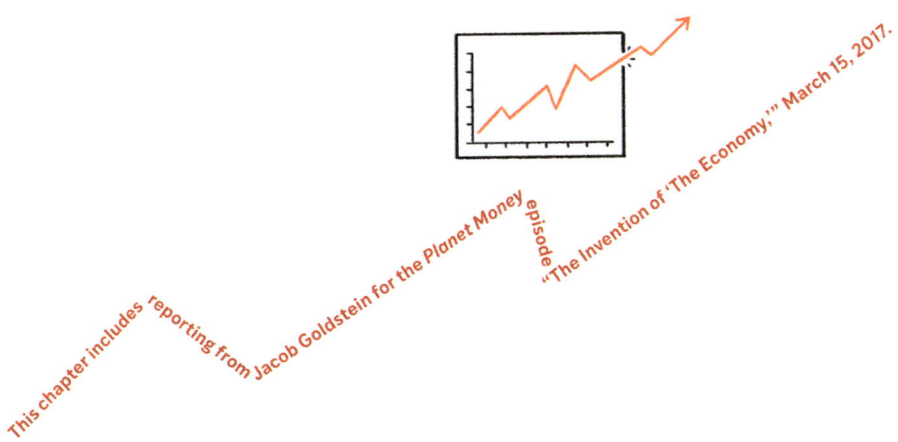

This chapter includes reporting from Jacob Goldstein for the Planet Money episode "The Invention of 'The Economy,'" March 15, 2017.

PART TWO
WORK &

CAREER

6

How Desi Invented TV

Owning a piece of primetime

Like many young scions, Desiderio Alberto Arnaz y de Acha III was born, in 1917, into a life scripted by his family. He attended fine schools, enjoyed the use of a personal boat and car, and was to study law at Notre Dame. His father was mayor of Santiago, the culture and music capital of Cuba. His mother was reputedly one of the 10 most beautiful women in Latin America. And his grandfather was upper management at Bacardi, the rum company.

"The world was my oyster," he told biographers. "What I wanted, I only needed to take."

That all changed in 1933, when military officers, supported by student activists, overthrew the Cuban government. Desiderio, or Desi, was 16 when a mob burned his home. He and his mother fled with $500 and their Chihuahua. They spent that $500 freeing his father, who had been imprisoned for being part of the prior government, and moved to Miami, arriving close to penniless. Arnaz recalls his father killing rats with a baseball bat each night before they went to bed.

Young Arnaz made money by cleaning poop from bird cages, then by driving a banana truck, then by telling a band manager, falsely, that he could play the drums. But Arnaz sang beautifully. After graduating high school, he earned good money playing at clubs. He started his own band, quite possibly introduced the conga line to America, and performed on Broadway, which led him to Hollywood.

That's when Desi Arnaz met a redheaded comedian who could sing, dance, and make audiences swoon just as well as he could: Lucille Ball.

The romance was quick, tempestuous, and catnip for the media. The couple eloped in 1940 and bought a ranch outside Hollywood that they named Desilu (a mashup of "Desi" and "Lucille"). They traveled constantly, Ball for films and Arnaz for his band, but wanted children and a family.

So they hatched a plan to spend more time together—they'd costar in a TV show. You may know the rest: Their show, *I Love Lucy*, was a beloved smash hit. Within a year of its premier, one episode alone had an estimated 30 million viewers. Generations of kids grew up watching reruns.

But that's the boring version of the story. Behind the scenes, the challenge of forming a family and creating entertainment they'd be proud of led Arnaz to create TV itself. Not the technology of lights dancing across our screens, but the way people make money from TV, the very concept of the sitcom and reruns and series like *Mission: Impossible* and *Star Trek*. Television as we know it today exists because of Arnaz and Ball.

Along the way, the couple became wealthy media moguls. Despite their popularity and pioneering approach, such immense financial success was not inevitable. They profited handsomely because they made a bold decision: to leave the world of stable, salaried employment for the up-and-down world of ownership. Even for TV stars, the jump to ownership is the surest path to land a truly rich payout. But the jump is always risky.

"We'll gamble everything"

BEFORE *I LOVE LUCY*, Lucille Ball was the "B Movie Queen." Her breakout role came in a radio comedy called *My Favorite Husband*, which CBS asked her to develop into a TV show. She insisted that Arnaz play her husband.

The executives doubted that Americans wanted an interracial couple on their screens. Would audiences believe that Lucille Ball, the all-American girl, was married to a Cuban immigrant with an accent? They wanted the six-foot, blue-eyed actor from *My Favorite Husband*, who played a banker.

Ball and Arnaz knew better. To prove it, they planned a national vaudeville tour. (Still popular in 1950!) The tour was an incredible risk. They turned down movie roles and lucrative nightclub engagements to train, practice, and hire other performers. But it paid off. In theaters, Arnaz and his band electrified audiences, and the two performed skits that featured bits like Ball doing belly flops and barking like a seal. The star of the show, though, was the couple's chemistry.

In one famous number, Ball takes the stage to sing in front of Arnaz's band, dressed as a showgirl. On the line "chick chicky boom," she swivels her hips and Arnaz's hat falls off. Audiences loved it, and their vaudeville success convinced television executives and network sponsors their TV show would work as well.

Forming Desilu and pitching *their* show was the first of three decisions that changed television history, because they now controlled their destiny to an extent that was rare back then.

Until 1948, Hollywood was defined by "the studio system," in which Paramount, Warner Bros., and a few other major studios dominated moviemaking by both making films and owning the theaters where they played. They also hired movie stars as salaried employees, deciding which films they'd appear in, managing their image (Norma Jeane Dougherty, you're now Marilyn Monroe), and demanding they arrive to work on time, six days a week.

At CBS, then a radio network tiptoeing into TV, Ball and Arnaz were, similarly, part-time employees: Ball in *My Favorite Husband* and Arnaz as the host of a radio quiz show called *Tropical Trip*, which CBS offered him in order to please Ball. (Instead of their original plan: hiring Johnny Carson.) Ball also had a multimovie contract with Columbia Pictures.

In 1948, the Supreme Court broke the studios' iron grip by forcing them to sell their theaters and banning practices they used to block out competitors' films. Two and a half years later, when Ball and Arnaz were finishing their vaudeville tour, actors and directors had started working with multiple studios and getting paid per film, with stars eventually negotiating for a share of a film's profits.

Arnaz and Ball, though, were pioneers. Rather than wait for a call from studios, they pitched their show to multiple studios. Even as they talked with CBS about adapting *My Favorite Husband*, Arnaz courted interest from NBC. He even paid freelancers to write alternative show concepts and scripts so CBS would fear losing them.

While Ball and Arnaz's lives fascinated the public, Arnaz's business savvy went mostly unrecognized, in part because of the prejudice against Hispanic Americans. In a later interview with Barbara Walters, Ball decried the slurs he endured. "They would not believe that . . . he was doing this successful building of a very well-run empire," she said. "I was doing the acting and having the children. . . . I had no part of it. I took that on much later."

Ultimately, the couple made a deal with CBS that would earn them weekly pay and 50 percent of the show's profits and hand them lots of creative control. A sponsor, Philip Morris, would foot most of the show's budget.

CBS wanted a weekly show, which left no time for Ball's film work or Arnaz's bandleading. "We'll gamble everything on this show," Arnaz told Ball's agent. "The answer is yes."

Starring in a television show may not sound like a gamble. But in 1950, TV was so new that a few cities, like Denver, didn't even have stations yet. The Arnazes' friends thought they were nuts. The equivalent today might be leaving Hollywood to star in VR shows.

> Sign of the times: This was the era when smoking on planes and in restaurants was common. But if the Philip Morris name means nothing to you, it's because the cigarette maker became so derided that they changed their name to Altria in 2003 to avoid the negative brand association.

When they gambled on *I Love Lucy*, the couple left one world for another. Previously they'd lived in the world of wage labor. It's where most workers live, defined by set salaries or project fees, and it can be quite comfortable. In *The Millionaire Next Door* (1996), researchers Thomas Stanley and William Danko shared their findings that most American millionaires did not inherit their wealth. They achieved financial independence by living modestly, saving some of each paycheck, and accumulating a nest egg over decades.

With Desilu and *I Love Lucy*, Arnaz and Ball entered the other world: of ownership, or equity, defined by a share of any profits. The profits could be zero. They could rue all the money they'd spent on the vaudeville tour and freelance scripts and all the wages they'd turned down. But if *I Love Lucy* succeeded, their earnings wouldn't be capped at their current salaries. They wouldn't have to beg for bonuses. The financial upside would go straight to them.

This is a fundamental divide in the economy: People who get really rich have equity, not salaries. This is why one dollar is a prestigious corporate salary. It means your compensation is all stock or equity.

A really big deal

ARNAZ AND BALL WERE READY to make *their* show when CBS asked when they were moving to New York. The pair responded that they had no intention of leaving their comfortable California ranch.

The Risk-Reward Spectrum

Imagine you're a hotshot making a six-figure salary at a big, venerable company. One day, a start-up founder starts wooing you. You like her and the company, and she wants to hire you as her second employee. Unlike most start-ups, which can't pay as well, she can match your salary. Should you go?

Maybe not! The start-up could quickly go bankrupt. You're taking a big, uncompensated risk. This is why most founders offer employees partial ownership through shares or stock options. It's like getting little lottery tickets alongside your salary, which pay out if the company succeeds.

This is a truism across the economy: More risk comes with greater (potential) rewards. When investing, lending Microsoft money (by buying a bond) will make you a little money with very little chance that Microsoft won't pay you back. Whereas buying Tesla stock could multiply your money 10 times, but there's a very real chance that Tesla's stock instead drops 50 percent. Like Arnaz and Ball, you've gotta risk it for the biscuit. And keeping this risk-reward trade-off in mind may change how you view risk and failure:

 Risk is not inherently bad. When making decisions, consider both the potential upside and the odds of success. A 10 percent chance of earning $10 million has an **expected value** of $1 million. A long-shot gambit to get your dream job still has high expected utility. Risky decisions can be good ones.

 Failure doesn't mean you made a bad decision. Just as elite poker players regularly lose hands when the other player gets lucky on the last card, anyone pursuing big opportunities will fail regularly. If your bosses reward success with promotions and fire employees for failures—without considering projects' risks and rewards—then they aren't truly pursuing big triumphs.

This caused a firestorm, because TV shows were broadcast and recorded in New York City. They had to be: They were recorded live, with the actors facing a single camera. It was like a little play—there were no close-ups, no retakes, no cuts from one scene to another. To replay shows later in California, studios recorded them with a kinescope, which filmed the camera's video monitor and produced a grainy, low-quality recording that didn't last. Not ideal! But it would be far worse if Desilu recorded in LA and CBS aired kinescope versions for the larger East Coast audience.

This was the second key moment that changed television history: Arnaz's and Ball's solution was to film *I Love Lucy* with three cameras and beautiful 35 mm film just like Hollywood used. They wanted three cameras so they could capture the ad libs and reactions that had worked so well on their vaudeville tour. And by recording on film, rather than broadcasting live and using a kinescope, the show would look great wherever it aired.

But three cameramen and all that rolling film wasn't cheap. CBS said it would double the show's cost and refused to pay. So Arnaz made a deal: Desilu would get paid less, and in exchange he and Ball would own the film.

CBS liked the sound of this. At the time, TV was ephemeral: It aired live, and maybe once more in other time zones. And that was it. Like a radio broadcast of a baseball game, if you missed it, you missed it. Owning the film did not seem like a huge concession.

For his part, Arnaz felt he'd gotten ownership of the show for a bargain. "He came from a family that was wealthy and powerful in Cuba," said NPR television critic Eric Deggans, speculating on Arnaz's desire for ownership. "They come to America and they don't have anything, but what they do have, I think, is a sense that they deserve to run things."

The ramifications of this deal, which, in hindsight, historians consider one of the biggest in the history of show business, weren't apparent

 The safe road is crowded. In the stock market, many investors want risky stocks and trades. But in everyday life, economists have documented that people have status quo bias and heightened risk aversion. We are loath to strike out on our own or move across the country, and we're more motivated by avoiding losses than achieving gains. Which means less competition for high-risk, high-reward opportunities.

until Ball got pregnant. Which led to big decision number three: Arnaz invented reruns and syndication.

With Ball pregnant, the couple wrote the pregnancy into the show. While Ball was giving birth, 70 percent of American televisions tuned into a prerecorded episode of *I Love Lucy* and watched Ball and Arnaz's on-screen counterparts become parents. Arnaz then signed licensing deal after licensing deal, so Americans could outfit their nurseries and homes with *I Love Lucy* merch.

But they couldn't film new episodes. Ball needed time to recover; they both needed time to be parents. They did have those old episodes sitting in a warehouse. Why not air some of them in the meantime? Just like that, the rerun was born.

Arnaz didn't stop there. He also invented syndication. Since they owned the shows, they weren't limited to airing them on CBS. They could sell full seasons of reruns to other TV networks. *I Love Lucy* episodes that used to make money one time, on the night they aired, could now keep airing and making money forever.

This long tail of income from reruns and syndication turned television into a gold mine. Now movie executives were jealous of television. It was the business model invented by Arnaz that drew studios like Disney to make their first TV shows.

By the time the last episode of *I Love Lucy* aired in 1957, Arnaz and Ball had created TV as we know it: the high production values of Hollywood; the profits that paid for star actors, directors, and writers; and the ability to rewatch shows again and again, with their creators profiting from each and every rerun.

After *I Love Lucy*, the unions that represented actors and writers negotiated for their members to receive residuals, a cut of the profits from reruns. (In 2023, these unions went on strike in large part to ensure they'd keep receiving residuals in the streaming era.) Residuals aren't full ownership, but they resemble equity. *The Shawshank Redemption* flopped in theaters, but actors like Bob Gunton, who played the mean prison warden (not a star role), eventually earned six-figure checks from the movie's enduring popularity.

When Arnaz shifted from bandleader to TV star, he exemplified how technology has changed the distribution of salaries and payouts for many

An Equity Stake of One's Own

Many forms of equity are attainable without great power or fame:

 At my local bookstore-café, the barista is the owner. So is the bookseller. And the person setting up open-mic night. The shop, co-owned by its employees, is a cooperative, one among a tiny but growing number of American workplaces. (In fact, the publisher of this book, W. W. Norton, is owned by its employees.)

 In 2005, Sean Parker asked graffiti artist David Choe to cover the offices of Facebook with murals. Choe asked for $60,000. Parker agreed, but offered instead to pay him in Facebook stock options. Choe accepted. When Facebook went public in 2012, his stock options were worth $200 million. You too can work for a start-up! Just remember that zero dollars is a more common outcome than $200 million.

 The gymnast Frederick "Flips" Richard does not own the Olympic Games or the University of Michigan, the institutions that helped him reach millions of fans. But he does "own" his substantial TikTok following, which allowed him to sign brand deals with Crocs and Marriott and to launch a clothing line. Even if you're a full-time employee, you can similarly "own" your relationship with your clients or your audience.

Millions of middle-class people have tiny (but personally meaningful) ownership stakes in Apple, NVIDIA, GM, and Berkshire Hathaway. That's what the stock market is for! And as we'll discuss in chapter 17, investing in these companies has become remarkably easy and low risk over the past few decades. It's the only known exception to the risk-reward trade-off.

 Many sports fans hate their club's owner or worry he'll move the team. Not Green Bay Packers fans! The team is a non-profit owned by more than half a million Packers fans. They don't receive any profits, but they pick a board of directors to pursue the fans' interest. Namely: a championship.

kinds of jobs. As a bandleader, when Arnaz could only play one show a night in one location, he was competing against the other bands in town that night. As a TV star, when he could be everywhere at once, and on repeat, he was competing against everyone who ever made a TV show. The possible payout is substantially more for TV, but so is the competition. Technology has created versions of this across industries, where the reach or impact or scope of work of one person can reach much further. The economist Sherwin Rosen called this the **Superstar Effect**: a small number of dominant singers, executives, and writers becoming incredibly wealthy. Meanwhile the average singers, executives, and writers make far less.

If your goal is work-life balance, you may want to avoid professions dominated by the Superstar Effect in favor of industries where the average worker makes a solid salary!

As *I Love Lucy* finished its run, Arnaz and Ball sold the show back to CBS for $4 million. That's more than $45 million in today's dollars, and it allowed them to buy RKO, the movie studio where Ball had once worked. They made it part of Desilu and became moguls. The shows they produced or filmed include *The Dick Van Dyke Show, The Andy Griffith Show, Gomer Pyle, Mission: Impossible*, and

Star Trek. While Arnaz had always been the dealmaker, Ball later headed the studio and personally green-lit *Star Trek*.

Arnaz's dealmaking created the financial conditions for the couple's creative success to make them fabulously rich. But it also gave them more say over their work. Before *I Love Lucy*, executives wanted Arnaz on-screen, but only to do what Americans expected Cubans to do: sing, dance, and play Latin music. They wanted Ball to star in a show about a typical, happy American couple. She and Arnaz power-played that into a show about an interracial couple! They became superstars.

This chapter includes reporting from Sonari Glinton and Robert Smith for the Planet Money episode "How Desi Invented Television," January 22, 2021.

The Zoom Boom vs. Happy Hour

Should my company let me work from home?

In 1994, Paul Spencer got a call from Chiat\Day. He was a young copywriter, and Chiat\Day was one of the hottest ad agencies in New York. They'd developed the Energizer Bunny into a memorable character; they had made Apple's iconic 1984 Super Bowl ad. And everyone was talking about their new office. Because Jay Chiat, the agency's legendary founder, had liberated everyone from their cubicles.

When Spencer arrived, the office was orange, taupe, and full of drawings and designs. No one showed him to his desk. He didn't have a desk. At reception, he checked out a laptop and cell phone for the day, which felt like being handed a .38 revolver in a police drama.

"I remember thinking, 'Wow, this is great. This is so beautiful,'" says Spencer. "It was like, wow, I'm going into creative battle."

Spencer said this to his new partner, an art director named Mike. In response, Mike rolled his eyes.

Jay Chiat had redesigned the agency's space after having a revelation: Workers spent too much time focused on internal politics and dreaming of a corner office. He would get rid of those corner offices—and of all the private spaces employees decorated with family photos. Like on a college campus, staff would float around an open area of collaboration and creativity. There would be no turf to battle over, nothing to distract from the work of selling more Taco Bell burritos and Apple computers.

Armed with his company-issued laptop, Paul Spencer got to work. Or tried to. By the afternoon, he couldn't focus. "The place is kind of scorching my brain," he says. He had to speak loudly to be heard over other conversations, and the orange walls felt like a migraine.

Spencer wasn't alone. Turf battles broke out as staff claimed conference rooms for quiet and privacy. Some staff went home to actually get work done.

"That was just a failure," says Spencer. "A noble experiment that failed." He went on to do his most successful work—coming up with the New York Lottery slogan "Hey, you never know"—at an ad agency where he had a private office with a couch. As open offices like Chiat\Day's became increasingly popular, he was relieved that going freelance allowed him to regularly work from home.

For decades, this was *the* office debate: Should offices be open, so coworkers can mingle, chat, and come up with the next big idea during serendipitous encounters? Or do people get more done with their own spaces, insulated from distracting noise? Is there some Goldilocks mix of the two that's best for everyone?

Then the pandemic struck, and millions of office types *had* to work from home. A new debate arose: Do we even need offices? Like Spencer and the Chiat\Day employees, many people found they were more productive at home; others missed the noise and socialization. Some people loved not having to commute; others missed the routine. Some managers worried their reports were slacking off. Others saw their teams making huge gains. In subsequent years, many executives ordered employees back to the office. By 2024, more than half of the pandemic-era's WFH days had reverted to standard office hours. But was this return to the office based on data and evidence? What have we learned from this enormous, accidental experiment in remote work?

What is an office for, anyway?

FOR MANY CENTURIES, most offices were appendages to the business they supported: often small, cramped spaces behind the shop, next to the factory, or by the port. In the 1800s, as telegrams, trains, and telephones became commonplace and as businesses grew in size and scale, companies needed more white-collar workers to coordinate everything. Offices no longer played a supporting role; they were the main event. They separated from factories and moved downtown. By the 1950s, the skyscrapers of Manhattan and Chicago were gleaming symbols of American enterprise.

From their Manhattan offices, oilmen worked all day without physically handling any kerosene or crude. Executives and middle managers of railways, department stores, and more similarly had less contact with daily operations. But even as offices distanced themselves from their respective stores, plants, and rail lines, they clustered into a kind of economic geography: tech firms in Silicon Valley, ad agencies on Manhattan's Madison Avenue, the movie industry in Hollywood. This is known as **agglomeration**.

Agglomeration makes it easier for companies to access industry-specific resources, such as the venture capital firms on Sand Hill Road that fund Silicon Valley start-ups, and to source talented workers, like New York City's legendary bagel rollers. Agglomeration also enables the exchange of information and ideas: Just as many early Impressionist painters developed their techniques in Montmartre's cafés and studios, start-up founders and ad executives network and swap tips at Bay Area meetups and Manhattan bars.

In the 2000s, videoconferencing, cloud computing, file-sharing software, and other tools made remote work increasingly accessible and challenged the logic of agglomeration. Economist Prithwiraj Choudhury, who has studied migration, wondered whether remote workers might now move back to struggling small towns that had for decades been losing talented people to cities. So when the U.S. Patent and Trademark Office (USPTO) rolled out a remote option in 2012, he teamed up with them to study the results.

The USPTO employs thousands of patent examiners who decide which new inventions deserve the legal protection of a patent. The job requires legal knowledge and, often, familiarity with topics ranging from pharmaceuticals to search algorithms. Since the USPTO introduced the remote program in phases, it allowed Choudhury to compare and contrast the experiences of the remote and in-person examiners.

Although his interest was in small cities and reverse brain drain, Choudhury soon found himself excited about remote work based on the benefits he observed:

- **Lifestyle:** The remote patent examiners replaced commuting time with leisure time, and they bought affordable homes in small towns. (Or moved closer to family.)

- **Employee retention:** Some staff told Choudhury the remote option motivated them to stay longer with the patent office.

- **Lower costs:** The USPTO did not reduce examiners' salaries if they moved to cheaper areas. But downsizing their offices saved the USPTO tens of millions of dollars per year.

- **Recruiting:** For remote organizations, the talent pool is not one city, or several, but the entire world. One USPTO executive gushed that they could now recruit in Eastern Europe, which has many skilled data scientists.

- **Productivity:** By looking at the number of patents reviewed each month, Choudhury and his fellow researchers found that productivity increased 4.4 percent. The examiners may have been motivated by a desire to keep their remote jobs; they may have been more focused away from office distractions. Maybe both!

In the 2010s, organizations ranging from AT&T to DreamWorks to software start-ups reported that they had employees working remotely for chunks of time. But despite the positive results that Choudhury documented, rates of remote work crept up only modestly: from 3.4 percent of all American workdays in 2005 to 7.2 percent just before the pandemic.

Why didn't more companies ditch the office? Economist Nicholas Bloom and others studied a Chinese travel agency that experimented with call-center employees working from home. The study spanned two years, from 2010 to 2012, and they noted that both workers and managers were initially uncertain about WFH. But like the USPTO, the company had positive results. Management decided to offer a permanent remote option, which many once-hesitant workers chose.

Bloom pointed to this uncertainty, along with a WFH stigma (it still seemed strange, and people joked about "shirking from home"), as key reasons that offices and agglomeration remained more popular than remote work. Plus, no one was certain whether WFH would work for executive teams and collaborative projects—unlike the discrete and solitary tasks of examining patents and fielding customer-service calls.

The office as a nursery

IN THE YEARS AFTER THE PANDEMIC, surveys conducted worldwide found that a majority of workers were pleasantly surprised by their WFH productivity. Even after a majority of Americans got vaccinated, some 35 percent of American workdays were still at home, and companies like Twitter and Amazon told workers that WFH was the new normal. One study of responses to Brazilian job postings found that workers valued remote work as much as a 15 percent bump in salary.

And then the share of WFH days began to fall, and the vibes shifted. Elon Musk bought Twitter, put beds in the office, and told workers who didn't want to come to the office to quit. Real estate firms, looking with panic at an enormous inventory of unused office space, also required in-office days. So did Wall Street firms. So many CEOs sent "return to office" memos and emails that RTO became a shorthand. RTO memos came even from companies like Meta that had previously embraced remote work.

Musk's RTO mandate suggests a not-so-secret motivation behind some mandates: Getting people to quit so the company didn't have to fire workers and pay them severance, and monitoring the remaining workers so they couldn't shirk.

But many RTO memos pointed to a consequence of WFH that manifested more slowly than its commute-slashing, focus-enhancing benefits: less training of new hires and learning from colleagues.

"The young generation is being damaged," JPMorgan's CEO said in leaked audio from a town hall meeting with members of the bank's staff. "They're being left behind."

Were the CEOs right? In late 2023, economists Natalia Emanuel, Emma Harrington, and Amanda Pallais investigated by studying an unnamed Fortune 500 company, specifically the productivity metrics and online interactions between software engineers who shared an office with teams who worked in different offices.

They found that the physically distant engineers, especially experienced ones, got more coding done. Fewer distractions for the win! But some of those distractions were questions from junior coworkers. The economists found that physically separate teams gave and received less feedback, even in written form. The short-term focus and productivity bump of remote work came at the cost of long-term learning.

This trade-off even showed up in pay raises: Young programmers who sat near coworkers initially got fewer raises, but they received bigger raises in the long run thanks to the human capital they developed in the office.

"Mentorship of junior engineers is not free," the economists write. And it's not equally shared. Among senior engineers, they found that women more often suffered interruptions in order to give feedback to younger programmers. The data showed gender expectations at work: women often being expected to, or more often choosing to, take on supportive, mentoring roles.

What the economists had documented was the **opportunity cost** of remote work. When you're choosing between different options, the oppor-

What's the Opportunity Cost?

Opportunity costs rear their heads in just about any either-or decision. If you practice spotting them, your decision-making gets a bit more rational, choice by choice. Some classics:

OPPORTUNITY	COST
Use your savings to pay off your mortgage early, so you save the 5 percent interest on the loan.	You can't invest that money in stocks that might earn a higher return than 5 percent.
Going to college.	Tuition and four years of lost income and potential promotions.
Agree to a project now, bird in the hand.	You're not available when a more lucrative one comes along next month.
Buying in bulk means you likely save money per unit.	You're tying up funds you could use for something else in the meantime and dealing with storing the big boxes.
Stay in your rocky relationship to see if the time you've invested pays off.	You are losing time you could spend finding a better match.

There's no easy guide to deciding between options, but you'll make a more rational decision if you accurately identify the costs of the road not taken.

tunity cost is what you could have gained from choosing differently. Like if you're deciding whether to attend college or get a graduate degree, there's the sticker price: the cost of tuition. But there is also an opportunity cost: what you could do with the money and time that you will spend earning the degree. Going to school means you might miss out on multiple years of income, training, and development at your current job. If you include the opportunity costs in your calculation, it might change your decision.

Compared to the upsides of remote work for workers and companies, such as avoiding commutes, living anywhere, and recruiting everywhere, costs like adapting to virtual meetings and setting up home offices may seem small. But if the opportunity cost is not learning the job as efficiently, not building professional networks, and not developing new skills, then remote work no longer looks quite as wise.

Many workers seem to have grasped this trade-off themselves: After lockdowns, younger and older workers, the mentees and mentors, returned to workplaces at higher rates than thirtysomethings (regardless of whether they had children). But many office workers also had the experience of shifting everything online due to just one remote coworker: Zoom meetings instead of conference rooms, Slack chats instead of deskside huddles. The study documented this too. Teams with a single coworker in the blocks-away building gave and received less feedback, which suggests that the office's learning benefits suffer from the slightest intrusion of remote work.

This, then, is what the office is for in the era of videoconferences and collaborating in the cloud: It's a nursery for developing employees, the place where learning happens through casual conversations and frustrating but essential interruptions to a person's productivity.

The office as an idea factory

WHILE MANY CEOS FRETTED about training in RTO memos, others pointed to another motivation for ending WFH: creativity and innovation.

"Collaborating and inventing is easier and more effective when we're in person," Amazon CEO Andy Jassy wrote in a 2023 all-staff memo. "Some of the best inventions have had their breakthrough moments from people staying behind in a meeting... or just popping by a teammate's office later that day."

Do eureka moments happen in person, not over Zoom? Once again, economists have some suggestive findings.

In the BC era (Before Coronavirus), Mike Andrews was an economics PhD hanging out in Joe's Place, the go-to bar for University of Iowa students. He was interested in the question of what makes people, places, and companies creative and innovative. Because, as we saw in chapter 5, countries rely on a never-ending stream of new technologies and productivity-boosting ideas to power their forever growth.

Over an ale, Andrews's buddy suggested he investigate whether people came up with more ideas at bars. This got Andrews thinking. A central premise of agglomeration is that proximity is crucial for creativity. If no idea is truly original, if all inventions build on other insights, then what you need is lots of people bumping into each other, chatting, and swapping ideas. Perhaps over a pint.

"If you press economists on why it matters that everyone's in the same city or within a few blocks, they'll say something like, 'People get together and talk at the bar,'" says Andrews. "But I don't think direct evidence of that had existed before."

Inspired by his bar talk, Andrews turned, coincidentally, to the U.S. Patent Office, which offers some of the only hard numbers to gauge innovation. If the office grants more patents, that's a sign of more invention and creativity. Andrews decided to look at what happened during Prohibition.

Not during national Prohibition though. In the decade prior, from 1909 to 1919, temperance activists had succeeded in passing prohibition at the local level, often by narrow margins. This shuttered busy bars and taverns overnight, even as neighboring towns and counties imbibed as normal. For Andrews, this was the holy grail of social science research: a natural experiment with control groups. He compared the number of patents granted before and after local prohibitions. When bars closed, did that show up in the patent data?

What he found was "pretty striking," says Andrews. Depending on how you measure, the closing of bars in 1920s America led to a roughly 15 percent reduction in granted patents. Which is on par with the drop of patents during the Great Depression.

Maybe tipsiness is the key to creativity. But Andrews believes the cause was the lack of conversation, not cocktails. He notes that patents barely dropped among women, who were less welcome at bars and taverns back then. And in a similar study, he found that Starbucks' expansion out of Seattle in the 1980s and '90s led to similar patent bumps—likely by providing Americans with a new venue for serendipitous conversation.

It's harder to study the impact of working together in an office—of adding a water cooler or, as Steve Jobs did at Pixar in 1986, putting the bathrooms in the heavily trafficked central atrium. Still, Andrews says, "If bumping into people and talking matters outside the office, then I think it makes sense that it probably matters inside the office too."

This suggests another opportunity cost of remote work: less creativity and fewer new ideas.

The creativity-versus-productivity trade-off, though, is more speculative. Innovation takes time to appear in economic data, and individual workers' and companies' creativity is hard to measure. If a group of remote-working producers and executives don't meet up in a bar and therefore don't come up with the idea for the next *Shark Week*, how does Andrews measure *that*?

It's entirely possible, too, that remote work can enable creativity and serendipity. In his Prohibition research, Andrews found that patent rates recovered within a few years, well before national Prohibition ended. "My guess is that a lot of the informal communication shifted to places like the church picnic, the public park, the barber shop, or the bowling alley," he says. Maybe we just need time to adapt to hanging out in virtual spaces.

The Goldilocks option

WHAT'S THE BEST WAY TO WORK? Should my boss let me work from home? There is not one right answer, and the cost-benefit calculation is annoyingly complicated. It depends on the nature of your work, where you are in your career, whether you're prioritizing the well-being of workers or success of a company.

The stakes are high for everyone. Remote work done right can help new parents stay in the job market and small cities to revitalize. Remote work done wrong can hurt young workers' career prospects and stifle the innovation and creativity that keeps the economy growing.

Since early 2023, rates of remote work within the United States have stabilized at approximately 28 percent of all workdays. (During the same

REMOTE WORK UNIVERSE CHARACTER SHEET

In this world of Zoom calls and asynchronous work, different kinds of workers receive bonuses and penalties that propel or impair their careers and personal lives.

THE C.E.O.

- +4 Access to global talent pool
- -2 Potential hit to innovation (double if in creative industry)
- -1 No corner office

THE NEW PARENT

- +2 Can launder lots of tiny clothes between meetings
- +4 Flexibility to do daycare pickup at 4pm
- -1 Don't stay hip by talking to young employees at happy hours

THE NEW GRAD

- -5 Fewer mentors and networking opportunities
- +3 Access to more companies without paying big-city rent
- -3 Constant fear of roommates blasting Taylor Swift during team meetings

WORKER WITH A DISABILITY

- +5 More job opportunities
- +3 Greater schedule flexibility
- +3 Can customize own workspace
- -2 Remote work tool still not that accessible

INDIVIDUAL CONTRIBUTOR

- +4 Fewer distractions
- +2 No commute
- -3 Fewer eureka moments

THE MIDDLE MANAGER

- -2 Has to learn to measure worker productivity in new ways
- -3 Workers less likely to feel team spirit without strong leadership
- +1 Can text about dinner plans during virtual all-staff meetings

period in Germany, 23.5 percent worked from home; in Canada, 20.1 percent.) Given these trade-offs, it's perhaps not surprising that fully remote companies remain uncommon. Instead, our big WFH experiment yielded the rise of hybrid work: A study in *Nature* showed that hybrid workers are just as productive as those who are in office full time, and they resign less frequently. "This study offers powerful evidence for why 80 percent of U.S. companies now offer some form of remote work and for why the remaining 20 percent of firms that don't are likely paying a price," said lead researcher Nicholas Bloom.

It's a modest change given the pandemic's scope and scale. But done well, hybrid is the Goldilocks option: Enough in-person time to train junior workers, exchange valuable information, and spark new ideas; enough time away from office distractions to focus. Plus a sprinkling of flexibility and commute-free days that help parents do child-care drop-offs and give everyone a bit more control over their lives.

This entire chapter, though, has been focused within companies. With less fanfare and debate, remote work has accelerated a long-gestating change: the waning of full-time employment and the rise of the gig economy. After all, if a job can be done fully remote, do you need to hire a full-time employee to do it?

This chapter includes reporting from Stacey Vanek Smith for the Planet Money episode "Open Office," August 8, 2018.

A Tale of Two Gig Workers

The pros and cons of being your own boss

In 2004, Gustavo Ajché said goodbye to his wife and two children in Guatemala to find work in the United States. Aided by a coyote, someone who smuggles migrants across the border, he endured 24 hours crammed in a van and three days and nights in a desert. He meant to stay with family in Chicago, but when they couldn't take him in, he flew to New York City to stay with a cousin.

"It was a dream come true," says Ajché. The seas of yellow cabs looked just like the movies.

One night, his cousin, who worked at a pizza parlor, said, "You're going to start work tomorrow." He had gotten Ajché a job delivering pizza.

For his first delivery, Ajché handed his pizzas to some boys on the corner. He realized the boys had tricked him when he biked back and his manager asked why he never made the delivery.

After six months, the owner sold the pizzeria. Ajché found work in construction, and when delivery apps like DoorDash and UberEats arrived in New York, he signed up. The money was good; the flexibility was great. He could make deliveries whenever his construction shifts ended.

Within a few years, so many customers ordered delivery through the apps that restaurants stopped hiring delivery workers. Emboldened by their market power, the apps "started to oppress the workers," says Ajché. New requirements pressured him to work faster, and Ajché and other workers say they increasingly received payments late or never got tips. "They said we were our own boss, but that wasn't the reality... They could track your location at any moment when you were using the app."

This is the well-known story of gig work: New tech companies hiring workers to deliver takeout, drive Ubers, and assemble IKEA furniture, not as employees, but as self-employed freelancers paid per delivery, ride, or screwed-together bed frame. The promise is freedom and flexibility; the reality can be precarious work without the protections of labor laws.

But gig work is more than DoorDash and Taskrabbit; it's an economy-wide shift. Established companies increasingly hire contractors and freelancers rather than employees, including for roles like marketer and "fractional" chief financial officer. New tools and technologies, along with our mass experiment with remote work, have enabled this transition. One study estimated that 36 percent of Americans were independent workers in 2024, up from 27 percent in 2016.

Forty-hour workweeks, full-time employment, companies: We treat them like the electrons, atoms, and molecules of the economy. But if current trends hold, they may not be the building blocks of the economy for much longer.

Through the story of two gig workers, Gustavo Ajché and software engineer Preethi Vaidyanathan, we'll see how this change is impacting different kinds of work and workers. And the ways Ajché and Vaidyanathan navigated this new work environment has a lesson for all of us: Be prepared to take more responsibility for managing your career.

The hire vs. fire calculation

REMEMBER THE PICKLE PROBLEM FROM CHAPTER 1? How it was more efficient to use prices, rather than central planning, to determine which food banks should get the latest donation of peanut butter?

In a landmark economics paper called "The Nature of the Firm," written in 1937, Ronald Coase pointed out that every company is similarly inefficient. Why do railroad and oil companies hire employees and create big, Soviet-style bureaucracies and workforces? Why not pay a monthly fee to Train Conductors LLC, or pay Pipeline Builders, Inc., to build your oil pipelines?

Coase's answer was that it would be a huge pain. It's costly and time-consuming to find people, negotiate contracts, and specify every little thing you'll need done. It's also hard to find companies to do bespoke tasks, like build 300 miles of pipeline, much less determine the right price for that work. In other words, the **transaction costs** are high.

At some point, the transaction costs of all those contracts and market-based solutions will outweigh the inefficiencies of bureaucracies. Better just to hire employees who will do whatever needs doing that day! Plus, while hired guns mostly focus on their fee, employees are members of an organization. This sense of belonging often endows them with feelings of psychological ownership; they are more invested in the company's success.

When Coase was writing, telegraphs and telephones had made communication easier and lowered the costs of managing big workforces. The inefficiencies of bureaucracy went down. During his life, he saw the growth of giant conglomerates like Sinclair Oil, General Electric, and the London, Midland and Scottish Railway.

Per Coase's **Theory of the Firm**, if a company hires you as a full-time employee, they are estimating that doing so is less inefficient than hiring a contractor. But if the transaction costs or efficiencies change, the company may switch to preferring a contractor.

Over the last four decades, new technology has had this precise effect: It's increased the ease and efficiency of hiring contractors rather than employees. Now that companies can constantly monitor a delivery truck's location, call the driver anytime, and choose the route, the driver doesn't have to be a trusted, full-time employee. Now that companies' finances and data are sitting in cloud-based spreadsheets, it's easier to contract with an outside accountant or data analyst.

In today's job market, contracting doesn't always mean hiring a gig worker. It often means outsourcing the work to another company. Train Conductors LLC is made up, but real examples abound. If you walk into a Marriott hotel, the housekeeping and front-desk staff may have been hired through a contractor like Crestline Hotels & Resorts, which partners with hotel chains. The cooks may have been hired through Danny Meyer's Union Square Hospitality Group (even if they're wearing Marriott name tags). The logic is similar for white-collar work: Companies have long outsourced public relations and legal advice to smaller firms because specialty work is often more efficient to pay for sporadically, as needed. Now agencies and freelance platforms exist to outsource just about any project, from analyzing a real estate deal to refreshing your brand and logo.

When companies switch from employees to gig or contract work for food delivery and other physical labor, it's not like a factory moving overseas. The work generally stays in the same city, or even the same hotel or workplace. So what changes when work moves outside the inner sanctum of the corporation?

Gig worker no. 1: Gustavo Ajché

WHEN AJCHÉ WAS NEW TO NEW YORK, he learned about a center that helped immigrants find jobs. It also offered workshops on labor rights. He enjoyed attending and meeting people. "A lot of people here have this concept of, 'Hey, you're an immigrant, you're Latino, you don't have many rights here,'" says Ajché. "But that's not true."

The instructors stressed speaking up and acting collectively. At construction sites, when Ajché asked for water or a break, he saw that it was more effective to get four workers to make the request together. It was a small lesson in collective action.

He found himself thinking of those workshops as the delivery apps got more demanding. During a snowstorm in 2020, his bike slid on black ice. He says he called the app to report the accident, and their first question was about the condition of the food. Could he still make the delivery?

Federal labor law requires companies to cover medical bills for on-the-job injuries and to keep paying hurt workers. But those laws were largely developed during the New Deal, designed for a world where big companies and full-time employment were the norm. So generally it is only full-time employees who are entitled to benefits and protections like health insurance or workers' compensation if injured on the job.

But Ajché didn't work for the restaurant, which contracted with the app company for delivery. He didn't work for the app company, which contracted with him for individual gigs. He worked for himself, a business of one. "I saw that a lot of people got into accidents, a lot of people died. [I had] friends who couldn't work for months because of serious accidents in the streets," he says. "And the apps didn't do anything about it, and didn't say anything about it."

His status as a gig worker hurt him in another way—it eroded the sense of fairness that in prior generations had bolstered low-wage workers' salaries. A worker's salary is the result of supply and demand in the labor market, which determines their bargaining power. If lots of people are willing and able to work as janitors (high supply), then companies can offer them a lower salary. In contrast, the pool of experienced, highly skilled engineers is smaller, and their work produces more value to the company, resulting in higher salaries.

But we are social creatures. Data going back to the 1960s shows that workers at large profitable companies, including blue-collar and "unskilled" workers like janitors, earned higher wages than comparable workers at smaller companies. Executives still made much more. But a broader sense of fairness within a firm ensured that the success of Ford and GE benefited its secretaries and janitors. Henry Ford paid his assembly-line workers so well that he got sued for not maximizing shareholder value!

The Slow Fade-out of Worker Power

The productivity of the average American worker has increased steadily for decades. But since the 1970s, rising productivity has stopped translating into healthy raises for workers.

Why? Economists have suggested a range of potential explanations, from technology and automation, to globalization (i.e., foreign competition and factories moving overseas) to lawmakers not increasing the minimum wage.

Another major reason? The decline of unions, which have long been workers' key tool for gaining bargaining power and claiming a fair share of profits. In the 1950s, at the peak of union membership, 33 percent of workers were organized. By 2024, just under 10 percent of American workers were represented by collective bargaining. The U.S. Department of the Treasury notes that, historically, the pay of union workers is 20 percent higher than that of nonunion workers.

During this period, many states passed right-to-work laws, first introduced in the late 1940s, which undercut unions' ability to organize. But the decline of unions is also a story of gig work and companies "shedding" jobs. It's much harder for hotel staff to unionize and negotiate when the cooks work for a catering contractor, the janitors work for a cleaning company, and bellhops work for a hospitality group. It's difficult for gig workers to collectively bargain, since they're technically not employees.

In a book on shedding, author David Weil summed it up: "Shifting work outward allows redistribution of gains upward."

But companies rarely extend this sense of fairness to gig workers or outside employees. In early 2020, Uber was valued at more than $50 billion, and its programmers and product managers made high six-figure salaries. But Ajché did not earn more as Uber's share price and revenues grew.

Companies often explicitly cite cost reduction as a justification for shifting to contractors. Just after the pandemic, Marriott laid off more than 800 staffers, mostly in food and beverage, and put out a bid for restaurant contracts worth $50 million. Amazon and Microsoft each laid

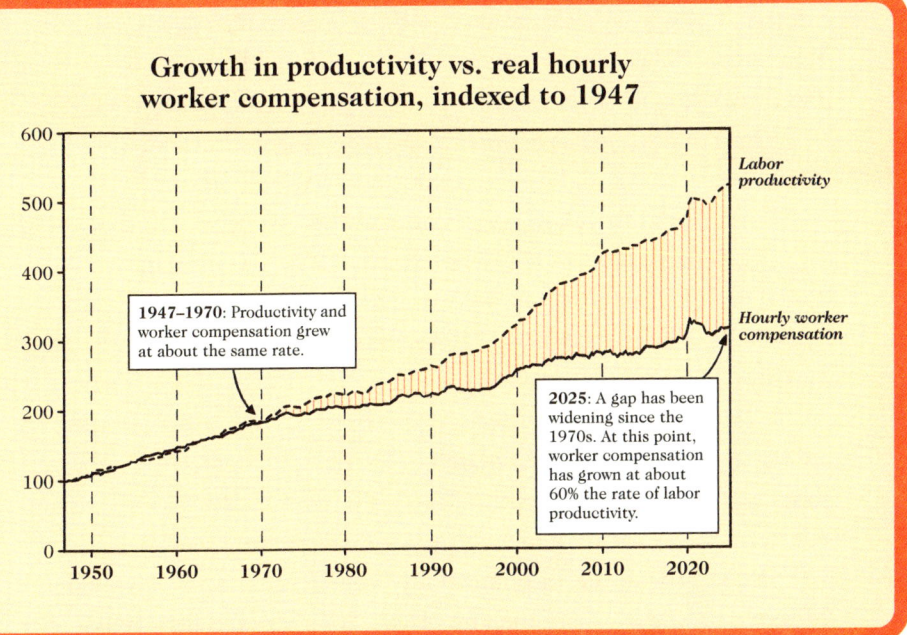

off workers, then offered to hire some back as contractors, all via third parties, with lower pay, no benefits, and fixed end dates. Various studies find that contractors doing jobs comparable to those of full-time employees make 4 to 24 percent less money, with less likelihood of receiving benefits like health insurance.

At the center's labor workshops, Ajché learned about another key tool for blue-collar workers: unions. For workers who lack coveted skills and experience, **collective bargaining**, backed by the threat of strikes, can empower them to demand better wages and safer workplaces. The organization "always told us . . . someone needs to speak up for the group . . . so that they don't exploit us," says Ajché.

Would this work in the gig economy? Delivery workers are an ever-changing group of contractors summoned into existence by apps. Ajché couldn't shut down the factory floor—everyone worked for multiple apps and thousands of scattered restaurants.

But Ajché was friends with a meaningful share of UberEats and DoorDash delivery workers. They met at centers like Worker's Justice Project, where he took those labor-activism classes, and while chatting during pickups. They formed WhatsApp groups and ate ramen together. "We connected as a group," Ajché says, and the apps seemed to notice if they didn't work. When a big group took an afternoon off to play soccer, their phones would ping with messages enticing them to make deliveries.

"Once that started to happen, that's when I saw that there was a huge labor force... you could see the community was really strong."

At Worker's Justice Project, Ajché explained his belief that they could organize delivery workers. He learned about a similar movement in California and the center's effort to organize New York's domestic cleaners. In 2020, he helped found Los Deliveristas Unidos to represent the city's roughly 65,000 food-app delivery workers.

A key tactic for Los Deliveristas was to get the attention of press and politicians. During their first march in October 2020, they told reporters about not having access to bathrooms, restaurants insisting they wait outside in freezing weather, and making below minimum wage.

"We went to speak to political representatives... and we would say, 'Hey, we need this, that, and the other.' Sometimes, a little while later the organization would tell us, 'Hey, we got their support,'" says Ajché. A U.S. senator even biked alongside Los Deliveristas in 2021.

Ajché believes being viewed as "essential workers" during the pandemic boosted their profile and persuasiveness; they were in the news almost every week. He also cites the importance of having facts and figures to give reporters and lawmakers. It was a "drastic change" when Los Deliveristas Unidos produced a report with Cornell University, "Essential but Unprotected: App-Based Food Couriers in New York City." In 2021, the City Council passed laws mandating a minimum wage for workers like Ajché, along with access to bathrooms and other protections.

It was a different playbook than the standard strategy of striking (or using the threat of a strike) to negotiate a better contract with one's employer. Los Deliveristas' success looked more like the strategy used by California fast-food workers who got the state government to mandate the creation of a fast-food council. Its representatives (some workers and some executives) now negotiate wages for line cooks and cashiers across California.

This strategy—of negotiating for better wages and treatment for the workers of an entire industry, rather than a single company—has a name: **sectoral bargaining**. And it has a long pedigree: In France, for example, which has a similar rate of union membership as the United States (approximately 10 percent), 95 to 98 percent of French workers in 2016 were covered by collective bargaining, with sectoral-bargaining agreements providing most of that coverage.

This approach addresses two collective-action problems. One: Many workers are scattered among so many disparate workplaces (or as gig workers) that it's hard to band together. Two: No one company wants to take the step of raising wages alone. If they do, they may have to raise prices, losing business to competitors. But if they all do it together, it works.

Still, the delivery apps fought the new laws. Ajché recalls receiving messages from the apps that said the laws would be disastrous for workers, and DoorDash, Grubhub, and Uber sued to prevent the most important change: a minimum wage of almost twenty dollars an hour.

"We went to court, and we saw that those people had an army of lawyers, and we only had one attorney from the city. And I thought, 'Okay, those people have already won,'" says Ajché. But the city beat the apps' legal challenge and then an appeal. Ajché was home when the attorney called to tell him the new laws would go forward. "They are moments that I'll never forget," he says. "If you don't stop speaking out and you are consistent, you can succeed."

Being a Netflix engineer won't save you

ONCE UPON A TIME, Netflix was a company that mailed people DVDs. Then, in 2007, after lots of hard work, it launched a streaming service. People loved it. Streaming grew so big so fast that Netflix couldn't build data centers fast enough to keep up with demand.

Their engineers, who had built the streaming service, said they could solve the problem by building cloud-computing infrastructure, which would help Netflix flexibly respond to surges like the entire East Coast firing up the final episode of *House of Cards* at 8:00 p.m. But building cloud computing from scratch would take time. If Netflix instead paid Amazon or Google to use their cloud computing, then Netflix wouldn't have to develop a cloud or keep building and running so many data centers. It could solve its biggest problem for a monthly fee. So that's what Netflix did. The company's engineers soon had less work to do. Many went looking for new jobs before the inevitable layoffs arrived.

In MBA-speak, Netflix chose to focus on its **core competencies**. Netflix was not especially good at building data centers, whereas Amazon and Google already had big businesses that specialized in data centers and cloud computing. By contracting Amazon to manage all that, Netflix could focus on fine-tuning its recommendation algorithm and developing new seasons of *House of Cards* and *Orange Is the New Black*.

The gospel of core competencies has been preached to budding executives since the 1990s, and if you're wondering whether your job or team will be replaced by freelancers or an outside contract, your best bet is to ask whether your role is in the company's core competency.

As Netflix shows, the answer is not always obvious. Netflix was a technology start-up, and yet many engineers were replaced by a contract with Amazon since they didn't work on core competencies like creating and acquiring content that fit their users' interests and making superior TV and movie recommendations. Marriott is a hotel company, but it often outsources work like cleaning rooms and cooking French toast in order to focus on core competencies like marketing their brands and running customer-loyalty programs.

Hiring contractors instead of employees sounds a bit sinister. Sometimes it is. But not always.

Gig Worker no. 2: Preethi Vaidyanathan

WHEN PREETHI VAIDYANATHAN GRADUATED from MIT in 2015, she had no concept of freelancing. The options were grad school or a full-time job. She had watched the film *Armageddon* at a formative age, and she'd interned at NASA's Jet Propulsion Lab, whose campus was home to marvels like a simulated Martian landscape for the Curiosity rover. So she applied to SpaceX, drank the first coffee of her life during her big day of in-person interviews ("a really bad idea"), and got a job with a team that trained mission control.

"I've done it. I figured it out. My life is complete," Vaidyanathan recalls thinking. "I'm gonna work here until I retire." That's how her parents' careers had gone.

Instead, she changed jobs once, then again. In 2021, Preethi was burned out from a demanding start-up job. Eager for a break, she recalled a time when she'd hired a contractor. It seemed "like an interesting way . . . to set your own schedule," she says. She quit the start-up and found contract work as a software engineer.

Like Ajché's delivery jobs, her contract gig was enabled by remote-work tools like Zoom, the GitHub profile that demonstrated her coding prowess, and other technologies that lowered the costs for companies of finding and contracting talented engineers.

Unlike Los Deliveristas, though, who were treated as interchangeable by the delivery apps, the cost for the start-up of not hiring *her* specifically was high. She had specific skills that the company needed right away, and waiting to find another equally qualified worker was costly. The start-up was getting more traffic to their website and usage of their software than expected, she says, so needed help managing the load and the servers. She'd done exactly that at her previous start-up job. As a result, she received great compensation and fair treatment—and had the leverage to demand both.

"I would've thought I would get treated like, 'Oh, I'm a second-class citizen,'" she says. "But it really felt like the opposite." Employers, she noticed, whispered sweet nothings while recruiting you: Friday happy hours, 401(k) match. But once you were bound to them, their incentive was to wring work out of you and your fixed salary, appealing to team loyalty to sugarcoat asking for extra work. But Vaidyanathan now got paid by the hour, and both sides knew the other could walk away. "It was more like, 'Hey, we're so sorry to have to do this, but would you mind sticking around for an extra hour?'" And then she got paid for that extra hour!

"It was great," she says. "I couldn't have asked for anything better."

On weekends, she started coding a video game. She wanted more time to focus on that, so she reduced her contracting work to four days a week. The company agreed to it, and with that extra day, she finished and released *Gourdlets*, a game whose goal is to build villages for adorable vegetable people. Having the time to work on the game, Vaidyanathan says, "was totally life-changing."

Vaidyanathan's dreamy new situation came with two new challenges. One was finding the next gig each time a contract ended. The other was knowing what to charge. Should she just . . . divide a reasonable salary by the number of work hours in a year?

Silicon Valley companies often hire engineers at specific levels (a college grad is L3; a midcareer coder might be L6) that correspond to salary ranges. Vaidyanathan could look those ranges up on sites like levels.fyi. In salary negotiations, it's a useful tactic to ask your employer to match the going rate for your role—or perhaps exceed it because of your tenure or track record.

But salary information did not help Vaidyanathan, because her contracting gigs were bespoke. One big insight, which she learned during a free-range reading session online, was to stop trying to figure out a one-size-fits-all hourly rate. Instead she should figure out what her work was worth to the company, and then charge that.

Nifty! But still challenging. Vaidyanathan's clients had a good sense of how valuable her work would be. She did not. "There is no directory where someone can tell me what the actual right amount to ask for is," Vaidyanathan says. "You just get enough contracts and talk about price with enough people to learn [your work's value]."

To put this in economic terms: Ajché had to tackle the power imbalance between him and platforms like Uber, whereas Preethi's challenge was to overcome the **information asymmetry** between her and her clients.

After more time in the hinterlands of Google search results, Preethi stumbled on a potential solution: 10x Management, an agency founded by two guys who said they'd been agents for musicians like John Mayer and Vanessa Carlton and now repped elite engineers. Their job was to find good clients for freelance engineers and negotiate their contracts, in exchange for a commission. Vaidyanathan signed up.

Instead of having to constantly drum up new opportunities through her network (which is how she serendipitously found her first gig) or market herself and establish a personal brand (like a new small company), Vaidyanathan now received emails from 10x about vetted freelance gigs, which they found by attending tech conferences and networking. For the tech companies, 10x was like MIT or Y Combinator. Since 10x only represented vetted, accomplished engineers, their name signaled quality.

The other big benefit was that 10x overcame information asymmetry. Just as the repeated auctions at Feeding America revealed the true worth of cereal and peanut butter, the 10x agents' many negotiations on behalf of many engineers helped them discover the worth of the engineers parachuting in for important projects. For her first 10x-sourced project, Vaidyanathan's agent asked her how much she wanted to charge. "I would say my number, and they would say, 'Okay, I think we should charge a lot more.'" Her agent was right—for that contract and more that followed.

Vaidyanathan was experiencing how contracting reduced fairness or equity of wages, but in an equal-but-opposite way from Ajché. If two marketers or middle managers have the same job, but one is twice as produc-

5 Tips for Being Your Own Agent

If you don't have an agent or union, you can advocate for yourself with these proven techniques:

1. WHAT'S YOUR BATNA? Your Best Alternative to a Negotiated Agreement. Basically, it means to know your backup option. If the current negotiation doesn't go your way, what will you do instead? The stronger your next-best offer is, the more confident you'll feel negotiating. If you don't have a strong BATNA, you're more vulnerable, so you can't demand as much. Can you go get a better BATNA? It's easier to ask for a raise when a competitor just offered you a plum position!

2. KNOW YOUR "WHY": Back up your asks with data and explanations. Don't ask for more salary or vacation days without context. If negotiating your salary, you can find similar job postings that list the compensation range, or email peers to ask their salary.

3. KNOW YOUR "WHY," PART TWO: Researchers have found that women who proactively negotiate often face a penalty—likely for acting inconsistently with gender norms and stereotypes. But Hannah Riley Bowles, who's studied this extensively, finds that backlash is less likely when women explain their why by providing context and information.

4. GROW THE PIE: Consider nonsalary factors like flexible hours, mentorship opportunities, and sense of mission. Unlike a raise, which will either reduce the companies' profits or the salary budget remaining for other workers' raises, these aren't a fixed pie, and they often matter more to long-term flourishing than a salary bump. Bowles has also found that women are often more successful than men at asking for more work flexibility and other nonmonetary benefits, and face less of a negotiation penalty when framing their ask as a win-win.

5. BUDDY UP: One of the most important things an agent does is check in to ask, "How's work going?" Due to a bias toward the status quo, many of us wait too long to change jobs or address problems. So consider finding a partner and committing to monthly or quarterly meetups to reflect and play the role of agent for each other. And if either of you is frustrated with work, discuss a plan and possible options.

tive, the higher-performing one might get a slightly higher bonus or salary. But rarely double the salary. In surveys, many executives report offering essentially standardized salaries to maintain harmony and morale among employees. Plus many enterprises are team efforts in which it's hard to isolate a single employee's contributions, much less put a precise dollar figure on them.

For the clients, hiring a 10x engineer was more like paying for software or a consultancy: They paid the market rate, mediated by how important the project was to them. In cases like Vaidyanathan's, moving from a workplace to the marketplace did not mean a pay cut. The pay was just as good, if not better, even after accounting for health insurance and other benefits of full-time employment.

Some 10x engineers who found themselves missing office life and teamwork later opted for full-time employment—so much so that 10x expanded into negotiating their job offers. Vaidyanathan doesn't feel that way. Thanks to her in-demand skill set and her ability to successfully negotiate with employers for her full worth, Vaidyanathan hasn't experienced corporations' gravitation toward contractors over full-time employees as a negative. Instead it's an opportunity. When I ask if she'll ever go back to full-time employment, she responds quickly: "I really hope not."

Please hang this poster in the common area. Thx!
—Mgmt
→

Know Your Rights: Laws of the Office

BUREAUCRATICUS MAXIMUS

All employees have a right to understand the following **LAWS OF THE OFFICE*** which hereby explain several seemingly irrational habits and practices pervasive across corporate life. Bad bosses, long meetings, and poorly defined goals all follow the law of **unintended consequences**. By reading this notice, you formally acknowledge that workplace practices are often delightfully, frustratingly irrational.

*Not really law laws. More like Murphy's Law laws.

GOODHART'S LAW

THE BIG IDEA "When a measure becomes a target, it stops being a good measure."

NAMED FOR British economist **Charles Goodhart**.

WHAT IT MEANS When people know how they're being evaluated, they game the system to optimize for what is measured.

FAMOUS EXAMPLE When Britain's National Health Service made it a goal to see emergency patients within four hours, wait times dropped. But hospitals gamed the metric by asking patients to wait outside, inside in an ambulance, until they were sure they could see them within four hours.

ALL WORKERS HAVE THE RIGHT TO Question Key Performance Indicators.

EMPLOYERS MUST Pick their metrics and goals wisely. People will hit their targets, but you may not like how they do it.

PARKINSON'S LAW

THE BIG IDEA "Work expands to fill the time available for its completion."

ATTRIBUTED TO Naval historian **C. Northcote Parkinson**.

WHAT IT MEANS If you schedule 60 minutes for a meeting, it will take the full 60 minutes, even if the work could be done in 15.

FAMOUS EXAMPLE When Steve Jobs asked Corning Glass to make screens for the original iPhone, Corning estimated research and development would take two years. But Jobs insisted on six months. "Don't be afraid," he reportedly said. "You can do this."

ALL WORKERS HAVE THE RIGHT TO Set themselves ambitious deadlines.

EMPLOYERS MUST End meetings early. Taste the freedom.

FAILURE
TO RECOGNIZE THESE LAWS DOES NOT EXEMPT YOUR WORKPLACE FROM THEIR EFFECTS

COMPLIANCE CERTIFICATION
Failure to display this poster has no consequences.

POP QUIZ
- ☐ KPI
- ☐ ROI
- ☐ RFP
- ☐ SWOT
- ☐ SMART
- ☐ SMH
- ☐ WTF
- ☐ JFC

THE PETER PRINCIPLE

THE BIG IDEA "Talented people are promoted to their level of incompetence."

COINED BY Canadian management consultant **Laurence Johnston Peter**.

WHAT IT MEANS People get promoted for doing their job well, until they are promoted to a job they are bad at. (Most often observed when good employees become bad people managers.)

FAMOUS EXAMPLE Politicians are good at campaigning, but not always good at governing.

Michael Scott from *The Office* was a great salesman and a hilariously terrible manager.

ALL WORKERS HAVE THE RIGHT TO Management training upon promotion.

EMPLOYERS MUST Craft career paths that don't always require shifting to management. It's okay to just be good at the job you already do.

CERTIFICATION OF ACKNOWLEDGMENT

"I acknowledge this poster"

_____
Employee name

_____
Signature

_____
Favorite color

REPORTING VIOLATIONS
Complaints may be submitted to the Bureau of Human Nature Regulation:

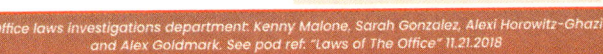

Office laws investigations department: Kenny Malone, Sarah Gonzalez, Alexi Horowitz-Ghazi and Alex Goldmark. See pod ref: "Laws of The Office" 11.21.2018

The Hopeful Tale of the ATM and the Bank Teller

Lessons from the life cycle of automation

What Angie Douglas remembers most of all were the payday lines. On Fridays, customers arrived at the local credit union in Onalaska, Wisconsin, to deposit their paychecks and get money for the weekend. As one of the bank tellers, Douglas watched the line form around 10:00 a.m. By noon, it snaked around the lobby, down the back stairway, and into the parking lot—even though the bank hired a part-time teller just for the lunch rush.

The customers were calm though. They chatted with their neighbors and even with the busy tellers. "One of the gals I worked with, I mean, she would know everything about their whole life," Douglas recalls.

This scene repeated most Fridays in the mid- to late 1980s, when Douglas, then in her twenties, was working her first "real" job. She associates the '80s with leg warmers, "Livin' on a Prayer" by Bon Jovi, and banking practices that now seem quaint: handwritten forms, the separate, air-conditioned room that housed the bank's mainframe computer, the "excitement" and "awe" of using a fax machine.

A few years into Douglas's banking career, the credit union installed its first ATM: an automated teller machine. A machine that did Douglas's job, the only job she'd had since graduating college.

Working in the modern economy means living in the crosshairs of job-eliminating inventions: robotic arms that replace assembly-line workers; self-service kiosks that replace cashiers; AI chatbots that replace customer-service reps and copywriters. Though workers have feared that machines will replace them since at least the introduction of the first mechanical loom in the 18th century, the economist David Autor traces our modern "automation anxiety" back to a 1961 *Time* magazine article about "The Automation Jobless" and their growing ranks. This anxiety has been supercharged by AI and large language models. Automation can hurt workers, upend lives, even end careers. The depth of the pain depends on the job, the stage of career, the pace of automation, and more. For many workers approaching retirement, automation means an early end to a career and a financially precarious old age. Workers unable to move from geographically isolated areas may never find another opportunity that matches their eliminated role.

But new technology does not always mean workers get replaced. When banks like Douglas's began automating her job, something surprising happened: They kept hiring bank tellers. In the United States, the total number of bank tellers grew slowly, year after year, well into the 2000s.

"We never looked [at ATMs as if they] would take our jobs," says Douglas. "It was more about like, 'Wow, that's cool . . . What will we have to do to make it work?"

Economic history abounds with examples of automation that led to worker prosperity rather than obsolescence. It's part of a pattern that is predictable, or, well, predictable-ish. As demonstrated by Douglas's experience, the threat posed by automation is widely misunderstood. And recognizing how new inventions and innovations tend to impact the economy and the workplace shows their opportunities are often underestimated.

The wave of the future: slow as molasses?

LIKE MOST NEW TECHNOLOGIES, the rollout of ATMs seems swift and inevitable in hindsight. But Douglas experienced ATMs, and then online banking, as a gradual process, "like stepping-stones," full of incremental gains and uncertainty.

Initially, ATMs barely automated anything. When customers withdrew money from ATMs, Douglas and her colleagues had to get the record of those withdrawals every day by picking up the phone, getting the ATM file over the modem, and updating customers' accounts. It took years for ATM manufacturers to add labor-saving features (like the ability to read checks and update accounts) and troubleshoot problems (like the credit union's downtown ATM freezing throughout the winter).

Instead, in those initial years, Douglas experienced ATMs as an additional service they offered. "They really were called TYME machines in Wisconsin," says Douglas. "Take Your Money Everywhere." Customers saw the machines not as a replacement for the bank branch, but as a replacement for traveler's checks. A common question, says Douglas, was whether the bank had more ATMs "up there" in north Wisconsin that they could use if they ran out of cash.

There was a learning curve with ATMs, too, which Douglas experienced as she moved from a behind-the-counter teller to working in the back office. Where should the bank place the machines: Around town or as a drive-through at the branch? What denominations of bills should they stock at each? Did people like video ATMs that let them talk to a teller? (They did not!) If they encouraged people to use ATMs, would customers never talk with tellers who could encourage them to apply for a loan or mortgage? (For years, banks limited ATM withdrawals to force customers into the branch.)

Most of all, customers were wary of automation. A little over a century earlier, entrepreneur Elisha Otis overcame the public's fears about his new elevator by staging a dramatic demonstration at the 1853 World's Fair, in which he cut the rope holding the platform to show that the safety break would control its descent. Similarly, bank customers needed to be wooed. Many banks gave their ATMs a human personality: Tillie the All-Time Teller. Their ATMs had an image of Tillie (brunette, friendly, cartoony).

Some banks put ATMs in vans and drove them around to show the public how they worked, and banking lore holds that ATMs only took off in New York City after a blizzard closed all the bank branches, forcing people to get cash from the machines.

"So many of the members didn't trust automation," says Douglas. "That took a long time for them to realize the convenience of that and to trust it. That their money was really still there." She tried to get her parents to use ATMs. To this day, her mother has never used one.

According to James Bessen, an economist and technologist at Boston University, the slow, stepping-stone uptake of new technologies has been common since the Industrial Revolution. In places like Lowell, Massachusetts, the invention of the power loom more than doubled the productivity of weavers compared to handlooms. But over the following 80 years, he notes, improving the power looms' design and workers' skills increased productivity twentyfold.

Sometimes major innovations take a long time to catch on. One of the first people ever to pay for digital spreadsheets—an accountant named Alan Snyder, who used physical spreadsheets every day—did not understand the software when he first saw a demo. Other times, the uptake is much slower than everyone expects. For example, many early internet users predicted commerce would one day migrate online. But after its founding in 1994, Amazon labored through a consistently unprofitable decade before enough people adopted ecommerce for it to become the "everything store." Throughout the late 1990s, prominent investors predicted its demise.

When industries change overnight, it's usually the result of a legal change, like trade barriers going up or down, Berlin Wall–style. When it comes to new inventions, the wave of the future is slow and steady.

The myth of de-skilling

A COMMON VIEW OF AUTOMATION is that it reduces skilled artisans to unskilled laborers. Instead of building an entire car from scratch, the worker just attaches three screws to a side panel all day. But that's not what the rollout of innovations typically looks like.

Instead, says Bessen, automation technologies typically create demand for new skills and adept workers. Those new Massachusetts textile mills, for example, did not hire cheap labor to operate their power looms. They recruited literate, unmarried women from around New England by offering literary lectures, a circulating library, and staff magazines as perks.

Mill managers needed these bright, young women because mastering the new power mills was challenging. One worker wrote a fictional account of a factory worker's first overwhelming experience:

> The next morning she went in the mill; and at first, the sight of so many bands, and wheels, and springs, in constant motion was very frightful. She felt afraid to touch the loom, and she was almost sure that she could never learn to weave; the harness puzzled and the reed perplexed her; the shuttle flew out, and made a new bump upon her head; and the first time she tried to spring the lathe, she broke out a quarter of the threads.

But the women improved steadily as they learned to operate the machines. Instead of "de-skilling" the workers, the new technology "up-skilled" them, creating more productive weavers with new skills. Bessen calculated that their output, in terms of yards of cloth woven per hour, tripled in just over a year.

"It is hard to find a clear example where a new technology was uniformly de-skilling during the 19th century," Bessen writes in *Learning by Doing: The Real Connection Between Innovation, Wages, and Wealth*. "... New machines such as the 'self-acting mule,' an automated spinning machine, begot the occupation of the 'semiskilled minder' who tended these machines, and the Linotype machine begot the skilled typesetter." Even interchangeable parts, widely seen as the development that replaced craftsmen with automatons, "depended very much on the skills of 'artificers' who adjusted the parts to make them fit, and these skills took considerable time and effort to develop."

Before he became an academic, Bessen experienced this himself when he developed software. In 1983, his company sold typesetting software to small newspapers, magazines, and catalog printers. Earlier software had required publishers to use code or markup tags like bold. Bessen's software was one of the first examples of "what-you-see-is-what-you-get," in which the printed document would resemble the page on their desktop screen. Easy! Intuitive! Bessen figured they'd sell the software and quickly pivot to adding more features.

Instead he received calls from confused customers. Some didn't have computer skills, so his company offered classes. Others said the software didn't work for them, so Bessen had to learn their specific needs and customize the product. The companies that bought his software had to learn how to adjust their entire workflow, with many companies making new, digital-first hires.

"All of these different kinds of learning meant that our company and our customers both made substantial human capital investments—often much greater than the cost of the technology itself—in order to use the software productively."

Inventions like the power loom and labor-saving software can certainly lead to layoffs, reduced costs, and a deskilled workforce. But their adoption can lead to the opposite: demand for new skills and major investments in both the invention and the workers needed to benefit from its use.

What should we do with this lump of labor?

"I TRUST THAT NO ONE who reads this today will look me up in the year 2000 in the event that my predictions have been totally inaccurate."

That's how the vice chairman of Wells Fargo began a prediction about ATMs and online banking in 1980. He expected such rapid adoption that bank branches would dwindle and the remaining have "few, if any, support staff members."

This is what many workers fear: The automated teller arrives, and suddenly the human teller is obsolete. Automation leads to layoffs and languishing wages. But this is such a famous misconception that economists gave it a name: the **lump of labor fallacy**. It's the assumption that there's a fixed amount of work that needs to be done, so automating some of it means less work and fewer jobs.

The experience of tellers like Angie Douglas is a demonstration of the lump of labor fallacy. As banks installed and improved ATMs—and Onalaska's payday lines dwindled—the cost of operating a bank branch went down. So, for decades, banks responded by opening more bank branches to pursue new customers. (Until the number of branches started falling in 2009.) Even if there were fewer tellers per office, there were more tellers overall.

"Because of automation," Douglas says, "we could open more branches and serve more members."

Bank teller was not a fast-growing occupation—since the U.S. workforce was getting bigger, bank tellers over time made up a smaller share of Americans' jobs. But instead of putting tellers out of a job, ATMs coexisted with them.

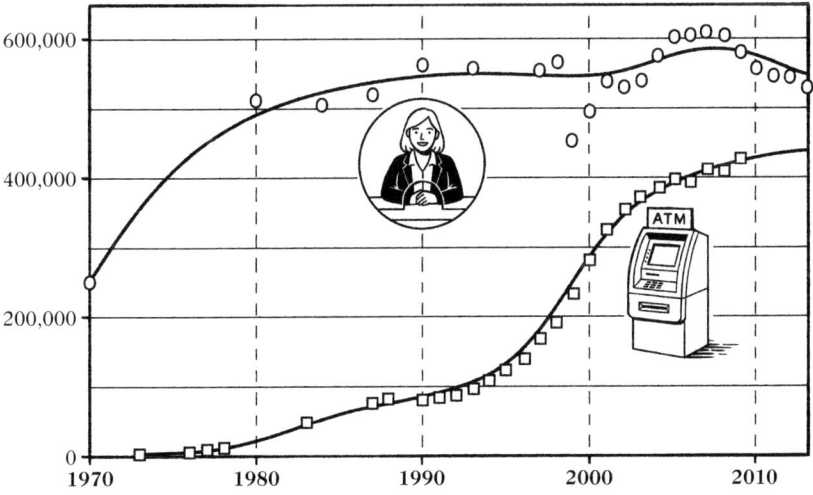

Number of Bank Tellers and ATMs

How a 160-Year-Old Economics Paradox Explains AI's Impact on Jobs

In the early 1860s, English politicians were worried about coal, which was powering the Industrial Revolution and Britain's economy. What would happen if it ran out? Maybe they should focus on developing engines that could produce more power with less coal?

But one economist didn't think that would solve their problem. In his book *The Coal Question*, William Stanley Jevons argued that greater energy efficiency would actually *increase* coal consumption. During his lifetime, for example, better steam engines made it cheaper to get power from coal. This made coal-powered work more affordable, which led to higher demand for coal and an increase in the number of coal-powered factories, trains, and steam ships.

This was the Jevons paradox. For about a century, it remained a mostly theoretical warning about resource consumption. Then, in the 1970s, the Jevons paradox regained the spotlight as governments tried to reduce the use of fossil fuels. Economists pointed out that:

Mandates to make cars travel farther per gallon of gas reduced the cost of driving, so people were more likely to drive to work or plan long road trips.

More-efficient light bulbs can reduce energy use, but also make lighting so cheap that people leave their lights on longer.

In 1947, Howard Aiken of Harvard, the principal designer of one of the earliest computers, estimated "that six electronic digital computers would be sufficient to satisfy the computing needs of the entire United States." But as computing got cheaper, people found a lot more uses for computers!

In the 1800s, cloth was so expensive, Bessen says, that the average person only had one set of clothes. "So there was all this pent-up demand." When factories started automating, the lower cost led people to buy more clothing. More demand for clothes meant greater demand for textile workers.

Much the same happened when spreadsheet software allowed accountants to perform complex calculations and analyses more quickly. When executives realized how fast their accountants could work, they began asking all sorts of what-if questions: What would happen to profits if we made our chocolate bars a little smaller? What about 2 percent larger? Demand for bookkeepers and accounting and auditing clerks went down, but demand for financial managers and analysts went up. The period of transition and adoption of the new tools is often painfully disruptive. That can't be dismissed in the name of greater progress, but neither should the progress be dismissed because of the disruption and pain. The task for society and workers is to find ways to manage and navigate these periods.

> This story may call to mind the Luddites of the early 1800s who famously destroyed machinery they felt was taking their jobs. But according to Bessen, Luddites were not really workers hurt by automation; they were individual business owners. So they were more like small tax-services companies that got outcompeted by H&R Block.

One saying goes, tasks get automated, not jobs. But, even in cases when entire jobs are automated, that doesn't mean unemployment will increase long-term. James Feigenbaum and Daniel Gross have investigated what happened when AT&T replaced the women who operated switchboards

> AI and large language models have revived talk of the Jevons paradox. By making white-collar work much more efficient, AI could reduce the need for human workers and cause job losses. But AI optimists see this as a coal-in-England situation. If AI makes workers more efficient, then the products and services they offer will be cheaper, and demand for them will increase.
>
> If that increase in demand is big enough, the result will be what bank tellers experienced when ATMs arrived: many years of more hirings than firings. But that's a big "if."

(they were almost all women) with mechanical switching technology. (In other words, with rotary dials on phones.) Back then, in the 1920s and '30s, AT&T was a monopoly with control of more than half of America's phone network. Their labor force was so large that 2 percent of all working women in America were AT&T switchboard operators. Automatic switching evaporated all those jobs. Yet there was such healthy demand for the young women's skills in other sectors, especially as typists and secretaries, that their unemployment rates did not rise overall or increase in the long-term.

"I think that's the big message that people get mixed up. It's that workers are fearful that their jobs are just gonna up and go completely," says Bessen. "And the real thing is the jobs are gonna change."

When a computer was a human

IN 1943, Dorothy Vaughan began her multidecade career at the National Advisory Committee for Aeronautics, which later became NASA. Women like Vaughan, known as computers, used slide rules, planimeters, and pencils to perform the many, many calculations needed to put astronauts in orbit—and get them back down.

You might know the name: Vaughan was profiled in the book *Hidden Figures*, by Margot Lee Shetterly, about NASA's unheralded African

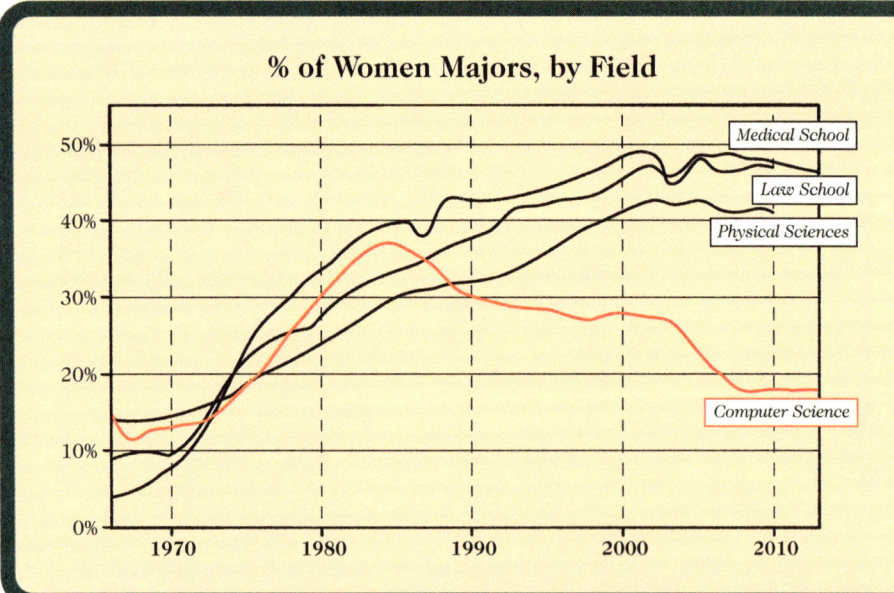

When Women Stopped Coding

Women played a pioneering role in computer science going all the way back to the mid-1800s, when Ada Lovelace wrote what is considered the first computer program (for a hypothetical general-purpose computer). In the 1960s, as computers arrived at NASA and offices around the country, many women took the lead in programming them. And when computer science became a career that increasingly required a college degree, the number of women in those programs was trending up.

Until 1984, when the trend reversed.

Today women hold just 35 percent of tech jobs in the United States. So what changed?

When Jane Margolis of UCLA asked this question, she found that the share of women in computer science started falling after personal computers started showing up in homes in significant numbers.

She believes this happened because computers became gendered. Ads for computers and video games targeted men and boys. Movies depicted programmers as nerdy guys. School computer labs were often male-dominated spaces. When Margolis interviewed students, she learned that families were more likely to buy computers for boys—even when their girls were equally interested.

So when these women took college courses in computer science, and the men had more experience with computers, it shook their confidence and made them feel they didn't belong. They also faced sexism and misogyny in computer science departments.

Economists believe that incentives drive behavior. But despite strong incentives to learn to code—computer science majors earned among the highest starting salaries throughout the 2000s—Margolis was seeing women with marks equal to those of men drop computer science. Feeling welcome and included can trump financial incentives. Which is why a new generation of economists is paying more attention to how discrimination can hold back the economy—and talented individuals.

American computers who played a pivotal role in the Space Race. The book was made into a film of the same name.

Vaughan is also a remarkable example of turning automation into an opportunity. As NASA started installing its first IBM computers, Vaughan, then the leader of a group of Black computers in a segregated wing of the campus, realized her team needed to adapt. She took courses on the FORTRAN programming language used to operate the computers—and encouraged her team to do the same.

"She intuitively understood that the most important part of the human capital that her team has is the ability to communicate with the scientists and engineers who need calculations performed," says labor economist Erica Groshen. NASA could have hired new FORTRAN programmers. But Vaughan convinced her boss that her team would do a better job, and they became the operators of the machines that would have replaced them. (A less out-of-this-world example: One study of Brazilian factories found that many workers whose jobs were automated ended up in customer service and support roles. After all, they knew the product and the company well, and hiring and firing is costly.)

As Vaughan's story shows, innovation automates specific tasks more often than entire jobs. And automating part of your job can make you more productive. Think of lawyers whose use of computers (to do research and draft documents) allowed them to take on more clients. Or, in the tellers' case, ATMs allowed them to spend less time counting cash and more time counseling customers and suggesting they sign up for the bank's credit card or a wealth-management advisor.

But just because the overall level of employment stays stable, that doesn't mean individual workers won't be burned. Eventually Angie Douglas's bank no longer needed the part-time teller who helped on Fridays, and not every teller adapted to the new job of steering customers toward banking products. With AT&T's phone operators, Feigenbaum and Gross found that the fired workers, especially older ones, were negatively impacted, facing periods of unemployment or ending up in lower-paid work like waitressing.

"There's a costly transition that's being imposed," says Bessen. "That's going to hurt some people."

To help workers adapt, Bessen advocates for policies like reversing America's defunding of public colleges—especially community colleges whose courses are, ideally, affordable for mid- or late-career workers, and that may partner with local employers on practical programs or apprenticeships.

"We used to have a system where we develop skills until you were 21 years old, and those skills were supposed to last you the rest of your life," he says. "Now... in many occupations, you've got to be continually relearning."

Even if technology progresses quickly, adoption and learning is slower. There's time to prepare and evolve, to surf the wave of technology change rather than be knocked over by it.

"When you're going through these things and you're living your life, you don't think that you're part of *innovation*," says Douglas as she reflects on her decades working with handwritten forms, then ATMs and direct deposit, and then online banking. "But you really look back now and you go, 'Wow, I really saw a lot of different types of innovation come into play.'"

The more things change...

TODAY AUTOMATION ANXIETY is centered on artificial intelligence. This uncertainty and looming sense of threat may seem unprecedented, but a lot of it fits our pattern.

- **New jobs and skills:** In 2023, Copy.ai, Anthropic, and Klarity offered six-figure salaries to hire "prompt engineers" who query chatbots to improve their AI products. Mocked as "types-question guys," these workers were deemed necessary to figure out best practices and unlock the new technology's value.

- **Growing pains:** Many innovations require years of investment and learning before they unlock real productivity. So far, the investments in AI research and data centers dwarf any productivity gains.

- **Jevons Paradox:** Translators top many lists of jobs endangered by AI. But the number of professional translators and interpreters keeps increasing! And is forecast to continue growing. Cheaper, faster translation done by computers has increased demand for human fine-tuning of machine-generated translation.

It's possible that this time is different, that AI will replace workers so fast and so thoroughly that we will all become lumps of labor. But many of NASA's human computers survived IBM computers. Many tellers did just fine in the age of Automated Teller Machines. Electricity, computers, and the internet changed how we live and work, and created winners and losers. They brought economic boons, not mass unemployment.

Most of all, economic history shows that the beginning of the innovation cycle is when opportunity tends to be greatest and immediate layoffs less likely. Textile factories eventually got so productive that making cloth even cheaper barely increased demand and labor-saving changes did reduce demand for workers. Ditto with our bank tellers. Eventually customers were so thoroughly served by ever-present bank branches (and banking apps) that banks hired fewer tellers and support staff. But that didn't happen until decades after the first power looms and ATMs appeared in factories and on street corners.

The fact that technology and automation tends to benefit the entire economy and the *average* worker is cold comfort if and when you're the unlucky one who gets laid off. In some cases, adapting or recovering can take years, or even a lifetime. But more automation is always arriving. You can only choose how to respond.

AI is an impressive technology with many unknown, unclear use cases. How can you use the magic box in your work? The only way to find out is with lots of trial and error. This is the period of the innovation cycle that has more ladders than trapdoors.

# PART THREE

LOVE &

10

The Labor of Finding Love

Every market has a designer

In 2019, Alden O'Rafferty was in her Stanford dorm. It was minutes to midnight, but every door was open. Students were running the halls and standing in doorways hitting refresh, refresh, refresh. Like almost every undergrad, O'Rafferty was waiting for an email. She'd been promised it would contain the name of her ideal match on campus. An hour earlier, she'd gotten a teasing email with that person's initials: KT. She heard a burst of noise down the hall. Someone's email had arrived.

"Someone goes like, 'Oh, I got a football player.' I run down to that side of the hall. And I'm like, 'Oh my gosh, let me look,'" says O'Rafferty. "And we're googling them. But then I'm still refreshing. Like, 'Oh, I got mine.' And then other people run over to me."

Her match's name was Kyra Dorado Teigen, and the email was from the Marriage Pact. The premise was different from dating apps, which encourage people to connect immediately. Instead, the Marriage Pact was a hedge. It would give you just one match per year, but your match would be so compatible that the two of you could make a pact: If you're both still single when you turn 30 or 40, then you should get married.

O'Rafferty and Teigen's email said they were in the 99th percentile of compatibility. So Teigen decided not to wait. She sent O'Rafferty a message on Instagram, and they met for a picnic. "There [are] little thermoses, and there's Pop-Tarts [and] squeezy applesauces," says Teigen. "I love those squeezy applesauces."

Matching through an app is now, statistically speaking, one of the most common forms of dating in the United States. What O'Rafferty and Teigen didn't know, though, is that the Marriage Pact was a Stanford class project, and that their 99 percent compatibility score was based on **market design**, a relatively new branch of economics.

For a long time, people have joked postbreakup that they are "back on the market." But there's truth there. Traditional economics defines a market as a place where buyers and sellers come together, whether in Baghdad's ancient marketplaces or Amsterdam's 17th-century stock exchange or on a mobile app. More recently, market design recognized that many other types of markets exist without buyers, sellers, and prices. These **matching markets** are systems that connect medical residents with hospitals, kidney donors with patients, and Teigens with O'Raffertys. Apps such as Tinder, Hinge, and Feeld have transformed dating by corralling the decentralized process of dating into centralized matching markets.

The Marriage Pact is an experiment in applying economic principles to design a better market for love. It's also a reminder that markets are not naturally occurring "free" spaces where optimal outcomes just manifest. Every market has some design or designers behind it, and those designers make choices that affect how the market works and who it benefits most.

The stable-marriage problem

THREE YEARS BEFORE Teigen and O'Rafferty's squeezy-applesauce picnic, another undergraduate, Liam McGregor, signed up for a Stanford class called Econ 136: Market Design. He was majoring in computer science, but his mom had looked through the course catalog and thought he'd like the class.

The professor, Paul Milgrom, explained that traditional economics embraced markets and the invisible hand over centralized planning (for all the reasons covered in chapter 1), so economists mostly discouraged politicians from meddling in markets. They saw governments' role as limited to just a few essential tasks:

- Ensuring physical safety, enforcing contracts, and protecting property rights

- Preventing monopolies, cartels, and collusion that would hinder competition

- Funding public goods that have positive externalities (building roads and sewers) and addressing negative externalities through taxes (high taxes on cigarettes or a carbon tax to combat climate change) or regulations (bans on fireworks in fire-prone areas)

- And if society deems the market outcome (too) inequitable, the government can redistribute wealth afterward

But some situations call for a different approach. Milgrom explained to the class that the field of market design arose to address two categories of markets that demanded more intervention and central coordination.

The first category was **unique goods**. Unlike products like iPhones or bananas, things like water rights or landing slots at airports aren't homogenous, and their supply is constrained in complex ways: Some aquifers take centuries to refill, and two planes that use the same landing slot might crash.

In class, Milgrom shared how he had personally been involved in this kind of market. In 1993, the U.S. government wanted his help selling an important natural resource: America's radio spectrum.

The radio spectrum is like an invisible highway: a range of electromagnetic waves (lanes), each best suited to different uses. And they are a finite resource (the highway is only so wide). Even in the early 1900s, ship captains complained about interference on their radios from amateurs using the same frequencies.

That's why the Federal Communications Commission allocates spectrum licenses (lanes). The FCC had previously doled these out to companies by application and by holding lotteries. But sometimes the lottery-winning company had a poor idea for the precious bandwidth, or speculators would win and resell the licenses. Plus, in 1993, the spectrum needed to accommodate new or growing uses like cell phones and wi-fi. So the FCC wanted a new system for selling licenses.

When Milgrom received a call about the spectrum, he replied, "I'm just an economic theorist! I don't know anything!'" But he was an expert on auctions, which are ideal for selling items too bespoke for supply and demand to establish the right price—a process known as price discovery. We turn to auctioneers when selling a champion breeding bull, and to Sotheby's when auctioning a sculpture of a bull preserved in formaldehyde.

According to classic economic theory, when it came to finding the right value for the spectrum, it didn't really matter how the FCC allocated licenses. If a speculator or mediocre company got valuable spectrum, a company with a better use for it could buy the license from them. Eventually the market would reach an efficient outcome.

But then private companies, not U.S. taxpayers, would profit from selling the spectrum. Additionally, reaching that efficient end state might take decades. A telephone company, for example, might spend years negotiating purchases of regional spectrum only to discover that national coverage would be prohibitively expensive.

This was a critical problem: Companies valued each spectrum license differently, and their value depended on whether each company could also purchase other parts of the spectrum.

So Milgrom and a colleague proposed one of the most complex auctions in history. Companies would bid simultaneously on every spectrum license. But to help them get a better sense of prices, there would be multiple rounds. After each, companies could evaluate their ability to buy their portfolio of licenses with their budget, and then adjust their bids.

But that would encourage strategic gaming of the system. Why would anyone be honest in that first round? If you're willing to pay millions, why reveal that information when you could wait until later rounds to outbid competitors?

This was a key takeaway for McGregor: Well-designed markets achieve efficient outcomes by incentivizing everyone to reveal their true preferences. If the rules give participants no incentive to lie about their preferences or willingness to pay, market designers say it's strategy-proof.

So Milgrom added rules that disqualified companies from bidding if they hadn't bid in prior rounds. Another rule said that each auction would end when no higher bids came in. If a participant feigned indifference, they'd lose out on that license.

No one had done anything like this before. Milgrom brought his models to the FCC on floppy disks, to reassure them with a demonstration. The auction ultimately earned more than $200 billion for the government. It was a windfall for taxpayers *and* a more socially optimal result. By selling each spectrum license to the company with the most valuable use for it, the FCC had unlocked billions of dollars of economic value. (While setting aside some spectrum for emergency services and nonprofit educational TV and radio.) For instance, this allowed a regional TV network to bid on multiple licenses at once, when otherwise they might have been too scared to bid for fear of ending up with an expensive but useless patchwork of licenses.

Markets selling unique goods require market design. But so do markets that don't have prices at all.

It's illegal to pay for a human organ in almost every country in the world. McGregor recalls learning how three economists designed a new system to match kidney donors to patients. "We've all just sort of decided that we don't want to do prices for some markets."

Without the traditional signals and incentives of pricing, economists turned to matchmaking algorithms to help willing "buyers" meet willing "sellers." "There's a sort of contrived example that's foundational to the course of market design," says McGregor. "It's called the **stable-marriage problem**." Developed by two economists in the 1960s, it involves six straight, single people on an island who want to get married.

A good example of the stable marriage problem is the reality TV show *Love Island*. There, the producers prod singles into coupling up after date nights, talent shows, and various shenanigans. On the economists' fantasy island, everyone sits down, ranks their interest in the other singles (first, second, third), and lets an algorithm make the matches. You can imagine the algorithm as multiple rounds of proposals:

Men propose to their first choice of women. Women accept best suitor.

Remaining men propose to their first choice of women. Women "trade up" if they prefer a new suitor.

Remaining man proposes to remaining woman.

This island of six singles is contrived and heteronormative. But the approach, known as the Gale-Shapley algorithm or deferred-acceptance algorithm, is more like a proof of concept. It demonstrates that you can make optimal matches in priceless markets by having everyone rank their preferences. When economists used a tweaked version of the algorithm to match 90,000 students to New York City

The outcome is always stable, but it's optimal for whichever side does the proposing. Meaning that on this island, the men are more likely to get a match in line with their preferences!

130   Love & Family

schools, for example, the number of students who got into one of their top-choice schools increased from roughly 50,000 to 70,000.

A collegial marriage market

A FEW WEEKS INTO CLASS, Milgrom told everyone to choose a topic for their final paper. McGregor and a classmate, Sophia Sterling, pitched Milgrom on doing a project instead. They had just learned about the stable-marriage problem, and they knew about marriage pacts. But what were the odds that they'd meet the best person to make that pact with before graduating? Stanford had more than 7,000 undergrads. You couldn't meet them all.

As McGregor recalls, their pitch was, "How will we find the best person for you to make a backup plan with?" It seemed like a fun thought experiment, and more fun to actually do it. Milgrom gave them the green light.

Their main challenge was that their north star, the deferred-acceptance algorithm, relied on everyone ranking everyone else. "But how on earth would you rank [so many] people, many of them who you don't know?" McGregor asks. Since Stanford's undergrads couldn't tell McGregor and Sterling their preferences, the pair would have to get students to reveal them. They decided on a survey.

Without realizing it, McGregor and Sterling were replicating past experiments in digital dating. Way back in 1965, Harvard's Operation Match fed punch-card questionnaires from singles into a washing-machine-size computer that spit out matches. When OkCupid dominated dating websites circa 2011, its users answered compatibility questions via online forms.

But the approach was novel for market design. "We've been aware for a long time that there was something wrong with just assuming people had preferences," says Milgrom. Or, put another way, that people knew their own preferences. In the stable-marriage problem, the singles don't go on dates. But on *Love Island*, the contestants need to hang out before coupling up, and in medicine, residents interview with hospitals and research their top choices. Market designers had ignored this whole courtship period.

With this in mind, McGregor and Sterling crafted a specific approach for the Marriage Pact questionnaire. Early on, Milgrom asked: What are the incentives for students to answer truthfully? In other words, how would they strategy-proof their market? Once students realized their answers determined their match, wouldn't they exaggerate to present themselves as more desirable? (Men, infamously, inflate their height on dating apps.)

Economics didn't offer a solution, but McGregor's mom did. She told him that shared values are what matter most for long-term relationships. Drawing on research from fields like psychology, McGregor and Sterling wrote questions like:

- Would you keep a gun in the house?

- I consider my friends quiet (Agree / Disagree)

- Is it okay for your child to be gay?

- If you're at a red light but no one is on the road, I would go (No way / Vroom, vroom)

The last one was maybe just for fun. But their value-centric questions both fit the premise of a marriage pact (are you long-term compatible?) and gave participants no reason to be anything but honest.

McGregor and Sterling could make a beautifully designed market, but if no one signed up, it wouldn't matter. Stanford was full of groups that wanted students to come to their improv show or fill out a class survey. Their pleas clogged campus inboxes; their flyers covered bathroom stalls. So McGregor and Sterling crafted a punchy message. Ideally students would hear about Marriage Pact so much that FOMO would kick in.

> Listen. Finding a life partner is (probably) not a priority [RN]. You hope things will manifest naturally. Fine. But (like many busy individuals)—years from now—you may realize that most viable boos are already hitched. At that point... it's less about finding "the one" & more about finding "the last one left." The Stanford Marriage Pact is here to cover the essentials. We know you have your noted non-negotiables. We know you're busy. We

also know Al Roth's Nobel Prize–winning deferred acceptance algorithm and a little linear algebra. We've used this to build the best (and only) market for finding your backup plan. Take our quiz & find your Marriage Pact match here.

McGregor and Sterling agreed they needed at least 100 students to make decent matches. Within two days, they had 2,000 sign-ups. By the end of the week, they had more than 4,000, which was more than half the student body. They even had to turn away students from other colleges. "That's when I felt I should probably implement the code," says McGregor.

The Marriage Pact fulfilled the three principles of well-designed markets, as articulated by Alvin Roth, a Stanford economist who won the Nobel Prize for his work on market design. A market must ensure safety, meaning that people feel safe to reveal and act on their real preferences, and won't see any reason to lie or deceive to gain advantage. It must be thick, meaning that it has enough participants to produce good outcomes. And it must avoid congestion, which is when people are overwhelmed by the options or aren't given sufficient time to make good choices.

The initial Marriage Pact drawing didn't go perfectly. The algorithm matched two siblings. A few students got womp-womp compatibility scores of just 4 percent. (Which meant they got matched with someone who answered the questions very differently, either because their responses were unusual compared to the cohort, or the people most similar to them were even more similar to other participants.) But the drama of match day gripped campus, so McGregor and Sterling decided to do it again the following year—even though Professor Milgrom had already given them an A+. They did it the year after that as well, at Stanford, Oxford, and an expanding roster of colleges.

That's when Teigen and O'Rafferty matched and met for their picnic. Afterward, O'Rafferty invited Teigen to her house and told her to close her eyes. "She leads me inside. . . . And then she puts kittens all over me because she fosters kittens," Teigen explains. As we talk, O'Rafferty interjects to claim, unconvincingly, that she didn't know any of this had date vibes.

The two didn't start dating. But they fell for each other in a platonic way. While they've dated other people, they say they plan on fulfilling the Marriage Pact one day. They've talked about their wedding ("There's going to be lights in the trees. We're not going to be wearing shoes. We're going to have flowers on our heads.") and what it means ("We're going to be friend-married for sure").

"It's a real marriage, you know?" says O'Rafferty. "It's just not a romantic one."

Teigen and O'Rafferty had their happy ending. Milgrom won the Nobel Prize in 2020 for his work on the spectrum auction and market design. Sterling graduated, accepted a job offer, and moved on to other projects. But McGregor wanted to keep working on the Marriage Pact, and he was hearing from venture capitalists who thought its explosive popularity on college campuses resembled Facebook's early days. A year after graduating, McGregor said yes to the investors and turned Marriage Pact into a business.

But venture capitalists didn't fund McGregor to send out annual surveys. Investors want founders to launch big businesses and apps that people use every day. As McGregor got started, he realized that building a well-designed dating marketplace clashed with the incentives of building a profitable dating app.

The dating app paradox

IF YOU RUN A DATING APP, you will face an inevitable problem: The better you are at matchmaking, the less money you'll make.

This shows up clearly in a key business metric: **customer lifetime value (CLV)** compared to **customer acquisition cost (CAC)**. In other words, does the dating app make more from the average user paying for premium features or clicking on ads than it costs to get them on the app through Instagram ads or other marketing? Every time you successfully match two (monogamous) singles, they will delete your app. The better you get at matchmaking, the faster your customers stop paying for services (lower lifetime value), and then you have to do more marketing to get new customers (higher acquisition costs).

The heads of dating apps generally respond that singles will only use their apps if they efficiently make good matches and offer a pleasant experience. But there's a strong business case *against* better matchmaking: One study by the consulting firm Bain found that companies that boost customer retention by 5 percent see increased profits of 25 to 95 percent. If you run a dating app, do you really want to pour resources into better matchmaking that might *reduce* retention 5 percent?

A defining feature of economists' successful market (re)designs is the absence of conflicting revenue goals. In the spectrum auction, companies wanted spectrum and the government wanted to sell it. The question was what the correct price should be. In the price-free kidney market, everyone involved wants more kidney donations and matches. Dating apps, in contrast, have incentives to match people just well enough to attract new users, but also to keep them waiting, and paying, as long as possible before a forever match. Customers presumably want faster, quality matching.

But even well-intentioned matchmakers can struggle to help singles. Under the hood, many dating apps are based on **collaborative filtering**. Companies like Netflix and Amazon use this process to track which movies you watch and which products you buy, and then show you TV shows watched or goods bought or liked by shoppers similar to you. But reality TV and scented candles don't have to like you back. So when dating apps do collaborative filtering, they try to predict how likely other singles are to like you back, and prioritize accordingly.

The problem, which many singles have experienced, is that liking a dating profile is not the same as liking a person. We all struggle to identify the traits we value in a partner. When researchers interviewed speed daters, they found that the singles' stated preferences (like someone's salary or friendly personality) did not predict whom they requested to date. Beyond a general preference for attractive people, many studies have found that we're surprisingly in the dark about what's important to us.

Dating apps provide lots of value by bringing so many singles together. This is especially true for LGBTQ daters, who are twice as likely to find a partner through dating apps. But after that, finding a good match seems to rely on luck and enduring a marathon of first dates. Data show we might find matches more efficiently by sniffing other singles' armpits (to get a whiff of their pheromones) than by reviewing dating profiles.

Asked about how he'd avoid this conundrum, McGregor said he never wanted Marriage Pact to be just about dating. On campuses, students in serious relationships signed up for it without guilt or subterfuge. The survey was fun, and so was being part of the event, single or not. Many students, like Teigen and O'Rafferty, enjoyed meeting even if they didn't date.

Marriage Pact did launch a survey-powered dating app. But McGregor decided instead to focus on a project called Matchbox, which allows people to run mini Marriage Pact events. Hosts send the survey to guests and then unveil the matches at a party.

The company originally created Matchbox to promote the dating app, but users clearly preferred Matchbox—and used it in ways McGregor never anticipated. A business conference matched mentors and mentees. A Bible study group matched Bible study partners. "Putting two people who are a great fit together is one of the fundamental problems of life, beyond finding your partner," says McGregor.

MARKET DESIGN AROSE TO DEAL WITH ATYPICAL MARKETS, and it has dramatically demonstrated its potential. Now some market design adherents are taking what they learned from auctions and matching to explore whether more traditional markets, like stock exchanges, might benefit from more intentional design. And once you study market design, you start noticing that "free markets" rely on lots of rules.

For many people, financial markets epitomize free markets and unfettered capitalism, and yet most of them have extensive rules. Stock exchanges (which are organized marketplaces!) have "circuit breakers" that halt all trading if prices swing too wildly in too short a period. In labor markets, companies can hire salespeople however they want, but professional football players have to be drafted, and lawyers have to pass their state's bar exam. In America's car market, most states force automakers to sell cars to dealerships rather than directly to customers.

In Alvin Roth's words: "For markets to work freely, they need rules that allow them to do so."

Unlike the spectrum auction or kidney-donation system, most markets were not set up in one go by socially minded designers. Their design and rules evolved over years, often through debate, lobbying, and compromise. Some important rules arose because motivated parties, like the car-dealership lobbyists, insisted on them; some are kind of random. Which is why it's so important to spot the designers behind each market and ask whose interests they're serving.

This chapter includes reporting from Sarah Gonzalez and Alex Mayyasi, included in the Planet Money episode "The Marriage Pact," March 5, 2021.

11

The Opportunity Atlas

The American Dream exists, it's just not evenly distributed

It all started with a flier. Lydia Grayson-Cross can't recall exactly what it said—she got it in 1995, when she was living in public housing in East Harlem. But she remembers what it offered. "Better living for people from the inner city," she says. "To get out of the projects' poverty, to have a choice to go somewhere."

That's what she wanted. She says cocaine use was commonplace in the housing project where she lived, a high-rise whose tenants were poor. She wasn't working. She struggled with drug addiction and relied on welfare and child support to get by. She had an unfinished college degree and ambitions to raise her three children somewhere safer. She had a cousin in Jacksonville, North Carolina, and she thought living there would offer better housing and job opportunities.

"I wanted to go to school," she says. "I wanted to finish college. I wanted to hold a full-time job and raise my kids there."

The flier promised financial support for moving out of public housing. She applied for it, and she waited. Because to get the support, she'd have to win a lottery. She told a public-housing employee that she was going to get it. "He didn't believe me. . . . He used to be like, 'Oh you can't say that, Ms. Grayson.'" (Back then, she was Lydia Grayson.)

But Grayson-Cross was right. She won the lottery, and with it a government voucher that she could use to pay the bulk of her rent if she found housing in a better neighborhood. She put her family's possessions in a moving truck and used some of her welfare money to buy Greyhound bus tickets for herself, her two-year-old daughter, and her two boys (both in elementary school).

"It was like a faith move," she says. Besides her cousin, "I didn't really know nobody down there. . . . I was a little fearful, but I just knew in the back of my mind that I had to do things to make things work."

When Grayson-Cross and her children moved to North Carolina, they became one of 4,608 families participating in one of the largest and most influential antipoverty experiments in American history. The Grayson-Cross family's move—and the program that funded it—forever changed their lives. And they, in turn, forever changed how economists, government officials, and other researchers understand poverty and the American Dream—the ideal that anyone, regardless of their race or background, can achieve a good life through hard work.

With rigor and precision, the study used the experiences of the 4,608 families to isolate which factors enable economic mobility—earning a higher salary and joining a higher income bracket than your parents and grandparents. Above all, it tested a hypothesis: Does where you live and grow up shape your economic destiny?

A grand experiment

A FEW YEARS BEFORE Lydia Grayson-Cross moved to Jacksonville, the housing lottery that sent her there was a radical idea to solve an intractable problem. One of the people who proposed the lottery was economist Mark Shroder. In 1991, he'd started working at the U.S. Department of Housing and Urban Development (HUD), whose mission is to provide affordable housing.

Every year, HUD and local housing agencies spend billions helping families like Grayson-Cross's afford a place to live. They provide apartments in housing projects for minimal monthly rents, and they distribute housing vouchers that subsidize families' rents in private apartment buildings. But since the projects concentrate extreme poverty in one area, they also concentrate crime, drugs, and other problems associated with poverty. Housing vouchers could theoretically help a family live elsewhere, but in practice, the landlords willing to accept the vouchers were in equally poor and dangerous neighborhoods.

Researchers and HUD officials had realized that families who lived in these areas rarely escaped them. This is one manifestation of a **poverty trap**. Sometimes people are hindered in the steps needed to escape poverty by the very conditions of being poor. It might mean dropping out of school because your family needs you to work. Or not being able to take a better job if it requires moving away from Grandma and her free childcare. And poverty had other debilitating effects. Psychologists who interviewed residents of certain poor neighborhoods compared its impact on children to living in a war zone.

Shroder and others suspected that moving families out of certain projects and unsafe neighborhoods could be life-changing—and they had good reason to think so. In the 1970s, the Supreme Court had ordered Chicago to desegregate its public housing. In doing so, the city had helped many Black families move into apartments in wealthier neighborhoods.

The Credibility Revolution

For much of its history, economics was an armchair discipline. Adam Smith sat around, observed how things worked, and developed theories. As late as the 1980s, economists who tried to test theories or track down data were second-class citizens within the profession.

The most influential economists mostly traded in theory. When people asked if raising the minimum wage was a good idea, they usually responded that it would kill jobs, because if the price of labor goes up, then bosses will hire fewer people. It sounded logical, and they had convincing charts.

Since then, economics has been transformed by the credibility revolution: an earnest attempt to track down data, use more rigorous statistical techniques, and test theories in the real world. A seminal moment came in the mid-1990s, when the economists David Card and Alan Krueger published their findings that modestly raising the minimum wage didn't kill jobs at all.

More findings followed that often overturned conventional economic wisdom. Card and others eventually earned Nobel honors. (Krueger passed away, so was not eligible.)

Card and Krueger reached their surprising result by exploiting a natural experiment: When New Jersey increased its minimum wage, they compared employment at fast-food restaurants on different sides of the New Jersey–Pennsylvania border.

Economists also copied an idea from medicine: randomized controlled trials, like the ones used to test new vaccines. Economists had often debated whether aid workers should freely distribute things like anti-parasite medication and bednets (to protect from mosquitoes and malaria) or charge a nominal price (to prevent waste, fund more aid, etc.). A series of famous studies tried both and found that free distribution worked way better, with huge health and financial benefits.

Researchers documented that those parents found jobs and saw their children graduate high school and college at higher rates.

The Supreme Court case was *Hills v. Gautreaux* (1976). Shroder had read about *Gautreaux*, and it made him and other HUD officials wonder: What if HUD did this around the country? Could they help poor Americans improve their lives by helping them move?

"If you really want to know whether this works, you need an experiment," says Shroder. That's where the lottery came in. Residents of public housing in five cities—Boston, Chicago, New York, Baltimore, and Los Angeles—received fliers like Grayson-Cross's. After they signed up, the lottery randomly assigned them to one of three groups.

The first was a control group: Those families would stay in public housing. Group two families would get a regular housing voucher—the ones they could use to subsidize their rent with any landlord willing to take it, but that most recipients used in neighborhoods with poverty rates around 50 percent. Families in group three, the experimental group, would get the same voucher, but only if they moved to a neighborhood with a poverty rate of 10 percent or lower.

Shroder and his colleagues called the program Moving to Opportunity. They hoped the experiment would show that HUD could do more than keep a roof over people's heads. Maybe a housing voucher could be a ticket to a better life. Maybe prosperous neighborhoods contained economic vitamins, some mix of essential ingredients that could help a family achieve the

> In chapter 18, you'll meet Emi Nakamura, an example of an economist going to great lengths to find new data to improve economic analysis—in her case, on why inflation happens.
>
> Other economists investigate prior research for fraud. Ironically, they found that a series of influential findings about honesty were based on fake data.
>
> Today the field has flipped, and the most admired work is empirical—it's based on cleverly assembled datasets, econometrics (math and statistics), and experiments. This change has made economists' findings more rigorous, and their tools and insights more practical and applicable.

American Dream: desegregated schools, safe streets, good jobs. Maybe they could even figure out which ingredients mattered most, replacing our hazy understanding of economic mobility with tested, data-driven strategies.

But many enrollees were less enthused about moving. "There were some people who were praying, literally praying, they would be in the regular voucher group," says Shroder. "They did not want to have to find another place that far away either socially or physically."

Grayson-Cross was an outlier. She not only prayed for a voucher that would help her move, but unlike most voucher recipients, who stayed within Boston, New York, or Chicago, she moved out of state. Like Shroder, Lydia Grayson-Cross saw the move as an opportunity.

Moving to opportunity?

THE FIRST MONTHS IN JACKSONVILLE WERE INAUSPICIOUS. Many landlords refuse renters with HUD vouchers, whether due to racism, classism, or other reasons. The Grayson family ended up in a rural, concrete house. They stayed warm with old kerosene heaters; they walked miles on country roads to the nearest store. "I didn't even have a clock," says Grayson-Cross. "I taught my kids how to tell time by the sun, believe it or not."

She initially found work in her kids' school cafeteria. But the terrible trade-offs of being a single parent followed her to North Carolina. Though she had attended some college, she says she humbled herself by taking hamburger orders at Hardee's. Sometimes she could drop her children at her cousin's, but she had to train them to sometimes stay home alone. "It was very challenging," Grayson-Cross says. "I wanted to pack up and come back up here [to New York], but I just kept . . . trying to persevere, you know, learning to trust God."

As researchers followed families like the Graysons—by collecting data on their incomes and children's grades, by interviewing some about their experiences—they found that the vouchers clearly helped people move to safety. Their new neighborhoods had less drugs and crime. People felt safer. Their mental and physical health improved.

Living in Jacksonville "allowed me to really calm my spirit down," says Grayson-Cross. "Because I, myself, I was kind of wild too, you know? It helped me settle."

But the researchers weren't seeing parents finding jobs and children thriving in school, in part because so many families struggled to stay in their new neighborhoods. Finding a rental was so challenging that only 48 percent of MTO families found a place in neighborhoods that met HUD's definition of low poverty. Even more had to move within a year or two due to landlords raising the rent or not maintaining the property.

After a year in the remote, unheated house, the Grayson family moved into a Jacksonville homeless shelter. Grayson-Cross recalls her son struggling in school and crying because other children teased him. "I just explained to him: 'We're going to persevere. We're going to move into a house and things are going to get better.'" But finding a house—a three-bedroom in a below-middle-class neighborhood—took another year.

While living in the shelter, Grayson-Cross worked at a nursing home, and she later worked at a military base, which offered good pay. She married a man she met through church, who was employed and helped with the children, and she completed a bachelor's degree.

Stability, though, proved elusive. The family kept moving, and her older son, who felt lonely in North Carolina, went to stay with his father in Florida, where he spent time in a juvenile detention center. Grayson-Cross says she could not always keep a job while balancing everything. In 2006, *The Wall Street Journal* highlighted her family as emblematic of the struggles facing Moving to Opportunity families, and researchers' and administrators' sense that families weren't benefiting as hoped. In 2011, when HUD released its final report on the program, it noted the health and safety benefits, but concluded that parents and children who moved "to opportunity" did not have higher incomes, test scores, or employment rates than families who stayed in public housing.

Maybe families couldn't move to opportunity. Maybe overcoming poverty traps took more than a change of address.

A generational project

IN 2014, researcher Nathan Hendren badged into the tenth floor of the Internal Revenue Service headquarters in Washington, D.C. The IRS had granted him and fellow economist Raj Chetty access to anonymized IRS data, and they were looking at income-tax data, studying people who *had* climbed out of poverty. Were there patterns among those people that might help others? One "vividly" memorable day, Hendren found a pattern that made him think that the final report on Moving to Opportunity had missed a success story.

First he noticed spots on a map: Families with upward economic mobility were clustered in neighborhoods across the country. He knew that mobility had declined nationwide, to the point that for every American who grew up to have a higher income than their parents, another American grew up to make less than their parents. But in cities like San Jose and Salt Lake City, the American Dream seemed alive and well.

This finding—that certain areas offer more economic opportunity—was the original hypothesis of Moving to Opportunity. "At that point, we [thought], well, geez, we should probably get the MTO data," says Hendren.

With the data, he and Chetty matched MTO families to their tax filings. (Again, all anonymized.) And they saw the same pattern: Many families' change of address led to improvements in their fortunes.

HUD's final report had concluded that MTO participants hadn't climbed out of poverty. But that report had come out before their younger children entered the job market. (HUD had issued its final report on Moving to Opportunity when Grayson-Cross's youngest was around seventeen years old.) Even though their parents didn't fare much better than parents who stayed in public housing, these younger children, who'd spent more formative time in their new neighborhoods, went on to graduate school and earn more income compared to the public-housing cohort. Families *could* move to opportunity, but it was a generational project.

Hendren and Chetty estimated that a young child who moved through MTO or a similar program increased their lifetime income by about $302,000. The key ingredient was how young they were when they moved. "You'd actually see higher outcomes on average for the four-year-old relative to the eight-year-old," says Hendren.

This was the experience in the Grayson-Cross family too. Her older sons have both struggled as adults, she says. They did not attend college, and they spent time homeless. Her daughter, though, who was only two when they moved to Jacksonville, earned an associate's degree and in 2024 was aiming to complete her bachelor's.

Lydia herself benefited from the move more as time went on. She met neighbors who made sure her children always had a ride to sports practices. She met people at church who helped out with babysitting or paying bills in a pinch. She earned her master's degree and, in 2018, returned to New York City, making a middle-class income as a substance-abuse counselor.

Reverse-engineering the American Dream

WHEN HENDREN AND CHETTY PUBLISHED THEIR FINDINGS, policy nerds shared them like a viral video. "Overnight, we were inundated," says Hendren, with emails from people who wanted to use housing policy to help poor children and families.

So that's what they did. Hendren and Chetty created a research organization, Opportunity Insights, to better understand economic mobility. "The big question is: Why is the American Dream more alive in some places than others?" says Chetty.

An initial step was publishing a map of economic mobility based on the IRS data. They called it the Opportunity Atlas, and made it freely accessible on their website. Moving to Opportunity had hypothesized that lower-poverty neighborhoods were springboards to better education and good jobs. But that's not what the Opportunity Atlas showed. In some prosperous cities, like Charlotte, poor people stayed poor, and the good, new jobs went to well-off transplants. Meanwhile, many small towns, such as communities in rural Iowa and North Dakota, had higher mobility than big cities.

With this in mind, Hendren and Chetty worked with housing agencies on MTO 2.0: housing vouchers that offered total freedom in where to move, paired with support and counseling about which neighborhoods had less poverty and more mobility. More than half the families chose high-mobility neighborhoods, spurring Congress to fund similar programs across the country.

Governments are also attempting to bring the lessons of MTO to public housing. Most prominently, Seattle's Housing Authority demolished and rebuilt Yesler Terrace, the city's first public housing site, completed in 1942, by replacing its public row houses with high-rises that mix market-rate apartments with affordable housing. The goal is to create a safe, desirable, mixed-income neighborhood without displacing poor residents. Some of the apartments boast the best views in the city.

Above all, Opportunity Insights and other researchers and officials want to understand what powered the positive results of MTO. "Is it because of resources available in the area, the quality of schools, the quality of jobs, public transit?" asks Chetty. If researchers could isolate the factors that matter most, maybe governments and local leaders could bring those key ingredients to poor neighborhoods, rather than making residents leave to access them.

In 2022, Hendren, Chetty, and more than 20 researchers came together to announce their biggest finding.

"What we found in a nutshell is that **social capital** . . . is one of the strongest predictors of differences in economic mobility," says Chetty. The idea is that your connections and contacts are an asset that pays regular dividends (by telling you about relevant job openings, for example), similar to how **human capital** refers to skills and education that can power your career.

According to the data, having lots of friends and connections isn't by itself sufficient for escaping poverty. But Chetty and his team identified a specific type of social tie that did help people climb the income ladder: interactions and friendships between low- and high-income people.

Just as MTO confirmed and clarified a common belief about economic mobility, the studies by Hendren, Chetty, and their collaborators used new data to investigate how social capital shapes our economic fortunes. Namely, they crunched data from more than 70 million Facebook users with 21 billion friendships. Not every Facebook friend is a real friend. But the data was a map of social capital and connections within a town or city, and it showed that areas that had unusually high levels of social capital and connection between richer and poorer people were the places with high mobility. They were the areas where the American Dream is alive and well.

"I was actually amazed to find in our data that the number of bowling alleys is strongly correlated with differences in upward mobility," Chetty noted, referencing social scientist Robert Putnam's famous book *Bowling Alone*, which documented the decline of social organizations in the United States. Putnam's iconic example was the local bowling club, where people from across the community might socialize, unlike in their more class-stratified workplaces.

Chetty and Hendren don't know exactly why cross-class friendships boost mobility. Maybe high-income people help their low-income friends get jobs and internships—sharing opportunity widely, rather than just within elite circles. Maybe there's some sharing of social habits or role modeling. The data doesn't say.

But their findings match up with other research, especially on segregation. When economist Rucker Johnson researched American schools that desegregated due to court orders, for example, he found that the Black students had higher graduation rates and incomes—all without a reciprocal cost to the white students.

Chetty and Hendren's Facebook-aided findings show dramatic effects: If a child from a disadvantaged background moves to a community with more intermingling between rich and poor families, their income in adulthood will be, on average, 20 percent higher.

Despite all his research on the importance of place, Chetty does not believe zip codes are destiny. He points to the success of immigrants who, on average, have higher income mobility than people born in the United States. Many immigrants do move to neighborhoods with high mobility. But that only explains part of the gap. Perhaps a key factor is the drive and determination often found among people who leave the world they know to seek opportunity.

That's huge! It's comparable to the income boost of a four-year-college degree.

When I ask Lydia Grayson-Cross if she has any advice for people who, like her, want to turn their life around, she responds quickly. "You have to be your own cheerleader. . . . I could say that several people in my corner helped me get there. But in the end, you're the one that has to do the footwork. It's up to you to get to the finish line."

Sure, the research shows that some neighborhoods offer more access to social capital, but motivated people can build social capital regardless of where they live. One impressive MTO participant, a 73-year-old grandmother who lived in public housing as part of the control group, pushed her adopted children to attend competitive charter schools. She kept herself and the family busy with afterschool and church programs, weekend cookouts, and college visits, connecting with people and potential role models. "There's no senior in this citizen," she told researchers who wrote a book about Moving to Opportunity.

According to another book that followed youth who grew up in poverty, many successful students who escaped poverty developed "identity projects," like an interest in medicine or joining the Junior Reserve Officers' Training Corps. These aspirations expanded their social networks and motivated them to finish school and pursue a career.

Chetty and Hendren have speculated that cross-class relationships may be a powerful source of role models. Remember Mike Andrews, the economist who studied patents during Prohibition? In another study, he and others found that a child who grows up next door to a doctor or lawyer is more likely to become a doctor or lawyer. But parents and teens who don't live next door to a successful professional can make their own luck by seeking out mentors and successful professionals.

After her return to New York City, Grayson-Cross suffered a setback. She needed multiple back surgeries, she says, after getting hit by a reckless driver. She can't work as much, and relies on disability payments to supplement her income. But she's proud of what she's accomplished: turning her life around in Jacksonville, getting a master's degree, and heading a women's organization on Staten Island.

"I think my story is still going to be rags to riches one day," she says. "I haven't given up on that."

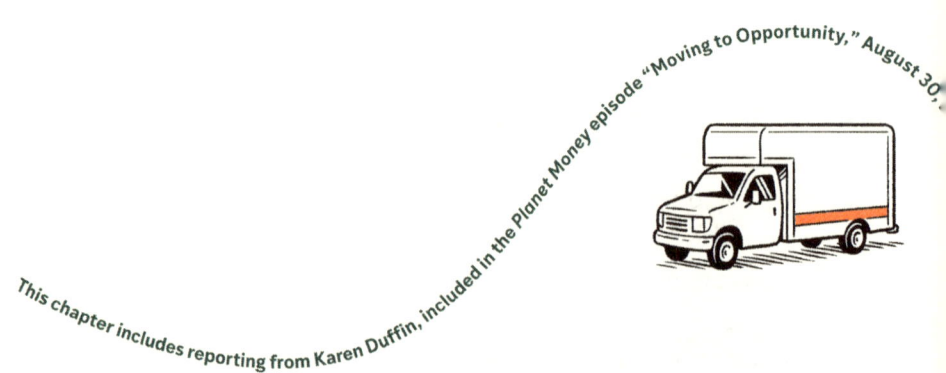

This chapter includes reporting from Karen Duffin, included in the Planet Money episode "Moving to Opportunity," August 30,

12

The Rent Is Too Damn High

The Squamish Nation's impossibly simple solution to the housing crisis

If in late 2024 you walked the shoreline in Vancouver, Canada, beach to beach, through the laid-back and well-off Kitsilano neighborhood and past the museums in Vanier Park, you'd arrive at a construction site where eleven residential towers rose from new foundations. The adjacent Burrard Street Bridge leads to downtown and Vancouver's striking skyline. But this cluster of high-rises and skyscrapers—squeezed between the bridge and the water, neighboring parks and single-family homes—looks like a second downtown packed into just four blocks. It feels distinct from the rest of the city.

That's because this site is not part of Vancouver. The development, Senákw, which roughly translates to "the place inside the head of False Creek," is a reserve that belongs to the Squamish Nation (Skwxwú7mesh Úxwumixw), who have lived in North America since long before the arrival of Europeans. With 250 to 300 of its rental apartments reserved for Squamish families, Senákw's construction represents an incredible moment of return: No Squamish had lived on this land since 1913, when residents were forced out and the provincial government burned the original Senákw village behind them. After a decades-long court case, the Squamish reclaimed these 10.5 acres in the early 2000s.

No one else can build like this in Vancouver—or almost anywhere in North America. Literally! In San Francisco, Boston, and other parts of Vancouver, zoning regulations have historically limited the height and density of new buildings, often to single-family homes with a yard. Reserves like Senákw, though, are not bound by these regulations.

The return of Senákw is a meaningful act of reconciliation and recompense. It also shows, in visually striking terms, how broken the housing market is in cities like Vancouver. It embodies how the desire for a place to live, especially among younger generations, has been blocked by cities' policies and choices. The demand for housing in Vancouver was overwhelming; the need for homes was, and is, desperate: An annual report on housing affordability ranks Vancouver as the third most expensive city in the world.

In 2022, Prime Minister Justin Trudeau attended Senákw's groundbreaking ceremony, as Vancouver's mayor praised the project. In addition to friendly diplomatic relations, the elected officials were enthused about Senákw's 6,000 new rental apartments. "We need to work together to provide more housing options for people," Trudeau said, "and that's what brings us here today."

We've seen how prices are signals and incentives. The high price of housing is a clear signal that these cities don't have enough homes. The rising of Senákw's towers shows how powerfully the incentive can mobilize people and resources to solve that shortage—if towns and cities stop sabotaging themselves and let people build as ambitiously as the Squamish Nation.

A fishy deal

PAÍTSMUK, a Squamish Nation Elder who also goes by the name David Jacobs, grew up in Homulchesan (X̱wemelch'stn), a reserve roughly six miles from Senákw, in the 1950s. He did not have plumbing, running water, or electricity until he was forced to attend a residential boarding school by the government. Like thousands of Indigenous Canadians, he was separated from family so he would assimilate.

"They took away my language," Paítsmuk says. "In our longhouse, we had to relearn." Despite the forced isolation—policies the Catholic Church and Canadian government have since apologized for as "cultural genocide" and "evil"—Paítsmuk grew up hearing stories of Senákw from family, including his father's grand-uncle, August Jack Khahtsahlano, who had watched Senákw burn in 1913.

In the 1860s, Senákw was both a village and gathering place, situated by seasonal salmon runs and bounties of duck, elk, and cedar trees. Vancouver did not yet exist, but the British had built a small mill town and timber sites nearby, amid the homelands of the Squamish, Musqueam, and Tsleil-Waututh. Despite their minor presence, the British claimed enormous swaths of land—all of it, really—reserving just 0.3 percent of British Columbia for First Nations. The village of Senákw and 82 surrounding acres became Kitsilano Indian Reserve No. 6, named after Paítsmuk's ancestor Khatsahlano. In 1886, when the transcontinental railroad arrived, the mill town incorporated as Vancouver and grew quickly.

Even though the British had designated Senákw a reserve, many colonizers still coveted the land. A Canadian railway company laid tracks across the reserve, then built another line a decade later, all without the permission of Squamish residents. Then, in 1913, the provincial government offered Senákw residents money to leave.

"They were walking around with envelopes with money in it," says Paítsmuk. "A lot of people didn't understand." According to contemporary reports, the province's attorney general told villagers that if they refused they would "get nothing at all for your land, not one cent."

"Once they accepted that, they said . . . 'You have to leave,'" says Paítsmuk. "The government brought a barge up to the beach . . . They weren't on the barge very long [before] they were burning their houses down."

After a period of bureaucratic delay, the Canadian government made the sale official, and Senákw and Kitsilano Indian Reserve No. 6 ceased to exist. That land became the approach to the Burrard Bridge; it became a wharf and marina; it became national defense buildings, city streets, and rental homes; it became, ultimately, the 40 acres of Vanier Park and its multiple museums. Despite having sold a large, prime piece of land, the Squamish Nation lacked funds for its members and for reserves like Homulchesan, where Paítsmuk grew up without essentials like plumbing.

In the 1960s, Paítsmuk joined Nexwsxwnı́w̓ntm ta Úxwumixw, the Squamish Nation Council. Early in his tenure, he says, an elder member said that there was "something fishy" about the land deal. They asked a legal adviser to investigate.

"The lawyer came back in a bit, and he said, 'I think we have something here,'" Paítsmuk recalls.

The Squamish never signed a treaty with Britain, but per British law, which stayed in force after Canadian independence, "the Crown" oversaw the reserves that they forced Native people onto and had a duty to represent Indigenous interests. This "honor of the Crown" principle is patronizing, but legally binding.

The lawyer's research revealed a history of the Crown failing its legal obligations to the Squamish as British and Canadian groups acquired Senákw through subterfuge and at below-market prices. The Canadian railway company had built its tracks across the reserve without paying reasonable compensation and without the permission of Indian Affairs, the government body meant to represent First Nations' best interest on behalf of the Crown. In 1913, when families boarded the barge and left Senákw, they did so in response to coercion by the provincial government, which intentionally did not alert Indian Affairs, making the sale illegitimate. It was not until decades later, after years of legal limbo, of fending off bad-faith attempts to purchase the reserve, of the government legally appropriating parcels (undervaluing them each time), that the Squamish and Indian Affairs agreed to accept the sale.

After hearing this legal history, Paı́tsmuk̲ and the Squamish Council decided to sue the Canadian government. In 1977, the council initiated the Omnibus Trust Action, a series of legal claims. The land of Seṅák̲w was gone, but they hoped to receive compensation.

Living near the money obelisk

THE HOUSING CRISES AFFLICTING so many prosperous cities are the result of a fundamental tension. To homeowners, their house or apartment is a place they chose, at great cost, and where they've raised their children, learned their neighbors' names, and organized block parties. It's also a financial asset and nest egg. They're incentivized to block the construction of new housing, which might change the neighborhood they love and, by boosting supply, reduce the price of their home and most valuable investment.

For everyone else, though, the homeowners' neighborhood is a place with access to jobs, social capital, and other opportunities that cluster in big cities due to agglomeration. Living there is a springboard to economic mobility and prosperity. Because of the high demand for homes, the restrictions on new housing, and the access to economic opportunities, owning real estate in these neighborhoods is like living next to a magic, money-producing obelisk. The lucky few who are in range of its power get wealthier. But from society's perspective, shouldn't we build more homes next to the wealth-spawning obelisk? Shouldn't we help more families contribute to and benefit from all the prosperity that cities enable?

Cities struggling with high housing costs, like New York, Vancouver, and Seattle, have not banned new homes. But according to economist and housing expert Daryl Fairweather, they've drastically limited their construction in two main ways:

1. **Single-family zoning:** Many towns and cities, including metropolises like San Francisco, ban apartment buildings and even duplexes from most residential neighborhoods.

Along with other restrictions like parking requirements and setbacks (minimum yardage between the street and your building), this suburban-sprawl mandate prevents developers from building denser developments that would increase the supply of housing.

2. **Approvals process:** If a proposed building follows zoning codes, the developer can just build it, right? Nope! Most municipalities allow neighbors to weigh in and require a vote by a planning board or commission. The approval process can stretch on and on, and the delays and uncertainty deter new projects and construction.

Even when governors and mayors promise to build more homes, they are foiled by local politicians' responsiveness to current homeowners. The potential future residents who need the new housing—the college grad who wants to job hunt in the city, the family with a housing voucher striving for a middle-class life—aren't around to vote for the city council and advocate for duplexes and high-rises. So instead of denser developments and affordable-enough housing, cities build an insignificant number of large, luxury homes that meet zoning codes.

One infamous example: When San Francisco residents complained that wealthy Google engineers were driving up rents, Google proposed building homes on their suburban campus, in Mountain View. But locals derailed that by arguing that it would disturb burrowing owls in the area.

The technical name for this behavior is **rent seeking**. Somewhat confusingly, the term originally referred to, among other things, landowners charging tenants and workers rent. Beginning in the 1960s, economists began using it to describe any unproductive behavior that extracts value from productive parts of the economy. If a business monopoly overcharges for its services, that's rent seeking. If a corrupt politician gives government contracts to shoddy businesses in exchange for kickbacks, that's rent seeking. And if homeowners use their political power to prevent the construction of housing—thereby making their property more valuable—that's rent seeking.

Some residents who object to high-rises counter that cities should instead build affordable housing and subsidize rent. The problem is that if zoning codes ban all dense housing, and if neighbors veto high-rises, then each subsidized unit will be incredibly expensive. If we truly care about affordability, says Fairweather, it's important to upzone neighborhoods, to allow them to be denser, which will grow the city's economy and produce more wealth that can be used to subsidize housing and be redistributed to vulnerable people.

"You can't really stop the economy from growing... or wealthy people from buying homes," she says. "The only thing we can do is try to build an abundance of housing so that the most vulnerable people aren't competed out of their housing."

But that's not what Vancouver's residents chose to do. And so, as the Squamish Nation's lawsuit navigated Canadian courts in the 1980s and 1990s, their rent-seeking behavior created the affordability crisis that would make Seṉákw's towers so badly needed.

"We're using their own paper against them"

AT COURT, the Squamish had to play by British and Canadian rules. The First Nations had no tradition of property titles. But the law required them to document their property interests and prove they had been wronged by a system they'd had no say in developing.

According to Alexandra Flynn, a law professor who previously represented other First Nations at the law firm Ratcliff LLP, which represented the Squamish Nation, this is one of the most challenging aspects of Indigenous land cases: assembling mountains of evidence to prove a century or more of land use. Since most First Nations have an oral tradition, their law firm had to track down maps and documents from archives and hire anthropologists to record oral accounts of Seṉákw.

"The evidence that was produced for the court case came from a lot of our old people, and our old people don't lie," says Paítsmuk. "This is what happened. This is who it happened to."

But the lawyers and researchers did not come cheap. Paítsmuk's colleague on the council, his cousin Squamish Nation hereditary Chief Gilbert "Gibby" Jacob, recalls the moment when they informed their people how much they'd need to spend. That money could go to programs and services. Pursuing the lawsuit was a huge risk. They asked the community: Should they proceed?

"People just said, go, go," says Chief Gibby. "Go fight whoever you gotta fight."

The research and motions took years. But the delays had two unexpected benefits.

First, when Canada amended its constitution in 1982, it "recognize[d] and affirm[ed]" First Nations' treaty rights. Over the next decade, courts pointed to the amendment to clarify that the Crown (i.e., the national government) had a fiduciary duty to manage reserves in Indigenous people's best interest.

Then, in 1989, the railroad company tried to sell the 10.5 acres of Senákw it once used for rail lines. The land was multiple city blocks, all undeveloped, along the water, with skyline views. A dream listing for any real estate agent. And an opportunity for the Squamish Nation. They sued for its return.

Paítsmuk and Chief Gibby spent many days in court. What Chief Gibby remembers most is staff wheeling in all the evidence each day. "There were over 10,000 documents," he says. "I was sitting there thinking... 'Thank God the white people don't throw out anything. We're using their own paper against them.'"

As the case progressed, Paítsmuk felt they "had the government on the ropes." They'd proven that Senákw's sale and acquisition had been illegal and against their interests. In 2000, after more than two decades in court, the government agreed to a $92.5 million settlement to compensate the Squamish, and a judge separately ruled that the Squamish should get back those 10.5 acres of Senákw. To celebrate, Paitsamuk went and got "a good mug of beer."

"Here we go, guys," he said. Many people had worked on the case, and the return of the land meant they had plans to make and more work to do.

Plan for seven generations

WHEN THE COURT CASE CONCLUDED, Sxwíxwtn Wilson Williams was a young man in a prominent Squamish family. He remembers hearing every house's phone ringing because everyone wanted to share the news. "It was like a shock wave," he says. "I just remember the pride... the happiness."

The Squamish leadership had long ago decided that they'd never sell the land. But how should they use it? Many people wanted to simply rebuild their village, says Williams, who began serving on the Squamish Council in

Redlining and Reparations

In 1933, employees at a new U.S. government entity, the Home Owners' Loan Corporation (HOLC), created a series of color-coded maps. It was the Great Depression, and families were losing their homes. HOLC's mission was to prevent this by providing families with new, government-subsidized loans. The following year, a new agency, the Federal Housing Association (FHA), was created. Together, HOLC and the FHA determined that homeowners who lived in areas shaded in green, yellow, or blue were eligible. But in neighborhoods outlined in red, homeowners couldn't get those federally insured mortgages.

The point of the maps was to tell banks which neighborhoods the FHA considered too poor and risky for their low-interest, government-insured mortgages. In practice, writes historian Richard Rothstein in *The Color of Law*, the maps outlined "state-sponsored segregation." With few exceptions, areas with nonwhite residents were coded red, and the presence of Black people was assumed to reduce property values and threaten the neighborhoods' stability.

For decades, the FHA and federal government channeled subsidies to white families and neighborhoods while depriving nonwhites of those investments by:

 refusing to insure mortgages in minority neighborhoods;

 subsidizing the construction of new neighborhoods and developments, but requiring that developers only allow white people to buy the new homes;

 constructing highways to improve access to mostly white suburbs, and building them through politically weak Black neighborhoods, or locating them between Black and white neighborhoods as intentional barriers; and

 updating their maps to redline neighborhoods that Black and nonwhite families started moving into.

> Policies like these cut Black families off from lowering their housing costs and enjoying the wealth-building benefits of homeownership. They created prosperous, racially segregated suburbs and impoverished ghettos. By the time the Fair Housing Act of 1968 outlawed redlining and racial covenants (clauses in homeowners' property deeds or in contracts made between neighbors that banned them from selling to nonwhite individuals), prosperous areas' high rents and mortgage payments, along with the restrictions on new housing, effectively excluded most minorities.
>
> Today, some legal scholars argue that paying reparations to Black families for redlining would be a standard application of law, compensating people for past harms. Much like the case of Senákw.

2013. But an elder councillor transformed the conversation, he says, by repeating an Indigenous saying that's believed to have originated in the Haudenosaunee (Iroquois) Constitution, and that has a long history in Squamish teachings and culture: Always prepare for the next seven generations.

As they discussed and debated, they faced a unique economic situation: All the local zoning codes and land-use regulations—like other laws that weren't national law—did not apply to the reserve. Since Senákw was liberated from zoning, the rent-seeking behavior by Vancouver homeowners was an opportunity rather than an obstacle.

When the council studied the land's potential—with the intent of generating as much income and employment as possible for Nation members, including future generations—the signal from Vancouver's housing market was clear: Building residences had the most potential to generate long-term income.

The development came with plenty of challenges. Since it's illegal under Indigenous law to seize reserve land, the Squamish could not use the land of Senákw as collateral to get loans. But they received a $1.4 billion low-interest loan from a national government fund meant to create new rental units. Senákw needed to connect to Vancouver's streets, sewage, and electric grid, so they negotiated a services agreement with the city, which did not demand any changes to the Senákw plan. Neighbors in Kits

Point sued the city for being secretive when negotiating the agreement—and suggested, patronizingly, that a small, parklike development would better align with Indigenous values. A judge rejected their challenge.

It was a remarkable turnaround. A century ago, Squamish leaders pleaded for the government to protect the specks of land they'd not yet taken. Now Canadian leaders were praising their "government-to-government" relations with the Squamish, while prominent developers were vying to partner with them.

"I'm always a half glass full [guy] . . . I felt that there were always good intentions on both sides," says Williams. "In this spirit of reconciliation today, the city of Vancouver [has] really seen the light, in like, 'Hey, this is your village, we want to help you be back there.'"

As Senákw's towers rise, 50 percent of the workers are Indigenous, with 15 percent Squamish representation, according to 2024 data. Many received training in trades such as hoist operation, construction safety, and mechanical design. Once the buildings are finished, Senákw's revenue is forecast as upward of $10 billion over coming decades, which will help the Squamish Nation build public housing on other reserves, assist homeless members, and achieve financial sustainability. Williams feels proud he's helping complete a project that his parents' generation started, and that will benefit seven generations.

When it opens, Senákw's 6,000 apartments are projected to more than double the number of new rental units added to Vancouver's housing supply that year. It's a meaningful contribution. By itself, though, the development will only slow the growth of housing costs in Vancouver. Senákw is unique; it can't solve Vancouver's housing shortages or be a universal model. But it does offer lessons.

Senákw's scale and size show the resources ready to be marshaled to solve the housing shortage. Just four blocks of Vancouver were returned to the Squamish, and therefore freed from zoning restrictions, and the result will be 6,000 new homes. Loosening zoning codes across entire cities would not look as dramatic as Senákw—a sprinkling of new duplexes among single-family homes, the occasional sprouting of a high-rise. But all together, they'd transform people's lives.

It's also telling that Senákw faced opposition from a neighborhood association, but received support from the city government, mayor, and prime minister. Our current system, which gives neighbors so much say

Trickle-Down Housing

A new "luxury" housing development may not seem like a win for housing affordability. But as housing economist Daryl Fairweather pointed out, if it increases the number of homes in the area, it can play a crucial role. Without it, the affluent people willing to buy or rent the expensive new homes will compete with less-wealthy families for existing housing.

A 2021 study, for example, by Evan Mast, an assistant professor of economics at the University of Notre Dame, looked at the construction of new, market-rate housing in 12 American cities. Mast estimated that every 100 residents who move into new, market-rate units open up space in existing buildings in (sometimes entirely different) lower-income neighborhoods for 45 to 70 people. These are the "migration ripple effects of new housing," he writes, that "affect a wide spectrum of neighborhoods."

But there's another reason that building market-rate housing is important for housing affordability: Today's luxury housing tends to become tomorrow's affordable housing.

This process is known as filtering. As buildings age, wealthier families often move out and are replaced by families with lower incomes. One study estimated that from 1985 to 2011, families moving into aging buildings had incomes 2.5 percent lower (for rentals) or 0.5 percent lower (for owned homes) each year.

Building affordable housing can be prohibitively expensive. But letting developers build new, market-rate homes costs taxpayers nothing, and, over time, a steady share of those homes will transform into affordable housing.

over new construction, has a veneer of participatory government. But it's more like leaving decisions in the hands of a landed gentry. Tellingly, politicians answerable to the wider electorate pursued their collective interest in lower housing costs by supporting Senákw. Homeowners' desire for their neighborhoods to stay the same, and to increase the value of their homes, has to be balanced with giving more people access to the cities and regions that are engines of prosperity and sources of opportunity.

Vancouver has started to move in the direction of balance: In 2023, the provincial government of British Columbia voted to end single-family zoning, and Vancouver's city council started allowing multiplexes with up to eight units.

The housing crisis is a story of economic incentives, but also of empathy. "I wish that communities had the mentality that it is their responsibility to grow, because we know there's going to be future generations that are going to need housing," Fairweather tells me. "I [wish] that people cared more about future residents."

Relationship Advice from Economists

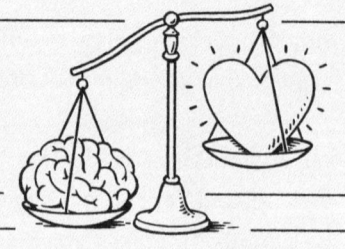

WARM HEARTS THROUGH COLD CALCULATION

Dear Love Economists,

Everyone my age complains they can't find someone looking for a serious relationship. But that's what I want, and I say so in my dating profile and when I meet someone. Why doesn't that seem to help me get to a second or third date?

—Bewildered in Boise

Dear Bewildered,

Your problem may be what economists call cheap talk: Anyone can *say* what they want. But how does the other party know they mean it?

The solution is to send a costly signal. For example, the economist Paul Milgrom met his wife at a dinner honoring Nobel Prize winners. She lived in Sweden, and he lived in California. When he got home, he said he'd like to see her again. He also offered to buy her a plane ticket to meet anywhere in the world. Expressing his interest through the time, money, and effort of his offer was a signal that couldn't be faked.

Dear Love Economists,

I feel like dating is so much work. I spend all my time driving across town for awkward app dates with strangers who lie about their height and talk about crypto. Should I just give up and get a cat?

—Dateless in Denver

Dear Dateless,

You are describing search costs: the work of sorting through options and prices before purchasing, say, new jeans or a car. When search costs get too high, people get exasperated and may not make a purchase at all.

In schools and universities, students have low search costs because they meet peers regularly in class. You can lower yours by joining clubs, giving speed dating a try, and doing things that involve regularly meeting new people. This applies to finding friends, too!

Dear Love Economists,

I've spent four years and $2,000 on couples therapy with a boyfriend who still does Borat-voice and has started talking about how marriage is "just a piece of paper." I would dump him, but then I'd feel like I wasted a lot of time and money. What should I do?

—Committed in Calgary

Dear Committed,

When economist Richard Thaler was a graduate student, he and a friend received free tickets to a basketball game. But the night of the match, a snowstorm blew in. "There is no way we are driving in this snow," his friend said. "But if we'd paid for those tickets, then we'd be going."

This is the sunk cost fallacy. Why drive through a snowstorm just because you paid for tickets? Or sit through a bad movie when you'd walk out if the tickets had been free? The money is already gone; spend your time on something else.

Similarly, the time you invest in a friendship or relationship is a sunk cost. It should not be the reason you stay in it.

Dear Love Economists,

When I open my dating apps, I always have lots of new matches and messages. This makes it easy to set up dates, but they've all been pretty "meh." Would I do better if I made the first move?

—Popular in Paris

Dear Popular,

Remember the stable-marriage problem? The Gale-Shapley algorithm matches people optimally, but there's an important asterisk. The side doing the proposing gets their best possible match! Everyone getting proposed to may have done better if they made the first move.

If you get asked out by someone you've gotten to know at church or in a college seminar, the Gale-Shapley algorithm doesn't apply. But dating apps resemble the multiple rounds and single "marketplace" of the Stable-Marriage Problem. So if you're on the apps, then maybe it's time to follow the wisdom of Sadie Hawkins dances and make the first move!

Dear Love Economists,

My partner and I just moved in together. We love it! But we're fighting about how to load the dishwasher, how often to clean the countertops, and whether duvet covers have any purpose. Is there a formula to navigate these disagreements and achieve domestic bliss?

—Co-living in Caracas

Dear Co-living,

Economists have not discovered the optimal way to load the dishwasher, and even if they did, you or your partner might still mess it up. What economics can offer, though, is a mindset for identifying opportunities to expand your collective supply of domestic bliss.

To do so, focus on finding Pareto improvements: ways to reallocate resources (or chores or decision making) in a way that makes someone better off without making anyone else worse off. If you have different preferences over how often to clean the kitchen, there's no costless solution where you both get exactly what you want. But if your partner really cares about squeezing the sponge dry after use, and it costs you basically nothing in time or effort, why not just do it?

Dear Love Economists,

My spouse and I prefer different kinds of restaurants, and while it's nice that we compromise, that means we never go to my top choice. How do I better lobby for the restaurant I want to go to?

—Frustrated in Fresno

Dear Frustrated,

Time to deploy a decoy. Have you ever noticed subscription offers for magazines or software that offer three tiers: a cheap option, a premium option, and a third choice that is obviously a terrible deal? That's the decoy. It's there to make the premium option seem better by comparison.

When you're debating where to go for dinner, try throwing in a decoy option. First, suggest the average place you're tired of. Then the new spot with good reviews that you want to try, but that's a bit of a walk. And finally propose a similar restaurant that's really far away. You'll find your partner opting for your preferred, better-by-comparison restaurant.

Or just alternate who chooses the restaurant each date night.

The questions in this column are fictional, but the stories and economic principles in the responses are 100% real. Thank you to Tim Harford, who came on the *Planet Money* podcast in 2014 to answer listeners' love questions. And to Daryl Fairweather, for pointing out the search costs of dating.

13

The Global Conspiracy to Make Childcare More Expensive

Why goods get cheaper and services don't

For months, Wesley Wade and his wife, Giovonni Wade, ended their days the same way, asking themselves, "How is this so hard?" The task consuming their evenings—after Wade's days working as a mental-health counselor and Giovonni's as an attorney—was finding childcare for their baby, Ella.

"She is a very defiant child, which we love," says Wesley. "It's very fun."

But finding childcare? That was not fun. That was incredibly difficult. Wesley, who was studying for his PhD, made an Excel spreadsheet while his wife kept a paper list of options. Seemingly every childcare center in Durham, North Carolina, the big university town where they lived, had a wait-list. There didn't seem to be enough spots. They went searching for hidden childcare: no website, maybe an ambiguous name like Jay's Jungle or the Blooming Room. But still, no spaces. The couple had money for childcare, but they couldn't find someone to give it to.

"I can't even say the words 'reasonably affordable,'" Wesley says. "None of it is reasonable at all!"

Eventually, Wesley quit his full-time job to take care of Ella. "I don't know how other people figure this out," says Wesley. ". . . I think my dissertation research might have been a little easier."

Why can't two successful professionals living in one of the wealthiest countries in human history find workable childcare? Why do we nod along when parents with good jobs and sound finances say they can't afford a second child, or a first? Why is raising children so expensive and getting more so? The answer is waiting for us at a dining-room table in 1990s New Haven, Connecticut, where a professor tinkers with a light meter.

Four thousand years of better, cheaper stuff

FOR MUCH OF HUMAN HISTORY, we spent a lot of time in the dark. The sun set, and that was it. People invented many strange and creative light sources to fend off the night: campfires, capturing fireflies in a lantern, making candles from salmon or cow fat, or even, according to some sailors' accounts, pushing a wick inside an oily seabird and lighting it. But getting consistent light was too much work for everyone to afford it.

The story of light and how people made it is one way to tell the story of human progress, of why daily life has materially improved over centuries. And, as we'll see, it's a way to understand what we might now call the cost of living, including for things like childcare in Durham, North Carolina.

In the 1990s, Yale economist Bill Nordhaus got interested in artificial light and energy efficiency. He borrowed a light meter from campus staff and, in his dining room, pointed it at different lamps and bulbs. He tracked their efficiency differences: how some produced more light (measured in lumens) when powered with the same amount of electricity.

"I just became more and more interested," he recalls. "Simple curiosity."

Nordhaus's light tinkering became serious research. At the time, economists were puzzling over a big question about how to measure cost of living. With inflation, prices go up most years, but so do salaries. That doesn't mean that everyone is richer, nor that everything is less affordable. It's hard to accurately quantify how much better or worse off someone is using salaries and prices.

Economists adjust for inflation by tracking, for example, that a gallon of milk cost 3.4 percent more in 2021 than 2020. But over the long run, these comparisons become absurd. How can one compare the cost of a new Ford Model T in 1910 to the cost of a new Honda Accord in 2025? Or the price of Pony Express messengers with the price of sending an email? Many economists suspected they were overestimating inflation-driven price increases by failing to account for how technology improved the quality of goods.

Nordhaus realized that he and his light bulbs could test this hypothesis, because artificial light was an ideal yardstick of changing prices. Humans have made artificial light since prehistory, but our technological improvements from fire pits to candles to light bulbs can be quantified: A wax candle might emit 13 lumens, while a modern LED light bulb might emit 800 lumens.

This became Nordhaus's quest: to figure out how much it cost people throughout history to create light, to ward off the night with candles or oil lamps or light bulbs. Which meant he needed literally ancient price data. The wonderful thing about academia is that Nordhaus just bumped into someone on the Yale campus with

This is a great example of how having smart people near one another produces innovation.

exactly that. "It's just unbelievable," says Nordhaus. "She actually had wage data and price data from the Babylonian era, so 4,000 years ago."

To compare the cost of lamp oil in ancient Babylon's markets with a 20th-century utility bill, Nordhaus made two adjustments. First he had to know exactly how much light those Babylonian lamps produced from a set amount of oil. So he bought an ancient-style terra-cotta lamp from a catalog, got it burning with the cold-pressed sesame oil used by Babylonians, and measured its brightness with his light meter.

"I would just measure it and write it down, just the way you see in the old movies," says Nordhaus. He measured re-creations of other light sources, too, like prehistoric fires.

The second step was to price the cost of those lumens in a universal currency: time. How much light could the average person buy with a day's wages? The answer in ancient Babylon, where a standard wage was one shekel per month, was not much. A full day of work bought 10 minutes of light.

"Maybe 10 minutes," says Nordhaus. "It was really expensive."

Nordhaus's work allowed him to chart a timeline of the "true" price of light, which confirmed economists' suspicion that they overestimated increases in the cost of living. Because the cost of light, at least, had dropped remarkably over time:

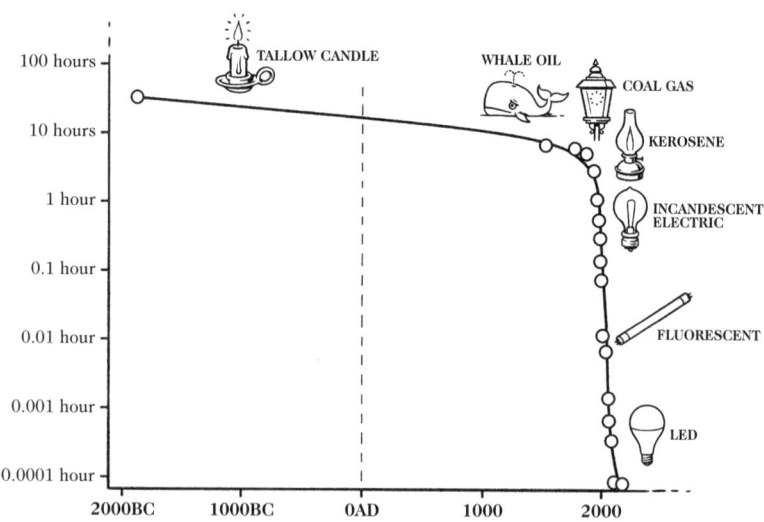

Throughout history, how long did a person have to work to afford to light a room brightly for an hour?

Nordhaus's chart is of light prices, but it charts an economic history of the world. For most of history, people barely improved on ancient Babylonians' light sources, which remained expensive. In the 1700s, the cost of light declined a bit when whaling became a global industry. (Unfortunately for whales, their massive fat stores made them big, floating sources of lamp fuel.) But the economy of the 1700s, like lighting technology, resembled ancient Babylon more than today. A majority of the population was subsistence farmers; well-lit dinner parties were an aristocratic luxury; and the max speed of travel and communication was that of a galloping horse or sailing ship.

Then the Industrial Revolution happened. "You can see it so clearly in lighting," says Nordhaus. "It's just an enormous change in the pace of improvement." Scholars begin to apply the scientific method to problems. Before, universities had mostly just preserved and passed on knowledge; now they began to create new technologies. The number of corporations exploded and financial markets provided funds for railroads, telegraph lines, and research and development.

Around 1850, a Canadian named Abraham Gesner figured out how to turn coal or oil into kerosene, which seemed like magical lamp fuel: brighter, cleaner, and cheaper. "You work a day, you get about an hour of whale oil. Kerosene, you get about five hours," says Nordhaus. ". . . Kerosene lit the world and saved the whales." When John D. Rockefeller created the Standard Oil Company, which evolved into a corporate behemoth unlike anything the world had ever seen, the main product was kerosene for lamps. When Edison and the light bulb came along, further driving down the cost of lighting, Standard Oil feared for their business—until they found a new market in gasoline-fueled cars. Edison was not the last word, of course. People obsessively worked on light bulbs and the systems that powered them, finding little improvements year after year.

Cheaper, faster, more efficient: This is how aristocratic luxuries like light, books, and refrigerators became widely affordable. It's how millions of people left the farm to become plumbers and poets and paralegals. By the time Nordhaus published his findings on artificial light, a day of work bought around 20,000 hours of light.

> Another example of this pace of progress: In the original *The Fast and the Furious* (2001), the LAPD sent an undercover agent to foil Vin Diesel's huge criminal enterprise, which was . . . stealing DVD players, a technology that was approaching obsolescence when the 10th film in the franchise was released in 2023.

The global economy has many faults, but it's also a giant conspiracy to provide us with better goods at a lower cost. Someone invents the shipping container to make loading and unloading cargo at ports faster and easier. Solar companies team up with Wall Street so homeowners don't have to pay up front to install panels on their roof. An agronomist develops crops that yield more food every harvest. This process has elevated millions of humans out of poverty and given them the ability to travel, choose a career, and light up Times Square as bright as noon for years on end.

So why is childcare still so expensive?

You can't innovate your way to a three-person quartet

TO UNDERSTAND HOW GOODS GET CHEAPER OVER TIME, you go to Nordhaus. To understand why services like childcare get more expensive over time, you read the work of the late Princeton economist William Baumol.

The origin story of Baumol's most famous theory is that he was asked by John D. Rockefeller III and President John F. Kennedy's cultural adviser, the philanthropist August Heckscher, to investigate why so many theaters and artists were struggling financially in the 1960s. Like Nordhaus with his dining-room experiments, Baumol, himself an avid painter and sculptor, and his Princeton colleague William Bowen, an assistant professor of economics, tracked down data, poking around backstage, sending questionnaires to theatergoers, and interviewing Broadway producers. Baumol soon developed an explanation, an elegant, data-backed theory that explained much more than why artists were starving—so much so that economists have since spent decades unpacking its implications.

Later dubbed **Baumol's cost disease**, the theory explains why raising children becomes increasingly expensive in rich societies. The essential insight is that while a single farmer produces far more food today than a century ago, the performing arts have not generally gotten more productive. "The output per man-hour of the violinist playing a Schubert quartet in a standard concert hall is relatively fixed," Baumol and Bowen wrote, "and it is fairly difficult to reduce the number of actors necessary for a performance of Henry IV, Part II."

To oversimplify a bit: The economy is divided between sectors like growing corn and manufacturing shirts, which become more efficient and productive over time, and trades like haircuts, fine dining, and teaching toddlers, which require roughly as much labor as they did before the Industrial Revolution.

Sadly, this doesn't mean that corn chips and halter tops get cheaper while plays and anniversary dinners remain the same price. Auto repair, plays, restaurants, and teaching toddlers get *more* expensive. These sectors are the victim of the wider economy's success:

1. As the corn chip and halter-top industries get more productive, they can make more product without an increase in costs. Profits up! The chip marketers and halter-top designers capture some of the productivity gains by getting raises and bonuses.

2. The violinists and teachers see those higher wages in the corn chip and halter-top industries and start switching careers.

3. The theaters and schools respond by raising their own wages to keep their staff.

4. But now, costs are up for theaters and childcare centers. Profits down! They raise prices to make ends meet. Or cut costs and reduce quality.

5. The end result is that theater and childcare *are* more expensive. Corn chips and halter top prices stay the same, or even drop because of productivity, while a concert and the babysitter you need to go see it have gotten relatively more expensive.

This cycle of Baumol's cost disease explains situations where productivity gains in one sector of the economy lead to rising costs in another sector that can't achieve the same efficiency improvements. Usually this means labor-intensive services, since human time and attention are the essential feature. As Baumol pointed out, it's difficult to make Shakespeare more efficient, or for a childcare worker to safely watch additional tod-

Tooth Fairy Inflation

Behold, tooth inflation! For more than two decades, the insurance company Delta Dental has polled a representative sample of 1,000 American parents. Their question: How much do you, as the tooth fairy, leave under your child's pillow for each lost tooth?

Their data reveals that the Tooth Fairy has been getting increasingly generous. In 2001, a lost tooth was worth, on average, $1.70. Adjusting for inflation, that's about $3.00 in 2024 dollars. But in 2024, parents deposited almost $6.00!

The kids don't need this extra money because of cost disease. In fact, they're *benefiting* from the global conspiracy that makes a kid's top purchases (sour candies, toys, stickers) cheaper and cheaper. The data doesn't lie: Kids are more spoiled nowadays.

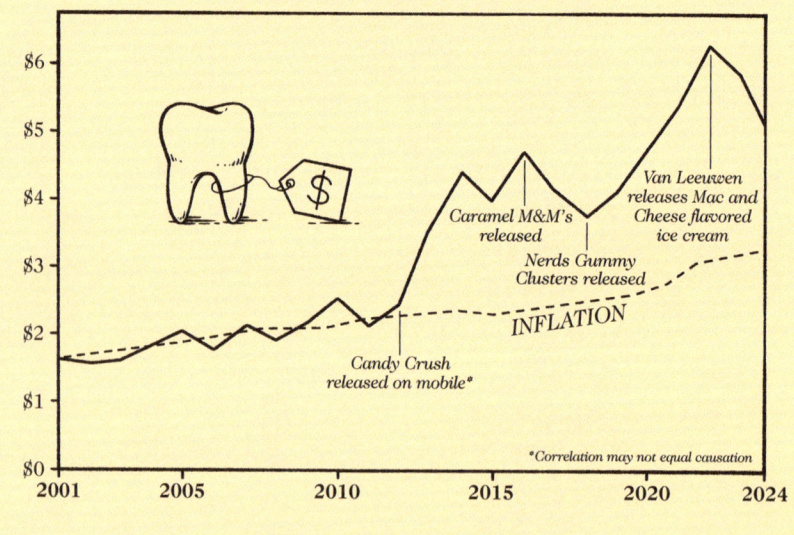

dlers. Baumol's cost disease is why health-care costs keep rising, and why your doctor may rush you out trying to see more patients per hour. It's why college keeps getting more expensive. Professors can still only teach one class and grade one paper at a time. Or why opera houses and theaters are nonprofits that ask wealthy patrons for donations, even as the ticket prices make your head spin.

This leads to a paradox. From a parent's perspective, the high price of childcare—$11,000 per child per year, on average, in the United States—suggests that childcare centers must make a killing. But the opposite is true: The staff tends to earn less than nearby burger flippers, and the owners barely make a profit. Given the shortage of spots, childcare centers could raise their prices. But they know that if costs go too high, then a chunk of parents will pivot to quitting their job, like Wesley did, hiring a nanny, or finding a neighbor or family member to watch their child. So childcare centers slightly underprice their service and keep wait-lists, which ensures they'll never lose out on revenue from a parent pulling their child last-minute.

While the global economy has conspired for decades to bring down the cost of dolls and footballs, the biggest expenses of raising kids—childcare, summer camp, music lessons, babysitting, college tuition, health care—all suffer from Baumol's cost disease.

In combination, this adds up to an average price tag for raising a child of more than $300,000, without including college tuition. In 2017, the federal government estimated, based on projected inflation and expenditure data, that raising a child born in 2015 would cost, through 2032 (when the child reached age seventeen), $233,610. That's more than $300,000 in 2025 dollars.

Three hundred thousand dollars is daunting! No wonder people are having fewer children. Securing a spot in childcare already pits new parents against each other like the Hunger Games. College tuition already looks like the Mount Everest of responsible budgeting. And the implication of cost disease is that the only way the cost of raising and educating children will stop going up is if the economy crashes. Sounds bad!

The good news is that wealthy countries have a simple cure for cost disease: subsidizing services like childcare. Baumol did the math: The increase in productivity from other parts of the economy creates enough new wealth to subsidize education, health care, and other sectors afflicted by cost disease.

The bad news is that if people are miserly—if executives and high-paid professionals pat themselves on the back for their high salaries and demand politicians keep taxes low—then other people will have to drop out of the workforce because childcare costs too much and schools suffer from teacher shortages. We seem to see this in the United States, which offers unusually little support to parents compared to peer countries. Due in part to this lack of state subsidies, many couples delay having children until their salaries increase: In 2016, American women in their 30s had more babies than women in their 20s.

Many Americans are famously resistant to tax increases, but this is the road to pauperdom. Since governments mostly provide labor-intensive services like education, policing, and health care, their budgets will inevitably be squeezed by cost disease.

The price of a successful economy is your taxes going up, forever.

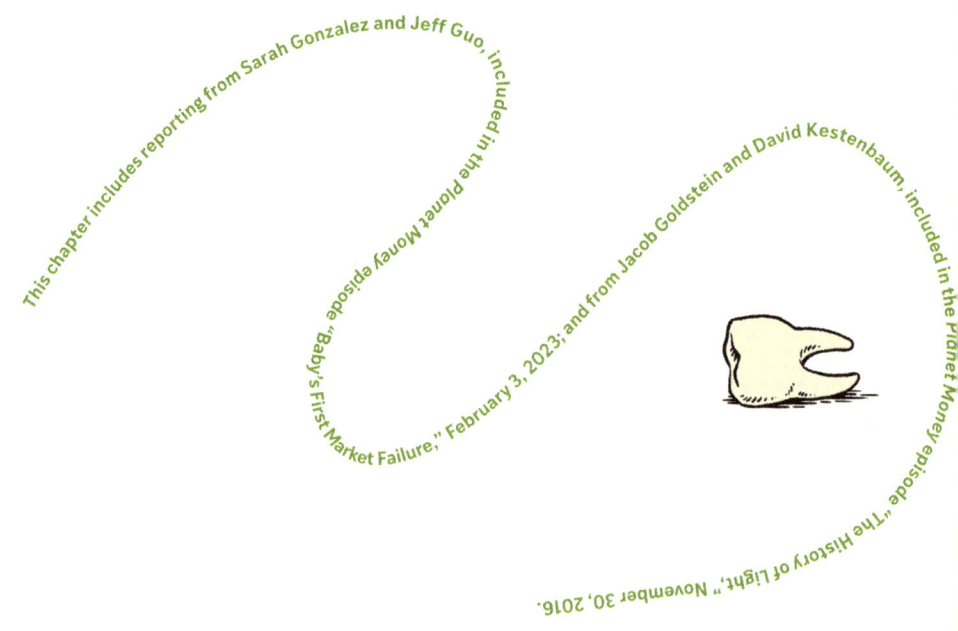

This chapter includes reporting from Sarah Gonzalez and Jeff Guo, included in the Planet Money episode "Baby's First Market Failure," February 3, 2023; and from Jacob Goldstein and David Kestenbaum, included in the Planet Money episode "The History of Light," November 30, 2016.

PART FOUR

SAVING &

14

Bobby Bonilla Day

The "worst contract in sports history" is a blueprint for retirement planning

For New York Mets fans, July 1 is a sad holiday. It's the day when their bumbling baseball franchise sends a $1 million check to Bobby Bonilla, a retired player who last put on a uniform decades ago. If you ask Mets fans about what's now known as Bobby Bonilla Day, they'll laugh, they'll cry, and they'll tell you, "July 1st is probably the worst day for the Mets, ever."

In 1999, Bonilla was an aging slugger for the Mets. The ball club owed him $6 million, but they wanted that money for other things. So they renegotiated. Bonilla agreed to a delay—if they paid him more. A lot more. Instead of paying him $6 million, the Mets agreed to send him just over $1 million per year, every year, from 2011 to 2035. Which sounds absurd. That's $30 million for 25 years of nonplaying! During some years, the Mets paid Bonilla more than they paid a starting player.

At *Planet Money*, though, this is our favorite sports contract because it demonstrates one of the most powerful lessons in finance, a principle whose implications are so profound that we need reminders of its power. Bobby Bonilla Day is maybe our favorite holiday of the year.

The basic principles of **compound interest** make clear that the Mets made a solid decision. Maybe even a great decision? Because when money is put to use over time, like Bobby Bonilla's $6 million, it grows, and then compounds, more and more, until $6 million becomes $30 million.

Bobby Bonilla's situation was unusual, but his million-dollar checks reveal the forces that turn savings into real wealth. Inside his widely mocked contract lies an economic lesson that can help all of us retire comfortably—and one day enjoy our own version of Bobby Bonilla Day.

An all-star retirement plan

AS BONILLA REMEMBERS IT, he was called to the office of Mets owner Fred Wilpon during his final season with the team. Once he arrived, they asked him questions that he interpreted as prodding him toward retiring or walking away from his contract.

Bonilla made clear that wasn't going to happen. He felt he still had more years of baseball to play. More important, he knew the Mets would not have agreed in the opposite situation: Wilpon didn't want to pay Bonilla like a star after his disappointing season, but if Bonilla had played like an MVP, Wilpon would not have paid him more. Risk had been priced in for both sides when Bonilla signed the original contract.

Owners and general managers—whether of a baseball club or a widget factory—generally prefer to pay their employees less. But the Mets were especially eager to avoid paying Bonilla $6 million. The team had just come tantalizingly close to playing in the World Series, and $6 million was enough to sign a star player who could help win them a championship.

So Bonilla and his agent proposed an alternative: Bonilla would leave the Mets without receiving the $6 million they'd promised to pay him for next season. But the Mets—after spending that $6 million to win a World Series, ideally—would send Bonilla checks in the future.

"One of the fears that a lot of athletes have is losing everything," says Bonilla. He didn't grow up with money, and he'd seen players bankrupt themselves after retiring in their 30s. He'd told his agent that he wanted to be able to spend money in retirement like he had as a player. Which meant that Bonilla and the Mets agreed: They both wanted Bonilla's $6 million payment delayed into the future.

Bonilla could have simply agreed to receive his $6 million in 2011 or 2035. But that would be a terrible deal! Both sides knew the Mets needed to pay Bonilla for waiting. Economists call this intuitive idea the **time value of money**, and they point to three major reasons why getting money now is more valuable than getting it later:

1. **Uncertainty:** There was a chance that the Mets wouldn't have enough money to pay Bonilla in the future. Stuff happens!

2. **Inflation:** If the U.S. inflation rate hit 15 percent, like in the 1980s, $6 million might barely buy a midsize sedan in 2035.

3. **Opportunity cost:** Bonilla could instead take that $6 million and make money with it some other way, like investing it in the stock market.

This same reasoning explains why the mortgage payments on a $1 million house will eventually total much more than $1 million. Compounding is a double-edged sword.

Bonilla was essentially lending the Mets $6 million, and for these three reasons, he wanted to be repaid with interest, just like a bank.

So the Mets and Bonilla needed to agree on the terms of their loan.

During the 1999 offseason, the Mets announced their agreement: Bonilla would leave the team and, under the terms of a deferred-money contract, he'd eventually be paid almost $30 million.

The compound-interest snowball

AT THE TIME OF THE ANNOUNCEMENT, Jose Fernandez was a long-suffering Mets fan—and an economics major at the University of South Florida. His friends, he recalls, hated the deal. They "couldn't wrap their minds around" the difference between $30 million and $6 million.

But Fernandez, who is now chair of the Economics Department at the University of Louisville, thought the deal might actually work out for the team. "I said to them . . . 'There's this little thing called compounding interest, and a lot of things can happen over time if you invest.'"

Fernandez says to imagine if Bonilla had received his $6 million in 1999 and invested it in the stock market, which, historically, averages returns of around 10 percent each year. A common mistake is thinking that Bonilla would earn approximately 10 percent of $6 million every year. Which sounds pretty good! By 2011, he'd have more than doubled his money. This is called **simple interest**.

But what actually happens when you invest money in the stock market (or loan it out in exchange for interest payments) is that it grows like a snowball rolling down a hill. At first the little snowball gets a little bigger: Bonilla's initial $6 million gets 10 percent bigger in the first year. Now he has $6.6 million (his initial $6 million and the $600,000 he made in interest).

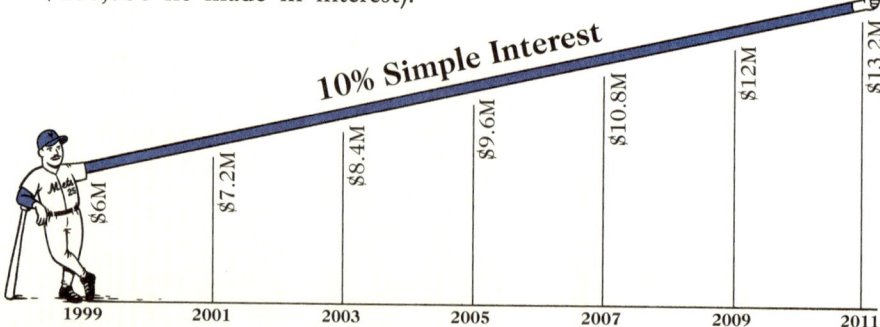

The next year he earns interest on the $6.6 million. The interest earns interest. It's like how a larger snowball has more surface area, so it picks up more snow with every rotation.

By the bottom of the hill, the snowball hasn't just doubled in size, it's grown exponentially. By 2011, Bonilla's $6 million is worth almost $19 million. By 2035, his $6 million is worth $185 million. That's not a typo!

The Mets did not want to give Bonilla the equivalent of 10 percent compound interest. Which was fair. Real-world investing comes with risk. Maybe a recession hits and stocks go down. Or growth is slow and stocks are sluggish. But, Fernandez says, the player and the team agreed on a reasonable rate of 8 percent. Accounting for the fact that Bonilla started getting chunks of money in 2011, the math shows that his $6 million is worth roughly the same as the $30 million the Mets will ultimately pay him. That was the time value of Bonilla's $6 million.

In other words: Vindication! Despite the annual self-criticism sessions by Mets fans, anyone with Microsoft Excel can mathematically absolve the Mets of the sin of Bobby Bonilla Day. All it takes is a little perspective to realize the truth that $6 million = $30 million.

It's good the math checks out, too, because Bonilla's deferred-compensation contract is the standard playbook for retirement. If you're currently working and you start saving for retirement, you are forming a little snowball at the top of a hill. Every day, while you work, sleep, and eat avocado toast, your retirement snowball is rolling downhill, increasing in size and speed, growing exponentially. Each time you add $100 or $1,000 you make the snowball a bit bigger and make it roll a bit faster.

"I'm comforted to know that the money was put away," Bonilla told us, retired, living

Financial Time Travel

Here's another way to think about the Bobby Bonilla deal: It's time travel. And like all time travel, financial time travel has strange effects.

Bobby Bonilla sent $6 million from his superstar-slugger years to his retiree years, turning it into $30 million.

The Mets wanted $6 million in 2000. So they sent $30 million in future profits back to the turn of the millennium.

The power of compound interest underpins the most basic but important advice in personal finance: Start saving for retirement as soon as possible! This may not feel helpful if you can barely pay your rent. But even a tiny investment can snowball impressively over time.

---

comfortably in Florida, and still getting paid like a superstar. Every July 1, he gets tons of texts from friends as the news of his contract reappears in sports headlines.

"I do get smiles when the tellers deposit [the check]," he added. Sometimes the teller has to get the manager. "I always get a kick out of that." He responds graciously, "Okay, take your time."

The deal was a win for the Mets too. The franchise essentially got a $6 million loan to fund a championship run and distributed the loan's cost across 25 future Mets teams (from 2011 to 2035). Which was especially helpful because of Major League Baseball's "luxury tax" rule that required high-spending teams like the Mets to pay penalties for exceeding a salary threshold.

After Bonilla signed his new contract, the Mets traded for Mike Hampton, an elite pitcher who helped them get to the World Series. They paid Hampton just shy of $6 million.

By getting to the World Series, the Mets, in theory, sold more jerseys and hot dogs, charged more for luxury seats and television broadcast rights, and won over a new generation of lifelong customers (that is, fans). These increases in revenue and team value should more than cover Bonilla's $1 million checks.

And while deferring so much compensation remains rare in professional sports—many leagues limit deferred-money contracts and other financial engineering—at least one other MLB team saw wisdom in the Mets' move. In 2023, the Dodgers agreed to pay superstar pitcher Shohei Ohtani $2 million a year for 10 years, and then $68 million per year from 2034 to 2043. Many commentators described it as a win-win move that would allow the team to surround Ohtani with star players.

Except ... the Mets made another financial decision in 2000 that, unlike Bobby Bonilla Day, actually was the most Mets thing ever. According to reporting by *The New York Times*, the Mets took every dollar from the Bobby Bonilla deal, and almost every other dollar the franchise earned from advertising deals and hot dog sales, and gave it to Bernie Madoff to invest. The same Bernie Madoff who was running the largest Ponzi scheme in history.

When Madoff was revealed as a fraud, the Mets lost a ton of money, and so did two Mets owners, who were close to Madoff and accused of knowing about the scheme. The Mets spent several years operating on a smaller budget, missing the playoffs, and giving fans the icky sense that their favorite pastime was linked to white-collar crime.

In 2020, the cash-strapped Mets were sold to Steven Cohen, a finance guy who has said publicly that he loves Bobby Bonilla Day. He and Bonilla have talked about Bonilla coming to the Mets stadium to celebrate the day. Maybe he can accept a jumbo-size check in person? Bonilla says he's open to it.

"I think it's just awesome that everybody's having fun with it," he says. "If it helps athletes really see the advantage of putting away money [for the future] ... I think it's a good thing."

So that's compound interest. But where exactly does its power come from? Why did the Mets give Bonilla 8 percent interest? Why are we all so confident our retirement savings will be worth more in 30 years rather than less? That's coming up next.

This chapter includes reporting from Kenny Malone and James Sneed, included in the Planet Money episode "Bobby Bonilla Day," June 25, 2021.

How We All Fell for a Confidence Trick

Banking in America, in three acts

here is no single origin story of banking. No one time and place where all the pieces were invented. If a prophetic person one day dreamed up a bank—in a world that did not have them—their peers would have dismissed the idea as madness.

Banks are too strange, too contradictory: They need us to deposit our money, but they also create money. They promise to keep our money safe, then risk our money on speculative investments. They are so important, we're told, that governments take extraordinary measures to keep them running. But they're also culprits in every downturn and depression.

So here is a story of banking, told in three acts, each chosen to explain why banks evolved into such odd institutions; why despite their many faults, they are essential to our collective prosperity; and how they are now changing, transforming, and, perhaps, disappearing.

Act I: Banks create money

WHEN FRANCIS RAWLE SAILED INTO PHILADELPHIA IN 1686, the city was a settlement of several thousand people. As a Quaker, Rawle had fled religious persecution. In Pennsylvania, he found prosperity. Within a few years, he was a merchant and landowner, active in local government and married into a prominent family.

The colony prospered too. Pennsylvania's fast-growing population was up to 30,000 in 1717. Philadelphia had shopkeepers, craftsmen, and a port that handled cargo for many colonies.

But the growing city suffered from a bummer of a business problem: There was never enough literal, physical cash. "Wee are full of Goods & Little or noe money to pass amongst us," a prominent Philadelphia merchant wrote to associates in London.

This was a problem across the colonies. American colonists used Britain's silver shillings. They used Spanish pieces of eight too: the silver coins minted in Mexico and Bolivia, which colonists received when selling goods in the Caribbean. (Or when pirates arrived in port.) But there was never enough of either: Residents regularly carted in crops to pay tax collectors.

In economic terms, the colonies had a **liquidity** problem. There was wealth in the colonies: the commerce of Philadelphia's busy shipyards,

New England's salted cod, Virginia's tobacco, and the enslaved people who also, shamefully, counted as financial assets. But without enough coins and money, colonists couldn't convert their wealth into a convenient medium for buying and selling stuff. Which led to two interrelated problems:

1. **Limiting trade:** In letters from the time, American merchants tell British trading partners that they lack gold to buy more British goods.

2. **Foiling everyday purchases:** Colonists' scarce gold and silver sailed abroad whenever they bought tea, furniture, and other essentials from England, reducing the currency circulating locally. Local politicians described families that "had lived well" but couldn't find a way to buy "Provisions for their [own] Support."

The entire economy was caught in a sand trap, slowed by high transaction costs. Lacking coins and silver, Philadelphians meticulously tracked their debts to each other, or paid with promissory notes (written IOUs) or commodities like beaver pelts or tobacco credits (a claim on a certain amount of tobacco from a local warehouse). They couldn't make change; they were never certain they'd be paid back. Transaction costs made everything more expensive and eroded the value of everyone's work—to the point that farmers sold entire harvests without earning enough to support themselves.

The colonies' lack of cash was not unique. Around the world, high transaction costs and coin shortages had defined economic life for millennia. Many empires thrived because of coinage: Ancient Athens' silver mines allowed it to mint coins, pay soldiers, and easily trade throughout the Mediterranean. When Marco Polo arrived in China, he was astounded that everyone confidently bought goods with pieces of paper bearing the seal of the ruler, Kublai Khan. But for centuries, no society managed to successfully copy the Khan's system of imperial paper money. In Rawle's time, European rulers envied Spain's gold and silver mines, and Britain banned their American colonies from minting coins because it wanted their silver and gold flowing back to England.

But the colonial constraints on the money supply led these rebellious British subjects to a world-leading insight: They developed an economy that ran on paper money created not from gold, silver, or copper, but by banks.

The first step came from wartime necessity. During wars with France and Native Americans, the lack of cash for soldiers and provisions led colonial assemblies to print **bills of credit**. They were government IOUs but resembled modern currencies: They came in denominations like a 20-shilling bill, featured artistic designs, and listed the issuing colony along with the signature of a trustee. Assemblies paid merchants and soldiers in bills of credit, who circulated them by spending their paper bills at shops, taverns, and markets. Since colonists could pay taxes with bills of credit, they knew they had value. And the bills made commerce easier: Buying ale and clearing a tab was simpler with bills of credit than hands of tobacco.

Colonies only printed bills during wartime, but they gave colonists a taste of paper money. And they wanted more.

"The wars would actually stimulate the economy because they were paid for in this paper currency, and you always saw these economic slumps following the wars," says historian Katie Moore. Colonists started asking, "What do we do when the war is over?"

Enter Rawle, who became Pennsylvania's paper-money champion, running for a seat on the assembly by proposing to print more. To advocate for paper money, he wielded the awesome power of the pamphlet, the mass media of the day, printed and sold for a pittance, and therefore as ubiquitous as social media or cable TV. The choice of gold, silver, and copper as money was arbitrary, he wrote. Currency could be based on anything of widespread value. He titled one pamphlet on paper money, enticingly, "Ways and Means for the Inhabitants of Delaware to Become Rich."

"Within a year," writes Moore, "most Philadelphia merchants had come around to supporting a paper currency."

Swayed by Rawle and his allies, Pennsylvania created loan offices known as **land banks**. Farmers could "deposit" their land, which meant taking out a loan, paid in paper bills of credit, with their farmland pledged as collateral. If they failed to pay back the loan, the bank could seize their land. But in the meantime, they spent the bills, which spread around Pennsylvania, providing cash and change.

This wasn't a modern bank, but land banks converted a common form of wealth (real estate) into liquid form (paper money) that could be easily spent.

They said "we're going to print money, put it in the treasury, and you can come borrow from the treasury," says economist Farley Grubb. It's like "if we took everyone's house mortgage, and we and chopped it up into little pieces and used that [as money]."

As the bills spread, they reduced transaction costs and boosted the economy. Benjamin Franklin wrote about Philadelphia as it recovered from vacant houses and general malaise to vigorous construction and trade. He credited the transformation to paper money.

Rawle's advocacy divided Pennsylvania politics along class lines. Today banks' extraordinary power to create money is associated with the interests of wealthy financiers. But Rawle represented poor farmers and new merchants, and his opponents were the British government, which feared a colonial currency would loosen their hold, and wealthy Englishmen, who preferred to demand payment in Spanish silver or pounds sterling.

At one point, the governor's council rebuked the publisher of Rawle's pamphlets. But Benjamin Franklin became a fellow pamphleteer, arguing for the superiority of banks that "coined" land, which was a far more dependable asset than gold or silver. Their ideas inspired protesters to petition and publicly confront assemblymen—and even throw bricks at the home of a paper-money opponent. Most colonies followed Pennsylvania in creating land banks, expanding the supply of paper money right up to the Revolution.

During this time, France was also experimenting with paper banknotes, and some paper currency circulated in England. But Grubb says that the colonies—despite being an economic backwater—were running on paper money more than any Western economy. In fact, Britain's efforts to constrain colonists' beloved paper money helped fuel their rebellion.

After independence, American leaders replaced land banks with private banks that accepted traditional deposits of gold, silver, and copper coins, now stamped at the nation's own mints. But these banks also printed paper money, expanding the money supply far beyond the volume of coins.

When a Philadelphia merchant deposited coins in the Bank of North America, he could withdraw banknotes. But his deposit wasn't done creating money. The bank kept a fraction of his deposit in reserve, but lent out the rest to another merchant, which that merchant might withdraw (as paper banknotes) and spend at shops. In turn, the shop owners would deposit that money at their banks, continuing the cycle. Each step created more money than the original value of the gold and silver.

This is called **fractional reserve banking**, and it's a core function of banks. The concept wasn't new: Bankers had realized centuries ago that they could lend out more money than they had, since not every customer would need their money back at once. But this is the moment when both England and the United States, the two countries that would dominate and establish the modern financial system, embraced banks and combined their moneylending function with the creation of currency.

By 1820, America had more than 300 banks that slowly expanded out from port cities. With banks growing the money supply, America escaped the sand trap of high transaction costs.

Act II: Banks put our savings to work

IN 1892, Jesse Binga arrived in Chicago with a taste for the wealth that finance and real estate could unlock. His mother and father had taught him their trades: real estate and barbering. After high school, he worked for a prominent African American attorney. Then, while traveling and working as a barber and train porter, he profited by buying and flipping land.

In Chicago, he found that the same racism that limited the prospects of Black men like him also presented an opportunity. This was the eve of the Great Migration, when 6 million African-Americans left the Jim Crow South, and the new arrivals strained the housing supply of Chicago's "Black Belt." Binga realized he could rent or buy property at a discount just outside the Black Belt—from white owners who refused to live with Black neighbors, or feared they would reduce property values—and then rent units at full price to Black families.

Binga "was breaking the borders," says Don Hayner, the longtime editor of the *Chicago Sun-Times* and author of a Jesse Binga biography. Since many landlords refused to rent to Black people, the new migrants had few housing alternatives. By expanding the Black Belt's borders, Binga expanded the supply of housing for African Americans. Unlike the neighborhood's many slumlords, he took pride in his properties, repairing and upgrading them himself. "Many a night I've worked all night on boilers and plumbing, and wiping joints and mending stairs, and hanging paper," he told a reporter.

It was a profitable enterprise that allowed Binga to build a real-estate empire. He became the landlord for more than a thousand Black Chicagoans, and he owned a 500-foot stretch of apartments and stores, known as the Binga Block, on State Street, which was the Black Belt's Broadway and Wall Street all in one.

In his biography, Hayner notes that Binga's tenants started approaching him for short-term loans—for emergencies, a rent payment, or a trip South. Binga became a kind of "street banker." Then he opened a real bank.

Binga could have just affixed a "Bank" sign to his office. But Binga was a man who always wore suits, spoke of himself in the third person, and preached the potential for African Americans to advance through thrift and hard work. When the Binga Bank opened in 1908, it was housed in a new, three-story building on State Street topped by a sign another two stories high that read JESSE BINGA BANKER. Binga liked to greet customers in the gleaming, 125-foot-long main room.

The bank's business model was typical. The fact that Binga was Chicago's first Black banker, employing a mostly Black staff and serving mostly Black customers, was unique. Which allows us to see how banks (when working well!) spur investment and economic growth, by helping idle piles of money find their way to productive use, making the pile grow.

Like all bankers, Binga was a matchmaker: between people with savings and local businesses and individuals who needed money. When Black families and businesses brought in their savings for safekeeping, Binga accepted their money and then, as soon as they left the building, gave almost all of it (except the fractional reserve) to someone else. He might lend one family's life savings to a young entrepreneur opening their first store. Or give money deposited by local businesses to young couples who needed help with a mortgage.

This is the textbook definition of banking: accepting deposits and making loans. It's also kind of bonkers! An entire industry devoted to making bets with people's life savings and the money businesses need to pay their employees.

To pull it off, Binga had to make lots of judgments about risk. Would that young entrepreneur succeed? Which couples would make their payments? He might insist that the first-time entrepreneur pay high interest payments, while an established business could pay a lower rate. Then, in turn, he had to offer customers interest on their deposits as a way to incentivize them to lend him their money.

By deciding on interest rates for different loans and bank accounts, Binga was one of many bankers collectively putting a price on money. Or, more precisely, the price of borrowing money. One reason Bobby Bonilla's $6 million became $30 million is because financiers like Binga offer interest that can compound over time.

If he set interest rates wisely, Binga would profit from the spread—the difference between how much interest he earned from loans and how much interest he gave depositors. If he did it wrong, he'd lose everyone's money and end up, as one minister put it, in an opening prayer at a bankers' convention, "behind the prison bars, or upon a scaffold." To further cushion the risk of any individual loan failing, Binga protected himself through diversification. By pooling together thousands of people's savings and making thousands of loans, he ensured that everyone's deposits would be safer, and would grow, even if a few loans failed.

Writing in 2010, economist Nick Rowe described banking and finance as a "confidence trick." Bank customers want their money to be perfectly safe and completely liquid (available to withdraw at any time). But the people asking banks for loans want to repay the money over five or ten years, not five or ten days, and not all of them will be able to repay. The two groups' desires seem incompatible, and whenever depositors worry the bank might be losing money and might not have everyone's deposits, this incompatibility can lead to **bank runs**: customers rushing to withdraw all their money at once. "It's surprising that Finance exists at all," writes Rowe. The confidence trick "all depends on trust."

Several Chicago banks had branches near the Black Belt. For Black residents, though, the Binga Bank differed in two crucial respects.

The first was their greater trust in Binga—because of his race, but also because of his reputation for honesty and business acumen. If he drank alcohol, it was a rare indulgence. One reporter described Binga as "the man that never sleeps when business is at hand or can be got by going after it." In an era when banks often failed—a star shortstop famously kept money in every bank in his hometown in case a few went bust—Binga's reputation enabled him to pull off the confidence trick.

The second was that white bankers rarely lent money to Black businesses, churches, and families, often because of racist beliefs that Black people were less intelligent or untrustworthy. Even those willing to lend charged higher interest rates and declined most loans. White bankers did not know the Black Belt. How could they assess the prospects of a promising, young entrepreneur? When Black Chicagoans entrusted their money to other banks, it flowed to segregated neighborhoods that excluded them. At the Binga Bank, their money stayed within the Black Belt.

Real estate and banking made Binga rich. In 1913, he became even wealthier, and part of the social elite, when he married Eudora Johnson, heir to a gambling-house fortune. Some of the city's most prosperous Black businessmen became shareholders in his bank. In 1921, when Illinois passed new banking regulations, Binga's bank met all the requirements and became the Binga State Bank.

Binga was "a giant," says Hayner, and his name symbolized wealth and success. His Christmas parties were the Black Belt's social event of the year, and he drove a high-end car. He lived in a large house on an all-white street that he refused to leave despite multiple bombing attempts. When a white mob surrounded a Black family moving into a house they'd bought with a Binga mortgage, he came to their rescue. "Binga waded through the crowd . . . and got his people out," says Hayner. "He was a courageous guy."

In Chicago, the prosperity of Binga's bank and real estate business reflected the fortunes of the Black Belt. He could not, by himself, fund all the mortgages that increased the homeownership rate, nor the development of all of State Street's shops and jazz clubs. But his bank "was like a beacon," Hayner says, that proved the feasibility of banking there. Another large Black-owned bank opened, and Black-owned life insurance companies started lending. By channeling the Black Belt's collective savings to people and businesses that needed funding, they created a virtuous cycle that enriched both sides.

Just as land banks' money creation in the coin-poor colonies demonstrates the importance of banking and currency for economic growth, Black banks like Binga's show the important role banks play in providing loans, or credit. Outside of Chicago, Black bankers in Harlem, Richmond, and Tulsa funded the development of those areas' "Black Wall Streets" and prosperous African American neighborhoods.

Even today, when economists study the arrival of banks and credit in places like rural India, they find reductions in poverty. And despite the prevalence of banking apps, neighborhoods without bank branches receive fewer mortgages and business loans, and their residents pay higher interest rates.

But that's when the confidence trick is working and bankers manage risk wisely. When it fails, we get bubbles, volatility, and recessions. In 1929, when the American stock market crashed, the resulting Great Depression wiped out Binga's finances. Like thousands of banks, the Binga State Bank was undone by a bank run. Many depositors blamed Binga for losing their money, but he remained a respected figure, revered by thousands who'd lost their savings, even as he ended up working as a janitor. To them, he was a paragon of success who, despite racism, threats, and bombings, put capitalism to work to build his own legend and the prosperity of Chicago's South Side.

Act III: Banks chase higher returns

DURING THE GREAT DEPRESSION, banking's confidence trick was exposed, and Americans' trust in banks vanished. And so, in 1933, President Franklin D. Roosevelt signed legislation to put the rabbit back in the hat. Its core was a powerful new backstop: the Federal Deposit Insurance Corporation (FDIC).

The FDIC is a government guarantee that depositors will never lose their money. Not by bailing banks out! Instead, banks pay fees to the FDIC, which provides deposit insurance. If a bank is failing, the FDIC takes over, uses the insurance money to restore customer deposits (up to a cap of $250,000, as of 2024), and then sells what's left of the ailing bank.

During the Great Depression, bakeries went bankrupt, cafés closed, and factories failed. Each was a tragedy with a human toll. So why didn't the government create backstops for them?

Because of the flip side of banks' economy-fueling powers: **systemic risk**. If there's a bank run, the damage can cascade like falling dominoes. Businesses that lose their deposits can't pay their bills and employees. Everyday depositors can't pay rent and buy groceries. The hurt spreads from the bank's customers to everyone in their economic radius.

Plus, financial anxiety creates a feedback loop. If other banks' customers see a run, they might worry, withdraw their money, and cause more bank runs. Soon no one can pay their bills or employees, the money supply dries up, and businesses are bankrupted by temporary cash crunches.

Ideally, the federal guarantee is like a circuit breaker: Since people know their deposits are safe, they don't rush the bank, ending the cycle of panic.

The legislation worked: Bank runs became much rarer after the Great Depression, and Americans increasingly viewed "money in the bank" as safe and secure.

But if you open a savings account, you'll notice that it does not offer the 8 percent interest rate that turned Bobby Bonilla's $6 million into $30 million. Those higher returns come from bankers and financiers seeking better profits and higher yields. This **search for yield** drove one of the most important financial developments of the past 50 years: the rise of **shadow banks**.

After the FDIC and financial reforms of the Great Depression, banking became stable and boring. The Federal Reserve Board set the maximum interest rate on savings accounts at 3 percent. This was well intentioned: It was thought that banks' competition for customers had led to unsustainably high interest rates, which contributed to bank failures. At first interest rates were well below the cap. But the regulation eventually proved to be a gift to big, established banks. From the 1950s to the '70s, people joked about the 3-6-3 rule: Bankers gave customers 3 percent interest on deposits, charged 6 percent interest on loans, and were golfing by 3:00 p.m.

What disrupted the status quo was inflation, which crested over 10 percent in the 1970s and '80s. The federal government raised the cap on interest rates, but not enough to match inflation. Americans' savings accounts still *lost* value each year. Anyone who could offer more interest would attract a lot of money.

In 1972, a shadow bank emerged that did just that—it offered 9 percent interest. Shadow banks sound mysterious, a bit nefarious. But millions of Americans have money in them. If you have any savings in a **money market fund (MMF)**, you do too. That 9 percent rate came from the world's first MMF: the Reserve Fund.

It's not news that you can make more money investing in stocks than from a savings account. But the Reserve Fund invested in the world's safest assets: short-term loans to the U.S. government, known as treasury bonds, which were paying a higher interest rate than a 1970s savings account.

The genius of the money market fund, though, was that it *felt* like a bank account—even though it was actually an investment fund and not bound by the cap on interest. The creators of the MMF made it easy to withdraw your money and gave people checkbooks so they could buy groceries with their MMF money. They also described the 9 percent rate as if it were interest on a savings account—even though it was technically an investment return that depended on repayments.

Banks lobbied furiously to ban money market funds. They lost. Congress removed interest rate ceilings on deposits, allowing banks to offer market interest rates. But without the costs of tellers and bank branches, MMFs could still offer a better deal, even after charging a fee for their services. By 2008, trillions of dollars were parked in MMFs.

Many kinds of shadow banks emerged. They come in esoteric varieties, but are all defined by doing things that banks do (channeling customers' savings to people and companies that need funding) without being formal banks subject to the drag and expense of government oversight and protections. From the regulators' perspective, their risks and transactions are in the shadows, and since they're not covered by deposit insurance, the money in shadow banks isn't protected by the government.

Is this a dangerous development? Or a good one? That's one of the biggest debates in finance and economics. All that oversight and insurance exists to maintain the confidence trick. One type of shadow banking known as **private credit** makes loans with money from life-insurance companies, pension funds, and other organizations making long-term investments and willing to take risks in exchange for higher rewards. These funders of private credit don't need their money back for years. Isn't that better than making loans with families' bank deposits? This way, there's no risk of bank runs. Right? Right?!

But shadow banks and traditional banks have gotten intertwined. In many cases, banks lend money to private credit, which these shadow banks then lend out. Do this enough times, and suddenly banks' health depends on the success of private credit; meanwhile, MMFs are already holding many families' emergency budgets and many companies' payroll. So are shadow banks systemically risky too? The Great Recession made clear that the answer is "yes." In fact, that very first MMF—the Reserve Fund—collapsed in 2008.

It collapsed because it gave people what they wanted: higher yield. Over the decades, as MMFs competed for customers, they offered better returns by making slightly riskier investments, like short-term loans to America's fourth-largest investment bank. Hard to imagine a large bank, founded in 1850, would fail to pay back some loans, right? But that bank was Lehman Brothers, which filed for bankruptcy in 2008. The Reserve Fund held $785 million in securities issued by Lehman, and the bankruptcy rendered the securities essentially worthless.

With Lehman failing, Reserve Fund customers worried about their money, which didn't have deposit protection, and rushed to withdraw it. It was a run on the shadow banks.

So the government intervened. The Federal Reserve and U.S. Treasury temporarily guaranteed money in MMFs (to any funds that opted into the program by paying premiums), bought troubled loans, and allowed the firms that ran MMFs to borrow money on generous terms. The impromptu rescue mostly worked: Most MMFs stayed solvent, and the Reserve Fund even managed to return more than 98 percent of customers' money when it was liquidated. After the recession, the U.S. government created some new oversight of shadow banks. But most new regulation fell on traditional banks, which reinforced the trend of money and money-lending flowing to shadow banks. Traditional banks aren't about to disappear, but their role in the economy is narrowing, and increasingly shared with shadow banks.

OUR PLAY IN THREE ACTS HAS, hopefully, shown just how strange banks are. Banks create money through fractional-reserve lending. Banks put our savings to work by providing credit and funding economic growth. Banks concoct new ways to boost returns while mitigating risk, which sometimes goes disastrously wrong. It's an inherently unstable combination that only works so long as we collectively trust that money in the bank—which, by definition, is not actually there—is perfectly safe and sound.

A Love Letter to Insurance

Dear Insurance,

I know what people say about you. They say you're too expensive, and never there for us when we actually need you. They say you bury exemptions and exceptions in fine print, so you never have to pay us. They complain you ruin a good time.

I'm not thrilled when I see monthly bills, and I don't like paying each year for one checkup and a flu shot. But I know that's not the full story. I appreciate you, insurance. In fact, I think I love you.

I love that, done right, you are a triumph of rationality. In the days of Achilles and Odysseus, people tried to avoid misfortune by consulting oracles and making sacrifices to vengeful gods. But your policies are based on the insight that we can predict the future. (Imperfectly, of course.) Even if we don't know which house will burn down or which of us will get sick, statisticians can predict how many homes will burn down and how many healthy people will soon need expensive care. Which means your agents can calculate how much everyone needs to pitch in to cover the cost of those inevitable tragedies.

Most of all, you are the best solution a market has to externalities. When the government requires insurance, you do the work of calculating the costs that would otherwise not be captured. You give discounts for better behavior—putting in smoke alarms or driving safer or building outside flood zones. Thank you for making markets work better.

I know you have qualities that people hate. You make it hard to file claims. You don't let people switch to a different plan when they realize their surgery isn't covered. You make us fix the wobbly handrail on our steps. You demand to know people's credit rating, then punish people with poor credit by charging more. You ignore people born with serious health problems unless you're forced to accept them. You can be cruel, inflexible and confusing.

But I understand that you don't have a choice. If you charge every one the same price, the only people who will sign up are the really sic people, or the worst drivers, or the people building homes in flood zones. I know that insurance only works to the fullest when everyone signs up. Because if only the riskiest people do, then this problem, of adverse selection, leads to a death spiral: such a high percentage of customers filing claims that you either go bankrupt or have to increase the cost to the point that everyone else cancels their policy.

(Is this why you charge so much for insurance on rental cars? Because people only buy it when they're driving off-road or in snowstorms?)

I love that you know your limits and don't try to insure correlated risks: single events such as a flood, war, or earthquake that could damage all the buildings in an area, bankrupting the insurers before everyone gets paid. So, sure, stick to uncorrelated risks like electrical fires or cancer, which are predictably random: a set number tend to happen each year, and a fire in Austin doesn't make a fire in Dallas more likely. Let charity or the government handle correlated risks.

I've also come to appreciate that while people see you as a downer—an extra cost, the corporate equivalent of a stern parent lecturing about life's dangers—they couldn't be more wrong. If anything, you are an enabler! Without insurance, what dive instructor would risk taking inexperienced, untalented me to a reef? Who would want to drive a car when an accident could mean bankruptcy? And how else will I, an inveterate worrier who pats my pockets three times an hour for my keys, ever put a big chunk of my net worth into a house that could burn down?

All to say, I've been thinking a lot about our relationship, and I now realize what I have, and what I've had all along: peace of mind and protection from catastrophe, all for the cost of a monthly subscription. You're not perfect, but neither am I. That's why I need insurance.

Forever yours,

xoxo Alex Mayyasi

P.S. I'm sorry I let my renter's insurance lapse right before my bike got stolen!

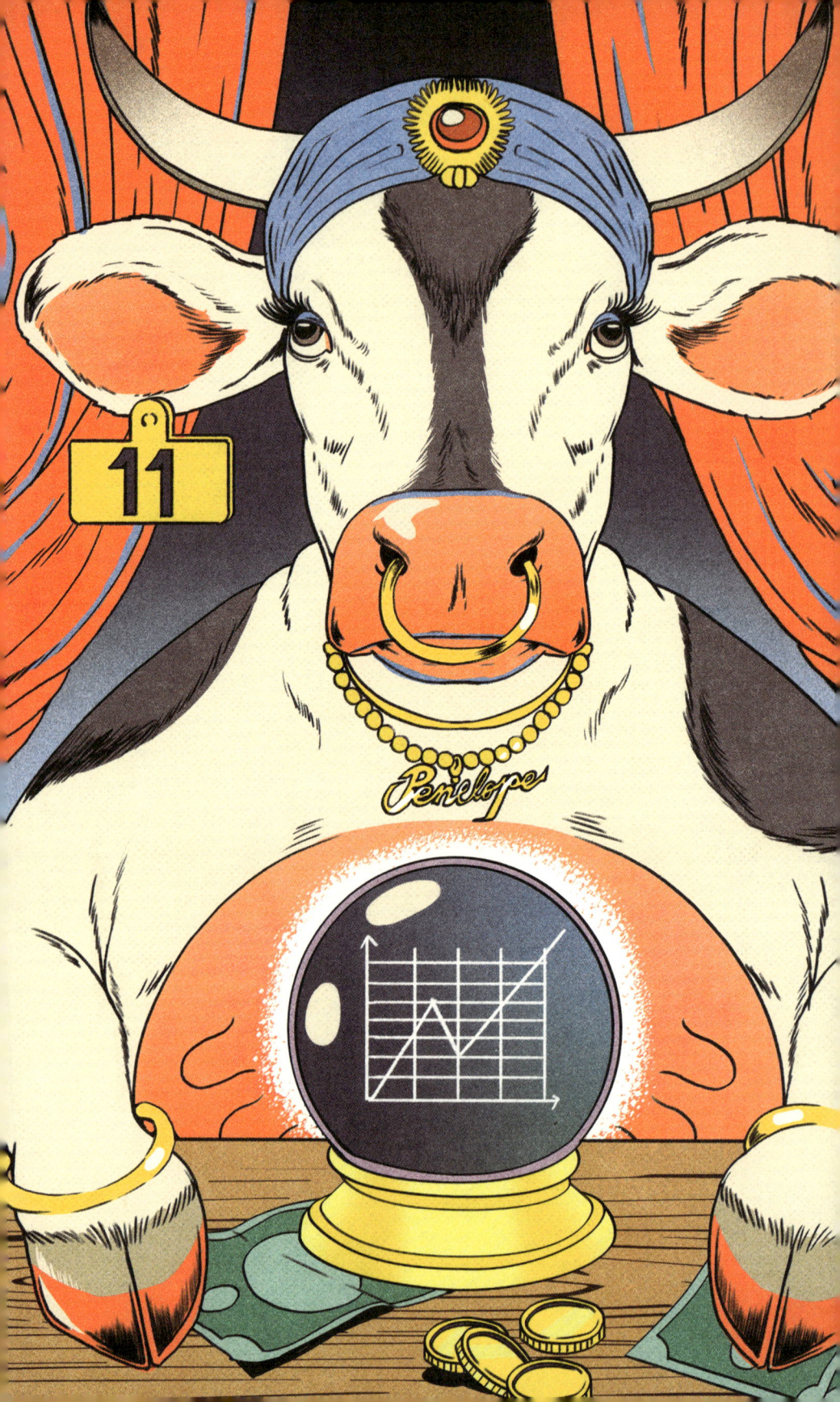

16
Weighing a Cow and Picking Stocks

Why it's so hard to beat the market

When Tony Mitchell read about the contest, he wanted in. A new company called Marketocracy had created an online game that allowed anyone to invest millions of (fake) dollars. Marketocracy's president was convinced he could find anonymous Americans who could invest just as well as, or better than, professionals. His fantasy football-esque game was his gambit for finding them.

Mitchell didn't have the résumé of a budding Warren Buffett. In 1999, he was a 40-year-old college dropout who worked long hours in hospitality and lived paycheck to paycheck. But he'd excelled at math as an undergrad, and finance had fascinated him since childhood, when he'd watched his father, a Ford engineer, check his stocks each day in the newspaper. Mitchell entered the contest, and Marketocracy gave him $1 million of faux money to invest. Thousands of other amateur stock pickers signed up too.

Mitchell took it seriously. He watched CEO interviews on CNBC and read business books like *One Up on Wall Street*, by the famous investor Peter Lynch. "A lot of guys are always... watching sports, and they know a lot about all the players in different teams and leagues," Mitchell says. "My hobby was investing and watching the market."

The Marketocracy contest tested an endlessly debated question: Can an average investor make money by picking stocks? Just how hard is it to beat the market? How rare a skill? The game changed Tony Mitchell's life, and because of the power of compound interest, learning the right lesson from his experience can shape yours as well.

What is this, capitalism for ants?

WHEN THE ORIGINAL CONTEST STARTED, in 2000, Mitchell was a restaurant manager, and he found it incredibly helpful to track expenses by making spreadsheets on the owner's Apple computer. The Peter Lynch book had advised him to "invest in what you know." (Lynch once bought Taco Bell stock because he was "impressed" by their burritos.) So Mitchell spent one chunk of his fake million dollars on Apple.

When he bought Apple stock, what was Mitchell buying? A teeny-tiny ownership stake.

In 1976, Apple Computers was a new company owned by Steve Jobs and Steve Wozniak. In 1980, though, the Steves took the company public through an **initial public offering, or IPO**: They divided ownership of Apple into millions of pieces and sold 4.6 million of those pieces on stock markets for around $100 million. From then on, any investor could buy a share from someone with Apple stock and become a partial owner, entitled to their share of Apple's profits.

A company doesn't have to go public. Jobs and Wozniak could have owned Apple forever, or found a few wealthy investors to buy the company.

But in 1980, Apple needed lots of money to fund their growth, and it's not easy to find ten people looking to invest $10 million each. Going public allows companies to get lots of money quickly, without taking on debt. And since investors can buy a single share, and easily sell that share if they later sour on the company or need the money, it's much easier to find buyers.

This alternative to public stock markets, of finding private investors or buyers, is where the "private" in private equity comes from.

Thanks to brokerage houses and stock markets and bond markets, anyone can be a tiny capitalist, profiting from money-lending and owning shares of companies. But you have to pick wisely.

A year into the contest, Mitchell's picks didn't look great. In 2000, the dot-com bubble burst. Many internet companies went bankrupt, and the price of his tech stocks, including Apple, plunged below the price he'd paid for them. But most of his competitors lost money too. He kept playing.

How much does this cow weigh?

WHAT MADE THE MARKETOCRACY CONTEST—and being a professional investor—so challenging is that it wasn't enough for Mitchell to grow his initial pot of $1 million. He needed to beat the market.

Remember how Simon Kuznets invented GDP to figure out if the collective economy was growing? Analysts have done something similar for the stock market since 1884, when Charles Dow and Edward Jones created the Dow Jones index. Each evening, they calculated the average stock price of eleven large companies. The index didn't capture every stock, but if it went up, most investors had likely made money that day. As Mitchell watched failing dot-coms drag down stock prices, the most popular index was the **S&P 500**, which tracks 500 of the largest companies listed on American stock exchanges.

Like many finance websites, Marketocracy used the S&P 500 as a baseline. If the value of Mitchell's portfolio increased 15 percent and the S&P 500 only went up 10 percent, he'd look pretty good. That extra 5 percent would be his **alpha**, or **edge** over the market by being smart and disciplined. (Or lucky.) But if the value of his portfolio only increased 5 percent, he'd have negative alpha: 5 percent of embarrassing unskill.

So how hard is beating the market? Out of the millions of investors who trade stocks each day, Mitchell only had to be above average, but that's more difficult than it sounds. To show why, *Planet Money*'s Jacob Goldstein and David Kestenbaum once went to the Burlington County Farm Fair in New Jersey.

At the fair, the pair asked the owners of a beautiful cow named Penelope if they could weigh her. By borrowing a truck scale, they found that she weighed 1,355 pounds. Then they posted photos of Penelope online, including a few with Goldstein standing beside her, and asked people to guess her weight.

The experiment was a re-creation of one conducted by Francis Galton, a famous statistician and scientist. (Who infamously coined the term *eugenics* and believed in racial hierarchy.) In 1906, he attended a contest to guess the weight of an ox. He asked to see all the slips, calculated the average of all the guesses, and compared the average to the winning guess.

He expected the average to be way off. He believed in the elite, in expertise. He figured deferring to a cattle rancher's guess would be the surest way to accuracy. Instead, the crowd triumphed. While many individual guesses were way off, the average of all the guesses was 1,197 pounds—off by just one pound from the ox's actual weight of 1,198 pounds. Almost perfect! In *Planet Money*'s re-creation, our internet mob, working from a few digital photos, was off by only 68 pounds, or roughly 5 percent. Pretty close!

Goldstein and Kestenbaum asked everyone who guessed if they had expertise with livestock, and some did. Multiple guessers sagely referenced the "absence of a visible udder." But the average expert guess was off by 83 pounds—notably worse than the mob.

This phenomenon, dubbed the **wisdom of crowds**, has been documented in situations ranging from election forecasts (calculating the average of multiple predictions is more accurate than any individual poll) to the quiz show *Who Wants to Be a Millionaire* (polling the audience gener-

What's the Deal with Bonds?

Bankers lend companies money and get paid back with interest. If any of your savings are invested in bonds, so do you. That's what a bond is: It's a loan to a company, government, or public utility. It's a promise that they will pay you back, and send you regular interest payments, but packaged up so it can be sold and resold, similar to a stock.

Why bother with bonds? Well, both sides can benefit from the bond market:

- **COMPANIES AND GOVERNMENTS** can typically borrow money at attractive rates. Since they're selling their debt to many people and organizations around the world, competition to buy their bonds leads to lower interest rates. If they were instead dependent on a few financial firms for funding, they'd have to pay more in interest.

- **INVESTORS** can diversify their portfolios. Since bonds offer that steady, dependable stream of payments, they're seen as safer than stocks, and bond prices tend to go up when investors flee risky stocks for the predictability of bonds. Having to hold on to a 30-year bond for 30 years might be a drag if you need your money back early, but investors are usually around to buy your bond. Plus, bonds' lower volatility makes them a classic choice for retirees who don't want to risk their portfolio losing 10 percent of its value just as they need it. (Ditto for people saving money to purchase a house.)

But bonds are not always safer or less volatile than stocks! Rather than buy bonds directly, many investors buy into bond funds or MMFs. And as you may recall, the original MMF, the Reserve Fund, collapsed when too many of its loans and bonds lost value simultaneously in 2008.

Buying bonds directly can be risky too. In 2019, *Planet Money* bought a junk bond: a loan to a company that was struggling financially. For $612, we bought a tiny percentage of an offshore oil services company's debt. If we got paid back, the yield was set to be 146.7 percent. (Due to the high risk, junk bonds offer higher interest payments, which means higher yields over the bond's lifespan.) Within a year, though, the pandemic struck, the company filed for bankruptcy, and we got back a measly five dollars.

Do Like the Rich Do: Tax-Loss Harvesting

You have income. You have wealth. You want more of both, but don't want to work more. What's the answer to this riddle? A good accountant! The tax code is a strange game, and accountants who push the right buttons reduce millionaires' tax bills by billions every year.

One of those buttons is section 165(f) of America's Internal Revenue Code. Section 165 has good intentions: Imagine a company that makes cashmere dog beds. Paris Hilton posts a photo of her tiny dogs looking cozy on cashmere; now everyone wants one of the beds. So the growing company, Cashmere Dog, buys a $20 million office . . . that they have to sell a year later for just $15 million when there's a recession. The real estate investment went bad, but they can deduct the $5 million loss from their tax bill, meaning their taxable income goes down by $5 million.

But the tax code is ground zero for unintended consequences. Accountants realized that a stock whose price has fallen is the same as Cashmere Dog's overpriced office: It's a capital asset that has lost money. And thus was born the ritual of tax-loss harvesting: Accountants scan clients' portfolios and advise them to sell the money losers and claim a tax deduction. That is, sell for a loss, and use the loss to counterbalance capital gains or your normal income. Common wisdom says to buy low and sell high. But in this situation, the client can sell low, lower their tax liability, buy a different stock—or even a nearly identical one, as long as it's not "substantially identical"—with the money, and profit when the economy improves. Poof. Tax benefits.

ally gets the right answer). It works because each person's evaluation is like an imperfect scale. Maybe one member of the crowd, Jason, will estimate how many humans equal one Penelope, while Janelle Googles the average weight of a cow. But even though Jason and Janelle and all the other guessers are wrong, their errors offset, leaving a remarkably good estimate based on all the bits of information contained in each guess.

To get accurate estimates or predictions, the number of guesses trumps expertise. So if you're trying to determine the financial value of a company, almost no mechanism would be better than a stock market in which millions of highly motivated people buy and sell shares every day, revealing their estimate of the company's value.

This, then, was the challenge facing Tony Mitchell, along with every other investor: not to be better than one mediocre investor, but to be better than the spookily accurate collective intelligence that emerges when the stock market synthesizes the guesses of millions of people.

Weighing stocks

WITHIN FINANCE, some people believe that stock markets so efficiently integrate all available information about each company that it's impossible to consistently beat the market. According to this **efficient markets hypothesis**, Mitchell's quest was quixotic. There are no bargain buys, no mispriced stocks to profit from.

But almost no one argues that markets are 100 percent efficient. There's a famous joke about this: Two economists see a $100 bill on the sidewalk, but don't pause to pick it up. One of them asks, "Was that a hundred-dollar bill on the ground?" The other replies, "No, if it was, someone would have picked it up already."

Nor are crowds always wise. They do best when each member thinks independently based on the information they have. That did not happen in the late 1990s, when analysts hyped internet businesses so much that Pets.com, which delivered pet food, losing money on each delivery, raised $82 million when it IPO'd in early 2000.

After the dot-com bubble burst, Mitchell saw opportunity in this kind of groupthink. Other investors seemed so scarred by the crash that they were ignoring technology businesses that seemed solid to him.

Like Priceline. Mitchell used Priceline to find deals on flights and hotels, and it was the only place he knew for that. He thought Priceline would rebound, so he faux bought it. And he was right. The company expanded, acquired additional brands and sites like Kayak and OpenTable, and now the company airs Super Bowl ads.

But there's a more fundamental caveat to markets' wisdom and efficiency. At the state fair, people have a clear goal: to guess Penelope's weight, which is an objective fact of the universe. But what does it mean for a share price to be "correct"?

Finance people have a few stock answers to this question. There's a jargony theoretical answer: Conceptually, all the stock shares should add up to the **present value** of expected future returns. As in, the money the company will earn in the future, valued in today's dollars. But that doesn't spit out a specific dollar amount everyone agrees on. So a common approach is to calculate a company's **price-to-earnings (P/E) ratio**. If Tesla's stock price is high, but its profits per share are much lower than Ford's, that suggests Tesla is overvalued (don't buy!) or that there is an expectation of lots of growth (buy!).

Mitchell thought it was the former. "I like the look of the car, but I just always thought the stock was overvalued." As Tesla matured beyond its start-up stage, he expected investors to evaluate Tesla like Ford or GM and conclude that it was overvalued. But Elon Musk superfans weren't thinking about P/E ratios or future cash flows. They kept buying the stock, so

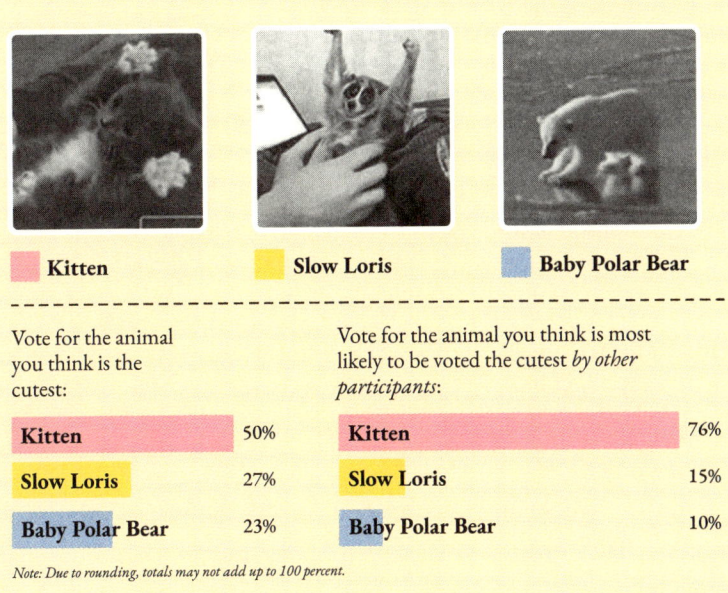

its price went up and up. Mitchell says that underestimating the enthusiasm for Tesla cost him the chance to profit from it.

This kind of stock picking is why the famous economist John Maynard Keynes compared the stock market to a beauty contest where everyone is trying to guess which stocks everyone else will think are valuable. Which is a recipe for groupthink, bubbles, and inefficient markets. Especially since stock-trading apps like Robinhood have turned the markets into a pocket casino. In this environment, some stocks don't have efficient prices; they have entertaining ones, such as the "meme stock" GameStop, a faltering chain of video-game stores whose stock rose more than 50 percent in a single day, January 22, 2021, during the pandemic. Shares peaked in late January at more than 10,000 percent over their price in late 2020, then fell almost 90 percent the week of February 1. This is the greater fool theory approach to stock pricing. People buying don't truly believe that the future returns justify the present price. They are instead betting that someone else will come along and buy the stock from them at a higher, even more foolish, price. Ride the momentum, sell before everyone else does.

Mitchell was tempted to short Tesla, or bet against it. If he had, he would have lost a lot of money. As Keynes is said to have observed, "The markets can remain irrational longer than you can remain solvent." (The remark is unattributed.)

So Mitchell kept looking for companies that, like Priceline, he believed were bargains and would rise in value. Most days he did not buy or sell, but he read every day and recorded business shows to watch in bed as he fell asleep. It was a lot of time and work, but he felt that "the more I could learn, the better I would do [in life]." He took classes part time to finish his college degree, then started working on an MBA. His salary went up, he accumulated savings, and he invested some of that money in his Marketocracy picks.

In 2014, Mitchell got an email from the founder of Marketocracy. Mitchell's (fake) portfolio was performing better than funds run by famous investors. Did he want to become a money manager on Marketocracy? Anyone on the Marketocracy website would be able to see his past investments and give him their money to invest. Their real money! In exchange, they'd pay Mitchell a small fee: 0.3 percent of every dollar they gave him to invest. (Marketocracy charged customers an additional fee.)

Mitchell would have to up his personal investment to $25,000. By now, though, he had the money and felt confident. "I was pretty excited about it." He still had a full-time job—in the liquor-distribution industry, repping brands like Skrewball peanut-butter whiskey. But now Tony Mitchell, slinger of novelty whiskey and onetime college dropout, was moonlighting as Peter Lynch, making money by investing his own savings and others'. He kept doing well, and he describes himself today, in restrained Midwestern language, as "a lot more comfortable." He no longer worries about water bills, and he can stop working if he wants.

But very few of us should try to be like Mitchell. Very few of us can be Mitchell. His story is a siren song.

The founder of Marketocracy, Ken Kam, died unexpectedly in 2019, ending the contest. Mitchell and several other investors teamed up to buy the Marketocracy name and restart the game, but the data and investing history was lost. So we can't know how many Marketocracy players consistently beat the market. But a few years after Mitchell discovered Marketocracy, another start-up, kaChing, launched a Facebook and MySpace game that had the same premise—it took an *"American Idol* investor talent discovery approach." Years later, in 2010, kaChing's founder shared that only seven out of their 450,000 gamers invested well enough that kaChing invited them to invest professionally on their platform. Seven!

If you buy and sell individual stocks, you're unlikely to do as well as Mitchell or kaChing's seven. You'll likely end up like those other 449,993 investors.

But if you want to beat the professionals, be financially savvy, and maybe even ride the stock market to retire as a millionaire . . . you *can* do it! Your best bet is a strategy developed by a Wall Street apostate that is the antithesis of Mitchell's hard work. It's lazy and boring. And it has a long track record of success.

The Biggest Bet of Your Life

How index funds took over

he rarity of Tony Mitchells in the Marketocracy and kaChing contests seems like an argument for entrusting retirement savings to professionals. Except... economists and finance types have known for decades that beating the market is shockingly rare among professionals as well. Even among those paid millions for their alleged prowess.

An initial famous finding came from Paul Samuelson, who in 1970 won the Nobel Prize in economics. In 1974, in a brisk paper, he wrote that, over the long run, most professional investors, or money managers, underperform the market. Sure, many do well any given year. But it's almost like asking 1,000 people to flip a coin. Some of them will get 10 heads in a row. But, ask them to flip 10 more times and way fewer of them will repeat their success.

The money managers' services were (and are) an even worse deal for their clients once you account for the fees they charge: often more than two dollars for every hundred they invest! So the cost of their fees and underperformance compounds every year. Middle-class families, wealthy families, the people managing the pension fund for all of Minnesota's teachers—they were all paying Wall Street traders exorbitantly to flip coins all day. Most professional portfolio managers, Samuelson wrote, "should go out of business—take up plumbing, teach Greek."

Samuelson didn't expect Wall Street to listen. What someone really ought to do, he suggested, was create an **index fund** that tracked the S&P 500. On average, the S&P 500 delivered an annual return of 10 percent each year. (Adjusted for inflation, the return was under 7 percent.) An index fund would allow people to pay super-low fees to broadly invest in "the market," and then sit back and profit from the whole market going up.

It would be the world's most boring and lazy investment strategy. But it should be more profitable. It should work. He challenged someone, anyone, to give it a try.

Rise of the Bogleheads

JOHN BOGLE WAS THAT SOMEONE. For 20 years, he'd been the kind of professional investor that Samuelson said should go out of business. But he'd just lost his big leadership position after overseeing a failed merger, and he'd taken Samuelson's class in college. When he read his old professor's paper, Bogle thought: Why not me?

In 1976, Bogle launched what would become the Vanguard 500 Index Fund. If someone saving for retirement gave him $500 to invest, Vanguard would buy them $500 worth of shares in S&P 500 stocks. Over time, Vanguard would buy shares of Etsy if it joined the S&P 500, and sell shares of Etsy if it dropped out.

And that was about it. Unlike Mitchell's **active investing**, Vanguard's index fund was **passive investing**.

The investing world greeted Bogle's index fund coldly. They called it a "sure path to mediocrity." Vanguard didn't strive for big paydays; it promised perfectly average returns, year after year. "Who wants to be operated on by an average surgeon?" a rival quipped.

Index funds also seemed to clash with money managers' core purpose. Sure, the low fees challenged their prime directive of making themselves lots of money. (A famous finance book, published in 1940, begins with a visitor to New York admiring the bankers' and traders' yachts and asking, "Where are the customers' yachts?") But many money managers view themselves, like Jesse Binga, as wisely allocating capital to productive companies. They don't fund them directly—traders usually buy Apple stock from another investor or market makers like a bank, not Apple. But prices are signals. A high share price helps companies borrow money cheaply in the bond market and recruit elite executives (often by paying them in stock or stock options). Without trading, investors can't anoint promising companies and expose posers.

> As a given stock rises in price—like NVIDIA during the early AI boom—its stock makes up a greater share of the index fund. Buying the S&P 500 means you end up owning a lot more in dollar terms of Apple, Google, and the most valuable public companies.

Customers didn't seem to like index funds either. Bogle hoped people would initially invest $150 million; instead Vanguard got just $11 million when it launched. Still, he promoted the fund with missionary zeal. In the book *Trillions*, financial journalist Robin Wigglesworth tells a story of Vanguard employees buying Bogle a priest outfit to match his evangelizing.

By 1986, after a decade of preaching, index funds were still a negligible share of the money invested in the stock market. But the bull market of the 1980s and '90s attracted Americans to investing. Plus, companies were phasing out pensions, in which companies invested retirement savings on their employees' behalf, in favor of 401(k) plans, in which workers invested for retirement themselves.

As millions of Americans contemplated stock markets for the first time, Bogle was there, offering simplicity and ever-lower fees. Since investing more money barely increased Vanguard's costs, adding more customers led to a virtuous circle of Bogle reducing the fees. Which attracted more customers. So Vanguard reduced its fees further. Today you can invest in Vanguard's S&P 500 index fund for less than 5 cents per 100 dollars invested.

Besides being cheap, index funds also benefit from what the Nobel laureate Harry Markowitz may or may not have called "the only free lunch in investing": **diversification**. (The remark is unattributed.) Every investment is risky, and the riskier ones tend to offer bigger potential payoffs (or losses). If you invest in different companies and sectors that have different (ideally uncorrelated) risks, your overall portfolio becomes less risky and you maximize your risk-adjusted returns. Tech sector in a slump? Your utility companies and snack manufacturers are doing fine. Global pandemic? Many companies are struggling, but not Google, Facebook, and Nintendo.

Bogle liked to explain that "the winning strategy for investing in stocks is to own all of the nation's publicly held businesses at very low cost." An S&P 500 index fund is close, but not the same as owning every public company. It's not a fully diversified portfolio. So Vanguard, along with competitors that started copying Bogle, created index funds for real estate, bonds, and international stock markets. They made it possible to create an entire, diversified portfolio through indexing, all without paying Wall Street's high fees. Vanguard invests $10 trillion on behalf of more than 50 million customers, and retail investors have more in index funds than in funds under active management.

When *Planet Money* reporters visited Vanguard's office in 2016, it was quiet and filled with oil paintings of sailing ships. (Vanguard is named after a Royal Navy flagship.) Bogle described Vanguard's strategy as "the essence of boredom" but painted most active investors as fools. "You're watching the market every day—up and down, 100-point, 200-, 300-, 400-point swings day after day. It's exciting, but it's meaningless."

Wall Street has changed a lot since Samuelson first threw the gauntlet that Bogle picked up. But number crunchers keep confirming that most active investors are deadweight loss. In 1999, for example, the economist Terrance Odean, working with data from 10,000 investor accounts

The Surprising GOATs of Investing

There's one group of active investors who do consistently beat the market: the managers of college endowments.

It wasn't always so. But in 1985, Yale hired David Swensen away from Wall Street to manage its $1.3 billion endowment. Over the next three and a half decades, Yale's annualized gains were 13.7 percent, 3.4 percent higher than the average endowment's. By the time of Swensen's death in 2021, Yale had investment gains of $57.6 billion.

His approach, which has spread to many universities, consists of a few key principles:

- **MAXIMUM DIVERSIFICATION:** Swensen didn't just buy tech stocks and energy stocks. He diversified into real estate, venture capital, private equity, and other elite funds.

- **PROFITING FROM ILLIQUIDITY:** Stocks and bonds are liquid; you can cash out anytime. That attracts lots of investors. Swensen believed that endowments, because they are large and borderline immortal, could patiently invest in nonliquid assets. Since few investors can make large illiquid investments, the companies offering them tend to pay better-than-market returns to attract investors.

- **WORLD-CLASS VETTING:** You and I can't demand that the world's best fund managers fly to our office, explain their investment process, and show us all their past trades and returns. But since endowments are huge and rarely ask for their money back early, even elite investors will offer special access.

The unfortunate secret of college endowments' investing success is that their huge scale (in both money and time) gives them unfair advantages. This also applies to big hedge funds, private equity, and famous investors like Warren Buffett and George Soros. They have access to much more than public stocks. It's not a level playing field.

The Biggest Bet of Your Life

at a brokerage house, found that investors consistently bought securities (stocks, bonds, and so on) that underperformed the securities they sold. In 2016, *The Wall Street Journal* reported that the manager of Nevada's public employees' pension fund invested every penny in index funds. He had no support staff, went home at 5:00 p.m. sharp every day, and had outperformed many of the country's largest pension funds over the previous one, three, five, and ten years.

One more: The psychologist Daniel Kahneman has described dining with "wealth advisers" who'd provided him with a spreadsheet of their financial performance over many years. He politely explained that their results were exactly what you'd expect from random chance, and they politely ignored him. Kahneman called this the "illusion of skill." When an investor (or anyone in any field) has a big success, we tend to ascribe meaning to it and to want to learn from it. Even when their success is just noise and a lucky roll of the dice.

Index funds' ultimate triumph, though, came when Warren Buffett publicly said he'd bet any professional investor that they couldn't beat an index fund. A hedge-fund guy, Ted Seides, heard about this, wrote to Buffett, and agreed to a $1 million bet. (The winner would choose a charity to donate the money to.) Buffett's champion was Vanguard's S&P 500 index fund; Seides chose a collection of hedge funds. After 10 years, in 2019, the bet ended in a rout: The S&P 500 had gained an average of 7.1 percent a year, and the hedge funds only 2.2 percent a year after fees. As the victor, Buffett sent the check to a charity in Omaha.

This bet now has the status of lore. (So much so that the publicity was probably worth much more than $1 million to Seides—a good trade!) But it was not a onetime bet between Buffett and hedge funds. If you have retirement savings or a college fund invested in the stock market, you have taken a side in this bet. Deciding whether to invest your savings in index funds or give them to active investors? That is the biggest bet of your life.

Not as lazy as it looks

INDEX FUNDS HAVE DEFEATED HEDGE FUNDS and proven their superiority over the average investor. But Warren Buffett is the world's most famous active investor. As the Motley Fool calculated, if you'd invested $10,000 in Buffett's Berkshire Hathaway in 1965, you'd have had about $355 million in

2023, compared with about $2.4 million if you'd invested the same amount in the S&P 500. Buffett definitely doesn't believe markets are so efficient that there's no profit to be made. Why not find a Warren Buffett who can invest your savings—like the founder of Marketocracy did with his contest?

The problem is that identifying the next Warren Buffett is almost as hard as beating the market. Sure, you can look at their past performance. But there will always be thousands of investors on a lucky run who are indistinguishable from genuine talents. In fact, if you're able to identify star investors, the most profitable move is to become a recruiter for hedge funds: recruiters make seven-figure salaries by identifying and wooing talented traders.

The secret ingredient of index funds, though, is that the world's best active investors are working for them, for free.

This is most evident through a thought experiment: Imagine if stock markets were 100 percent index funds. Everyone's fees would be nice and low, but the stock market would lose its collective wisdom. If Google's CEO put out a press release saying, "Eh, screw it, I'm going to fire everyone and go on a five-year vacation," Google's share price and market value would keep going up, because its presence in the S&P 500 (and other indexes) would guarantee that new index investors would keep buying Google stock. And if a tiny pharmaceutical company invented a cure for cancer, its stock price wouldn't rise much.

In the real world, this scenario would never last. Anyone paying attention would see huge piles of $100 bills on the ground. Eventually, they'd pick them up by selling Google stock to buy We Cured Cancer, Inc. As other investors copied the trade, Google would drop out of the S&P 500, replaced by We Cured Cancer, Inc., and index funds would sell Google and buy the pharmaceutical.

This mimicry by index funds happens in our world too. Passive investors essentially outsource the work of paying attention to the market and assembling their portfolios. Not to a single investor. But to the collective intelligence of the entire stock market, to every active investor who pushes stock prices up and down, into and out of index funds.

In the 1970s, when Bogle first plotted financial apostasy, most money managers did a mediocre job, mistook their luck for skill, and charged princely fees that made it harder for families to retire comfortably. Thanks to index funds, though, firms have felt pressure to lower their fees (or go out of business), and index funds are freeloading off the work of the remaining investors. Newer low-fee passive investing options have sprung up, like exchange-traded funds (ETFs), that offer similar products. To a remarkable degree, Wall Street has become a much better deal for the average investor, making equity, ownership, and compound interest more widely accessible—at least if you have the humility to accept you probably can't beat the market and you're okay accepting the benefits of being average.

Now all we have to do is account for the silent thief, inflation.

This chapter includes reporting from Jacob Goldstein and David Kestenbaum, included in the Planet Money episode "Brilliant vs. Boring," January 23, 2019.

Why Is My Money Worth Less Every Year?

A brief history of the battle against inflation

Inflation is a "silent thief." If it's 10 percent per year, the dollars you earned last year are worth less today, and the interest from a savings account or returns from the stock market would have to be 10 percent just to make up for the theft.

Ten percent inflation is bad. But in Brazil, circa 1987, the annual inflation rate was over 200 percent. By 1990, prices were almost doubling some months. Stores raised prices daily. Savvy shoppers saw employees changing price tags and ran ahead of them to grab groceries tagged with the lower price. Some brewers stopped making beer because by the time it was ready to drink it was worth less than the grain and hops used to make it. This was **hyperinflation**.

Whenever André Lara Resende, Edmar Lisboa Bacha, and Pérsio Arida got together, they bemoaned the government's inability to tame inflation—and discussed what they'd do instead. The three had become friends in the late 1970s and early '80s, when they had been fellow Brazilian scholars at MIT and Harvard. Back then, they participated in heady debates about economics with peers who went on to win Nobel Prizes. But once they returned to Brazil, their friendly debates no longer felt academic. Their country's economy was failing. Money felt like sand slipping through their fingers. Brazilians were living an economic roller coaster.

As anger mounted, in June 1987, the president announced the first of what became a series of price freezes on all goods. But Brazilians didn't believe the new ban on price increases would last. So companies stopped selling stuff, and shelves went bare while stores waited for the freeze to end.

The next president saw that banks were offering customers really high interest rates. They had to—if the interest rate was lower than inflation, people wouldn't deposit their money. But the fast growth of bank deposits fueled inflation. So the new president restricted people's access to their bank accounts. If people couldn't withdraw and spend the money they earned from interest, he reasoned, prices wouldn't go up so much. Brazilians were furious, and in September 1992, the president was impeached. The vice president took over and appointed a new finance minister. Who then called Bacha.

"He said, 'Well, I've just been named the finance minister. You know that I don't know economics, so please come to meet me in Brasília tomorrow. We need you,'" Bacha recalls. "Well, I was terrified."

Mythical Money Printers

If a country is drowning in national debt, can it just print more money to pay it off? The classic response is: Ack! No! Printing lots of money causes inflation. Soon, you're pushing a wheelbarrow of bills to the grocery store to buy milk. With your money worth less, the value of your currency drops, making it even harder to meet your next debt payment. (Although not for the United States, since its debts are in dollars.)

Does this mean that countries like Brazil caused hyperinflation by running literal money printers on overdrive? Well, no. Countries print banknotes and mint coins so banks can fill their ATMs. But physical currency is a minority of the money supply.

Instead, when people say a country is "printing money," what they usually mean is that the government is increasing the amount of money in circulation. They may raise money by selling bonds, but have their own central bank buy that debt. Or the central bank may buy bonds and financial assets from private banks (so they have more money to lend out) to spur lending and economic growth. (More on that soon!)

Real money printers don't go *brrrr* as they physically print dollars. They're not printers at all. They are unremarkable computers in the offices of central banks. And the sound they make is the click of a mouse or enter key.

Lara got a similar request. But they said no. Bacha didn't want to move to the capital, Brasília; Lara had started working in banking ("high treason [in] academic circles") and worried that politicians wanted another price freeze or quick fix. But senators called to promise them free rein. Bacha met the president, and when he asked for an autograph for his kids, the president wrote, "Please tell your father to work fast for the benefit of the country."

Luckily, the friends had a plan. It involved some simple ideas, such as reducing Brazil's debt. But the core of the plan was so novel, so perplexing and unorthodox, that they were surprised when Brazil's leaders approved it.

Lara knew it would work. Bacha was less sure. "It's one thing to do it at your office," he said. "It had never, never been put into practice anywhere."

The dramatic experiment they were about to run on their country is best appreciated with some context on where it fits in the history of the global fight against inflation. So let's take a little (de)tour around the world to some of the seminal moments that shaped our collective understanding of what causes inflation and what tames it. First, to Britain, just after World War II, when a crocodile hunter claimed he had a machine that could simulate the economy.

The big economic lever

THE MAN WITH THE MACHINE, Bill Phillips, was born in New Zealand and arrived in London after World War II to study sociology, eventually switching to economics. In addition to crocodile-hunting experience, he had been an electrical engineer and worked at a gold mine. So as he studied, his instinct was to build things. He tinkered in a garage and emerged with a fridge-size contraption that to modern eyes looks something like a Rube Goldberg machine, with water flowing back and forth between different tubs and chambers. He said it was a model of the British economy.

He showed it off at the London School of Economics (LSE), and, according to his friend economist Richard Lipsey, "all the staff came out to humiliate this upstart idiot." Phillips showed how water flowed from the Treasury tank to chambers representing health and education (as the government spent money) and then got pumped back to the Treasury more or less rapidly as you pulled a lever to tweak the taxation rate. "It turned out after ten minutes that he knew more than everybody there, and they shut up," says Lipsey. They offered him a job at LSE.

Phillips soon found himself drinking sherry with other economists and debating the principles of the newish field of macroeconomics—the study of growth and productivity not just among individuals, but on the level of entire countries. His obsession was figuring out how to make life in a market economy less chaotic.

Economic history is a story of booms and busts. Bubbles and bursts. Before World War II and the Great Depression, stock market crashes and various "panics" (the Panic of 1873, the Panic of 1907) occurred roughly

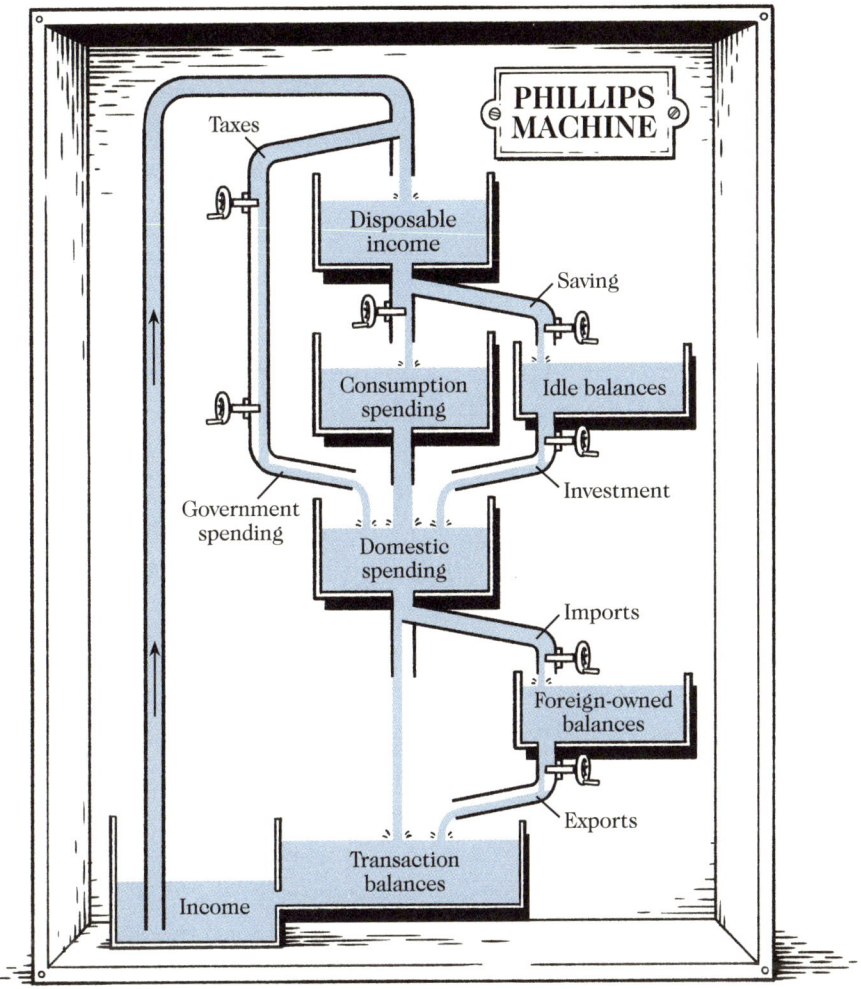

every 20 years, and then more often. Overall a lot of panicking, sandwiched between periods of growth, or even booming growth.

Economists call this yoyoing pattern of growth and contraction the **business cycle**. After the Great Depression, John Maynard Keynes, an economist whose personal life was full of love affairs with leading literary figures, suggested that governments could prevent, or at least moderate, these booms and busts. One of his chief insights was that the government itself could be a balancing force, increasing or decreasing its spending like a counterweight.

Is the economy irrationally exuberant, with tons of rapid, expensive hiring and new investment? Then the government should lower spending like a parent turning down the music at a raging party. Is the economy struggling, with layoffs and wary investors afraid to lend? Then the government should increase spending, contributing some new energy to perk up hiring and business activity. This is known as **fiscal policy**, or counter-cyclical spending.

But Phillips and his peers had a sense that inflation played a role, too, since it was linked to unemployment. When unemployment is low, workers have more bargaining power to demand raises. If Latin tutors and widget-factory workers get paid more, that pushes up the price of language classes and widgets, and you get inflation. This theory of inflation came to be called a **wage-price spiral**.

Another option for tamping down inflation and an overheating economy is increasing taxes so companies and families hire and spend less. Weirdly this idea has never caught on!

One day, a fellow professor told Phillips he had the perfect dataset to test the theory: 100 years of the UK's wage and unemployment data. Phillips took the data home and tinkered.

On Monday, he returned with a graph, which Lipsey describes as wowing the room. He'd plotted the data and created an elegant curve that showed an inverse relationship between unemployment and wage rate growth, which was a major contributor to inflation. It seemed to confirm a clear trade-off between employment and inflation, with changes in the inflation rate changing the employment rate, and vice versa. High inflation and low unemployment went hand in hand.

Phillips's graph spread. Other economists found the same curve in data from other countries, including the United States. In 1961, Paul Samuelson and Robert Solow dubbed it the **Phillips Curve**, and Samuelson put it in his textbook *Economics*. In the White House, advisers cited the Phillips Curve to describe this trade-off between employment and inflation. Governments began treating it almost like a manual—policymakers could pick a point on the curve and aim for it.

Its principal users were central bankers. In the UK, the central bank is the Bank of England. In the United States, it is the Federal Reserve. Generally speaking, it's central banks' responsibility to manage inflation. When Phillips first developed his graph, though, even central bankers had only a rudimentary understanding of inflation, because it was a new era for money itself. Up until the 1930s and the Great Depression, many countries had used the **gold standard**—allowing anyone to turn in currency for a fixed amount of gold—as a way to "back" a currency and ensure that it held at least a certain value. Today, we have **fiat currency**: money backed by nothing but faith that the government will manage the money supply responsibly and not screw up too badly.

Central bankers don't control employment or inflation directly. But they can control interest rates, which, by making it more or less expensive to borrow money, either spurs or slows lending, hiring, and growth. They don't turn a big dial that says "Interest Rates." But they can nudge the rate up or down by changing the interest rate they offer to banks, who keep some of *their* money at the central bank, or in other ways we don't really need to get into here.

Pulling the interest rate lever is known as **monetary policy**. Unlike fiscal policy (increasing or decreasing government spending), monetary policy doesn't require governments to pass legislation. Instead, like mechanics fine-tuning the engine of a Formula 1 car, central bankers tweak interest rates. The goal is to do so judiciously and achieve Bill Phillips's dream of reducing the big swings between an overheating economy and a depressed one.

Phillips's curve had become a manual for managing inflation. But in the 1970s, the American economy acted in ways that seemed to break the Phillips Curve, forcing economists to adapt and update the anti-inflation playbook.

You can think of this as, basically, inflation per year

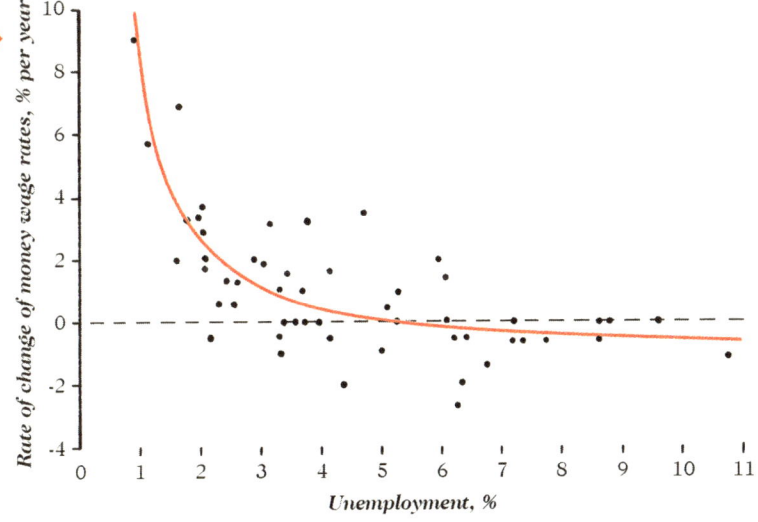

Shocking expectations

IN THE 1970S, Americans suffered through the Great Inflation, a period of increasing prices spurred by a supply shock in the oil markets: Arab countries cut oil production and stopped exporting to countries like the United States that were backing Israel in the 1973 Arab-Israeli War. The shortage meant that people who really needed oil were willing to pay more and more, driving up the price. Inflation, having hit 10 percent in the U.S., kept climbing.

But unemployment was high too: over 7 percent by December 1974. This painful combination of high inflation and high unemployment earned the name **stagflation**. And according to the Phillips Curve, it wasn't supposed to happen.

In 1979, the Fed got a new chairman: Paul Volcker. He didn't believe the Phillips Curve applied to the situation. His predecessors had aimed for a specific interest rate, hoping it would lead to steady growth, but inflation kept increasing. Volcker's approach was: I don't care what the actual rate is, I'm going to keep focused on managing the money supply, aggressively, until inflation drops. He didn't just nudge the interest-rate dial. He pulled it like a ship captain steering clear of stormy seas. Volcker increased rates radically, from about 11 percent to around 20 percent. Terrifyingly high by the standards of the day, and astronomical by today's standards.

The economy recoiled, just as the Phillips Curve predicted. Unemployment increased. Critics and politicians blasted Volcker. An armed man tried to abduct members of the Fed to demand lower interest rates. But inflation didn't budge—initially it went up—even though the oil crisis had been resolved. Stressed, Volcker paced his office over and over. Some other dynamic was keeping inflation high.

When *Planet Money* spoke to Volcker before his death in 2019, he still expressed skepticism of the Phillips Curve. "The more abstract mathematical models they make," he said, "the more they lose sight of [how] they're dealing with human beings and emotions, and those things change."

He says the real problem became clear to him when he met with a bunch of businessmen and told them the Fed would get inflation down. One of them responded that he didn't believe Volcker. In fact, he was so sure that high inflation would continue that he'd agreed to give his workers a 13 percent raise each year. These kinds of choices, repeated across the economy, would further increase salaries and prices. People's expectations of inflation were now a self-fulfilling prophecy.

Recognizing that inflation was in people's heads, Volcker continued pulling the interest-rate lever, but his focus was convincing the public that inflation would end. He told journalists he and the Fed were willing to torch the economy to control inflation. The economic pain grew. His pacing wore a hole in his rug. But over time, people realized that this intransigent six-foot-seven smoker of (mostly) cheap cigars was serious, and inflation started coming down. Volcker is now widely lauded as a hero, the knight who slayed the dragon of stagflation.

The Phillips Curve gave economists the comforting sense that they could follow a manual as they deftly pulled the interest-rate lever. The oil crisis showed them that they had to account for supply and demand shocks. Volcker's actions demonstrated that everyone's collective expectations played an essential role. So economists updated the Phillips Curve. Tweaked it. Added complexity to account for expectations and supply and demand shocks. By the 1990s, many economists and bankers in Washington, London, and elsewhere were again using their updated Phillips Curves like a manual to balance inflation and unemployment.

But in other capitals, where high inflation meant 1,000 percent, not 10 percent, even the updated curve didn't seem like a helpful guide. How do you whip inflation expectations when inflation is literally off the charts?

The Plano Real

WHEN ANDRÉ LARA AND EDMAR BACHA AGREED to tackle Brazil's inflation in 1993, the annual rate would exceed 2,000 percent. "I still believed in the Phillips Curve. There was good empirical evidence for the Phillips Curve," says Lara. "But not in Brazil."

Like Fed bankers, they believed Brazil's money supply was key. Lara, Bacha, and Arida told the finance minister they had to reduce Brazil's spending and debt.

But like Volcker, they believed they also had to change people's expectations, to convince them that inflation would come down and restore faith in Brazilian money itself. Since Brazilians expected the value of their currency, then the cruzeiro, to go down, they demanded huge pay raises, spent money as soon as they got it, and often quoted prices in U.S. dol-

The Secret Target

Why do central banks meddle with the money supply? Why not sit back, do nothing, and enjoy 0 percent inflation?

The problem is that there is supply and demand for everything, including money, and the supply of and demand for money causes inflation to go up or down. When banks make loans, that increases the money supply, nudging inflation up. If the economy slows down and businesses lay off workers, then fewer people buy goods, nudging prices (and inflation) down.

Sitting back isn't an option. So what inflation rate should central bankers aim for?

For decades, no central bank had an official answer. Then, in 1986, New Zealand bankers fighting high inflation asked the question. Five percent seemed too high. But if they aimed for 0 percent, they might get deflation (negative inflation), which most economists think is really bad. With deflation, your money is worth more in the future, so people wait to spend their money, and banks are less inclined to lend. Less spending and less lending means sluggish growth.

They gave themselves some wiggle room: They targeted inflation somewhere between, initially, 0 and 2 percent. Which they achieved! In December 1991, thank you very much.

This idea, inflation targeting, spread to other countries, including the United States, which similarly settled on a 2 percent target in 1996. But they didn't tell anyone for almost two decades. After all, targeting 2 percent inflation means *trying* to make Americans' money worth a bit less every year. It means being a silent thief!

This is why your money is worth less every year. That's the goal.

---

lars, since the value of a house in cruzeiros, for example, would change dramatically week to week. All of this pushed up prices. Brazilians' belief in inflation was a self-fulfilling prophecy cycling even faster than it had in the United States.

So Lara and his friends implemented their unusual plan: Brazil would create an entirely new currency, one that was stable, dependable, and trustworthy. The catch was this currency would not be real. It would not be printed. There would be no coins. They called it a virtual currency.

"We call it a unit of real value—URVs," says Bacha. "Yeah, it was a virtue that [it] didn't exist, in fact."

Brazilians would still use cruzeiros, but everything would be listed in URVs: their wages, their taxes, the prices in stores. And URV prices would be stable, because one URV would be worth one U.S. dollar. So if a gallon of milk cost 1 URV on Tuesday, it would cost 1 URV next Tuesday.

The milk would still be more expensive. Every night, the central bank published a memo updating the exchange rate between URVs and cruzeiros, which store owners could check in newspapers. So 1 URV might be worth a few more cruzeiros on Wednesday than it had on Tuesday. The trick, though, was to get Brazilians used to URVs and then eventually, once people trusted it (and not a minute before!), to make URVs the real currency. It would be like turning the currency off and then back on. A reboot.

Bacha said that when he explained the plan to a senator, "after a while, he said, with some anguish in his voice, 'Well, Bacha, if this is the only way that you tell me that it can be done, then we [will] follow you to the precipice.'"

When they launched the virtual currency, in March 1994, and started printing the exchange rate, many Brazilians were puzzled. But then they realized how useful URVs were. URVs were a service: a way to avoid changing price tags twice per day, and a way to enjoy the stability of U.S. dollars without actually getting dollars.

"We saw the [adoption] of URV very fast," says Lara. "It gained credibility more and more." He knew they were succeeding when his doctor billed him in URVs.

That's when they stood on the precipice, looked down, and took the most important step: getting rid of the cruzeiro and swapping URVs for a new, stable currency. On July 1, 1994, banks across the country started issuing Brazil's new currency, now called the real. Its value was the same as a URV; one real equaled one URV. Overnight, reals replaced URVs on price tags and in contracts. The day of the launch, Bacha remembers swearing to people that inflation would "end tomorrow." And it did. Monthly inflation fell from 48 percent in June to just 7.8 percent in July and 1.9 percent in August. The real even became, for a time, worth more than a dollar. "That was the coup de grâce," says Lara.

Stores used the real. Employees and unions did, too, and since the real was stable, they no longer needed big raises just to keep up with price increases. When people got new mortgages, the payments were based on the assumption of modest inflation. Now people's belief in the currency's stability was a self-fulfilling prophecy.

The friends were lauded as heroes—like Volcker, except they didn't cause a recession. Bacha was elected to Brazil's prestigious Academy of Letters, Arida became the head of Brazil's central bank, and Lara became a special adviser to the next president. That president, of course, was the finance minister who had trusted them to tackle inflation, Fernando Henrique Cardoso.

But a strange thing happened after the friends' triumph. Economists around the world lauded Brazil's achievement, but focused on the familiar part: how they balanced the budget and got the money supply under control. They saw them, like Volcker, as master mechanics who pulled the right levers, and overlooked the psychological coup of using a virtual currency to convince Brazilians that inflation would end.

The friends' Plano Real, and its thesis that people's expectations were the dominant cause of inflation (or at least the perpetuator of it), was ahead of its time. Today, though, economists are confirming this starring role of expectations. Not by studying the dramatic fights against inflation, but from studying the quiet victories of inflation that never happened in the first place.

The central bankers' new clothes

EMI NAKAMURA IS AN ECONOMIST of the new data detective variety. Growing up, both her parents were microeconomists: They studied how people and businesses make decisions. Big ideas in microeconomics include opportunity costs, monopoly versus perfect competition, and externalities, and microeconomists like her parents could test those ideas with lots of experiments and data (like comparing monopolists' profits with companies in more competitive sectors). Her parents liked to repeat a quote from a Jeff Goldblum film, *The Race for the Double Helix*, about identifying the structure of DNA: "There's nothing worse than a wrong fact."

Nakamura became an economist too: a macroeconomist. She immediately noticed that macroeconomists had less data and fewer case studies to work with. "The current monetary environment really has only been around since the 1950s," she says. "... Thankfully events like the Great Depression or the [2008] financial crisis, they don't happen often. But that does mean that we are in a situation of trying to extrapolate from relatively small numbers of events."

If Bill Phillips's instinct was to use data to build things, like his famous curve, Nakamura's is to ask how that data was collected. How are metrics like the inflation rate calculated, and what nuances might that single, clean number be hiding?

The only major inflation episode in modern America was the one Volcker grappled with in the 1980s. Which is why economists have analyzed it again and again. But Nakamura prospected for additional data. The inflation rate comes from a long, laborious process of government agents visiting stores across the country—or calling them up—to check on prices. They check the same stores for years, being careful to get the price for the exact same moisture-wicking, knee-length, white athletic socks each month. If the price of many items that Americans buy (athletic socks, romaine lettuce, gasoline) goes up each month, that's inflation. Every economist has access to overall inflation numbers. But Nakamura wanted the underlying data: the price of lettuce and athletic socks in each store. She found the information in the bowels of the Bureau of Labor Statistics. But only back to 1980 or so.

"I kind of realized at some point from some of the older people who worked at the Bureau of Labor Statistics that there were these dusty old cabinets filled with microfilm cartridges . . . of prices from the 1970s," says Nakamura. "But the last reader that could read these microfilm cartridges had actually broken."

It was like a paleontologist discovering a trove of Jurassic fossils. With the help of a Bureau of Labor Statistics employee and a student researcher, they eventually found a company willing to retrofit a machine to read the aging cartridges. Now they had a decade of new data from one of the most important periods in American economic history.

It allowed Nakamura to look at inflation state by state. Which helped her and her collaborators solve, or at least shed light on, a mystery that had consumed macroeconomics for a decade: the case of America's missing disinflation and missing inflation. During the Great Recession of 2008–2010, unemployment shot up, then fell to historic lows as the American economy recovered. But inflation barely budged, even though the Phillips Curve said it should have dropped and risen with employment. Economists suggested various fixes to the curve to account for this confounding stability of prices. Some wrote half jokingly that the Phillips Curve was hibernating.

Nakamura found a potential answer in her new Volcker-era, state-by-state data. For example, let's say Texas experienced higher inflation than California. The differences can't be explained by Volcker's changes to the national interest rate, since that rate applied to both states equally. So she looked to other factors. Maybe an oil boom in Texas increased demand for restaurant meals, boosting local employment, salaries, and prices.

With the new data, Nakamura and her collaborators could isolate and measure the effect of expectations on inflation versus the effect of unemployment-rate changes. Their state-based analysis said that when Volker pulled big economic levers, the effect was tiny: If you only looked at the impact of employment, the Phillips Curve was nearly flat. Instead, people's changing expectations did most of the work.

When they did a similar state-by-state analysis for the 2000s, Nakamura and company reached an equal but opposite conclusion: The reason inflation barely budged, the reason for the missing disinflation and inflation, was Americans' expectations. They'd just experienced 25 years of low and stable inflation. (A period dubbed the **Great Moderation**. Which, by the way, is a complete historical anomaly!) Their anchored expectations ensured inflation stayed anchored too.

After the COVID-19 pandemic, supply-chain disruptions pushed up prices, similar to the effect of the oil embargo and energy crisis in the 1970s. But in the United States—despite Phillips Curve–wielding economists, politicians, and journalists predicting a recession—inflation returned to modest levels without the Fed inflicting Volcker-esque unemployment and pain. The anchor of Americans' expectations appeared to hold.

"I think that if Americans' memory of inflation was replaced with Argentinians', price levels might jump a lot," says Nakamura. Over the past 30 years, while Americans enjoyed low, stable inflation, Argentinians experienced double-digit inflation, interrupted by bouts of deflation (during recessions) and hyperinflation (more than 2,000 percent in 1990). Such lived experience, she says, "forms our sense of what's possible. The central bank can influence that, but it's the baseline." Even as many Americans found new and better jobs during the Great Resignation, a period in

2021 when inflation was rising, they largely did not demand the kind of big, inflation-adjusted annual raises that can trigger a wage-price spiral.

Nakamura's spelunking through pricing data and Lara and Bacha's psychologically savvy virtual-currency maneuver show us that the job of the Fed and central bankers leans less toward mechanical fine-tuning and more toward storytelling or prophesying or economic psychology. Or putting on a performance of responsible monetary policy, like high priests of finance doing the Ritual of Low Inflation.

No country can tame hyperinflation if its budget is out of control and the central bank is "printing money" like crazy. When the central bank nudges interest rates up or down, that impacts the costs of mortgages and loans, which influences all our decisions and the state of the economy. Pulling those levers matters.

But when it comes to prices, those levers matter less than people's collective belief in the stability of money, and the bankers' and government's willingness to act to keep inflation low. It might be more effective for people to have misplaced faith in the Fed's competence than it is for the Fed bankers to actually be competent! After all, it's our trust and faith that enable them to tell self-fulfilling prophecies of stable money and strong economic growth.

This chapter includes reporting from Chana Joffe-Walt for the Planet Money episode "How Four Drinking Buddies Saved Brazil," December 2, 2015.

PART FIVE

LEIS

URE

19

Why Weekends Are Like Subways and Uber

A lesson in the power of networks

In 1929, Soviet leader Joseph Stalin decided that the weekend was bourgeois and inefficient. Sundays were for family gatherings, which promoted ties to kin rather than the Communist collective, and for religion, which the Soviet state disavowed. So he introduced *nepreryvka*, or the continuous workweek. The new Soviet week was five days long, with each worker receiving a single, randomly assigned day off. Now Soviet factories could keep humming 365 days per year.

On paper, this was a better deal for Soviet workers, who previously had only Sunday off. Before, they had worked six days and had one day off. Now they got their day off after just four days at work. (Stalin balanced the scales by canceling some national holidays, so workers had roughly the same number of days off each year.) All the same, workers hated *nepreryvka*. Rather than most of the country having Sunday off, now a random 20 percent of the population was free any given day.

"What are we to do at home if the wife is in the factory, the children in school, and no one can come to see us?" one worker griped. His free day was less valuable because his friends and family were working. "That's no holiday, if you have to celebrate by yourself." By 1931, Stalin backtracked, and the Soviet Union once again had a coordinated day off.

A Soviet-era calendar showing the *nepreryvka* schedule

monday tuesday wednesday thursday friday saturday sunday

Stalin's misadventures in calendaring reveal that weekends are not just days of the week. Weekends are a technology to organize time.

Like subways, the internet, and Instagram, weekends are a tool whose usefulness comes from **network effects**: They are valuable and useful because of all the other people using them, and they become more valuable as more and more people participate.

> Weekends are also one of humanity's greatest inventions, if you ask me!

Network effects are key to understanding the modern economy: the dominance of behemoths like Google and Meta, and their unprecedented concentration of power and influence. Network effects also explain why so few languages are prevalent on the internet, why so many people drink Chardonnay, and, most important, why leisure time today faces its greatest threat since Stalin.

History's hardest product launches

A FAMOUS AXIOM OF INNOVATION, attributed to Ralph Waldo Emerson, who never quite said it this way, goes: "Build a better mousetrap, and the world will beat a path to your door." The reality is that you not only have to invent the new trap, you have to convince stores to sell it and customers to buy it. But if you invent a network good—a product whose usefulness comes from network effects—the marketing challenge increases exponentially: You need to convince hundreds or thousands of people to start using your invention simultaneously. If customers only trickle in, the product is worthless.

This was the dilemma facing Samuel Morse in December 1842, as he walked into the Capitol Building in Washington, D.C., and stretched a long bundle of wire between two meeting rooms, connecting each end to a machine he'd invented.

He was pitching a wondrous new technology: a telegraph. At the time, it took more than a month for a message to steam by ship from New York around Cape Horn to San Francisco. Morse felt confident he could send messages quickly and accurately across continents, even across oceans.

But no one seemed to grasp the telegraph's potential. A painter turned inventor, Morse had for years "den[ied] myself all pleasures, and even necessary food" as he pitched world leaders for funding, without success. His

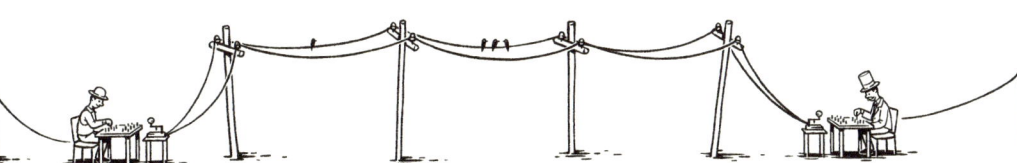

problem was that watching a single telegraph in action was like playing catch with yourself—he was demonstrating a network good without a network. That day in D.C., he tapped out a message in the system of dots and dashes he'd invented, then received it, via the wire, in another room. The assembled congressmen seemed skeptical; some ridiculed him.

Network goods aren't useful until you've built the entire network. Which is why Morse was pitching governments. Highways, railways, and, later, subways and electric grids require enormous up-front costs. Often governments are the only institutions with the money and power to build them. Historically, when private companies built network goods, they often relied initially on substantial public funding.

Despite the skepticism, Congress narrowly voted to fund Morse, who then built a telegraph line along the railway from Baltimore to Washington. Residents played chess matches over the wires. Baltimore police telegraphed a description of a criminal fleeing by train to D.C. so the crook could be arrested at the station. Someone messaged a bank to ask about a customer's creditworthiness. People started to get it.

Within a few years, Morse's company was racing to build telegraph lines as competitors sprang up and tried to do it first. With network goods, the race to build the network tends to be a winner-take-all situation. If a telegraph company wires an entire region and opens plenty of convenient telegraph offices, it becomes much more difficult for a competitor to build a separate, parallel network and win customers. What customer would choose to use the less effective, second-tier network?

In tech industry parlance, network effects are a "moat" that protect companies from competition. With his early lead, Morse established large, profitable telegraph lines that transformed him from "starving artist" to titan of industry.

A century or so after the telegraph wired much of the world, a new network arose (the internet), which enabled new kinds of network goods. The construction of these new goods was as simple and affordable as creating a website (thefacebook.com, ebay.com) or app (Uber, Hinge). But companies still had to convince people that their networks offered value to the customer. Why join Facebook if it doesn't have any users? Why download Uber if there aren't already lots of drivers or customers? The compa-

The Lifecycle of For-Profit Network Goods

1. An entrepreneur or company creates a network good, such as Google, Facebook, or Uber.

2. They successfully entice a critical mass of people to use their platform.

3. Network effects allow them to improve the service and reduce costs, making it more useful for customers, advertisers, and service providers.

4. The network grows larger, and the company establishes a strong moat that protects it from competitors.

5. The company is tempted to degrade the customer experience to increase profits. Maybe they cram more ads in the search results or users' social media feeds. Maybe they increase prices and share less revenue with drivers.

6. The lock-in of network effects ensures people keep using the platform even as the experience degrades.

7. Until eventually, maybe, a competitor successfully launches a new network good, like the AI chatbots starting to steal some of Google's search business, or TikTok becoming the new, dominant social media app circa 2019.

The tech writer and researcher Cory Doctorow has coined a catchy name for this cycle of networks and platforms degrading as their managers seek ever-greater profits: enshittification.

nies that solved this conundrum were rewarded with a deep moat and a network that grew increasingly valuable as more customers joined.

Investors and start-up founders love network effects. In the past few decades, a majority of the world's biggest new companies have risen, at least in part, thanks to network effects.

- As more people used Google, the data from their search queries became a competitive advantage that allowed Google to continually improve the search algorithm and ad targeting.

- As more people joined Instagram, the social network became increasingly useful and entertaining. (Or at least increased FOMO.)

- As more businesses sold their products on Amazon's "everything store," the increased selection attracted more customers, which attracted more sellers.

Due to the winner-take-all principle, however, just a few CEOs (and creators and influencers) determine our social media diets, and corporate profits are increasingly concentrated in the coffers of a few dominant firms.

Network effects are a powerful concept in business and economics. But they extend into many parts of our lives.

Schrödinger's Saturdays

DAYS, MONTHS, YEARS. These units of time arise from natural phenomena: the sun rising and setting, the moon waxing and waning, the return of warmth each spring. A week, though, is a human invention.

Why seven days? Resting every seventh day is deeply rooted in Abrahamic religious traditions, but leaders of other societies also created seven-day weeks, including the Mesopotamian ruler King Sargon of Akkad (2300 BC) and the Emperor Constantine (AD 321). In *Waiting for the Weekend*, Witold Rybczynski notes that by the third century, the seven-day week was the norm in Rome, and the concept then spread across its empire. But the innovation of coordinating schedules has a long, universal

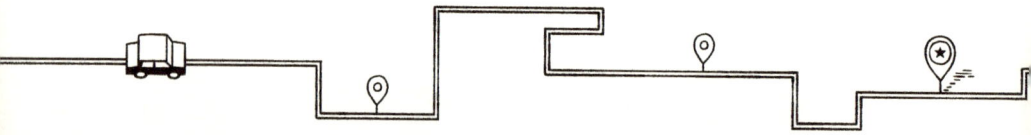

history: designating one day as market day, perhaps, or one day as a day of worship.

The idea of the weekend evolved over time, and began to be codified after the Industrial Revolution created a black-and-white distinction between work hours and leisure time. (In preindustrial agrarian societies, farmers rested when the day's work was done or when the sun set, not at five o'clock sharp.) The workers who marched into New England's textile mills and English coal mines generally had Sunday off as a religious day. They might also cheekily take Saint Monday, which was the euphemism for shirking on Monday to nurse a hangover. The weekend's official expansion had many protagonists and motivations: unions lobbied for capped hours and time off, Henry Ford believed that a weekend would encourage road trips and car ownership, executives used longer weekends to reduce hours during the Great Depression in order to cut costs and limit layoffs. In 1938, the United States' Fair Labor Standards Act established a 44-hour workweek (reduced in 1940 to 40 hours) and mandated that workers receive overtime after 40 hours, and the five-day workweek became standard.

The weekend meant more free time. It also created something new: weekly leisure time that the majority of the population enjoyed together. The late Rabbi Abraham Joshua Heschel described the Sabbath as a cathedral in time. The secular weekend is then, perhaps, a carousel in time. A Central Park in time. A music festival in time.

We've now lived with weekends so long that many of its network-effect benefits are invisible to us. Like Apple's app store (a classic network-effect business), the weekend became a platform for others to build upon. In England, the development of shared days off and the growth of the weekend contributed to the rising popularity of leisure activities, and entrepreneurs and business owners built dance halls, sports arenas, and country getaways to cater to weekenders. "The modern idea of personal leisure emerged at the same time as the business of leisure," writes Rynczynski. "The first could not have happened without the second."

Without weekends, you don't get many giant music festivals and 80,000-person sports arenas. A world of *nepreryvka* doesn't develop cute B&Bs for weekend getaways and restaurants that serve bottomless mimosas.

Network Effects Rule Everything Around Me

If you look for network effects in action, you'll start spotting them in many parts of life.

🍷 CHARDONNAY AND CABERNET

Vintners could make wine from thousands of different grape varieties, but just a handful dominate wine production. That's because customers seek out popular varieties like Chardonnay. Which leads winemakers to invest in growing more and ever-better Chardonnays. Which makes those wines even more popular.

NEW YEAR'S EVE PARTIES

A party with only one attendee is not a party. If you want to host New Year's, you're competing to get all your friends to RSVP by convincing them that *your* party will be the popular one. Send invitations early, or make sure your most social friends commit to your soiree—a tactic in platform businesses known as the "marquee strategy."

🤝 NETWORKING

Like any network, your professional network gets more valuable as it grows. But it's a two-sided market, so pay attention to how and why people join your network. The easier it is for peers to connect with you (maybe you post your email address online with a friendly note), and the more value you provide people who join your network (by making introductions and such), the faster it will grow.

Not everyone has weekends off, of course, and plenty of people prefer a free Tuesday so they can get chores done or enjoy uncrowded theaters, stores, or ski lifts. Overall, though, the value of collective days off is so strong that researchers Cristobal Young and Chaeyoon Lim found that unemployed people reported almost as big a happiness spike on weekends as people with jobs. "The essential characteristic of the weekend is not just the having of a day off," they write, "but rather that *other people* have the day off."

Yet even as the average worker has gained more leisure time over the last century, many people feel like they are busier than ever. In part, this is because the market has delivered us so many products and activities to spend our leisure time consuming—including social media, which devours our time and attention. But many workers have lost the clear demarcation between work and time off.

In the 1930s, physicist Erwin Schrödinger attempted to explain a counterintuitive principle of quantum mechanics (that a subatomic particle can simultaneously exist in two different states until the particle is

LANGUAGES

Every language has value, but it's most helpful to learn languages that many other people are using. This helps explain why the number of languages in regular use has declined, with some 3,500 expected to disappear before the end of the 21st century. Similarly, just a few languages, such as English, Chinese, and Spanish, predominate online.

♪♪ TOP-40 SONGS

Many popular songs are popular because they are good songs or total bops. They are also popular because they are popular. No matter how good an obscure song is, it's hard to compete with the joy of hearing a classic play on the radio, or thousands of people screaming every line of "HOT TO GO!"

observed) using the example of a cat in a box. In his thought experiment, the box contains poison that will be released depending on the state of a subatomic particle. Until you open the box and check, Schrödinger's cat is somehow both alive and dead.

Today millions of us have **Schrödinger Saturdays**—sure, we have the day off, but we're expected to check our work email, which might send us scurrying to review a contract or respond to our boss. Or we live according to the whims of just-in-time scheduling. Fast-food restaurants and clothing stores make workers show up, but then send them home if the scheduling software predicts a slow day.

The encroachment of work into free time reminds us of something fundamental about life. Economists spend lots of time thinking about money. But our most valuable (and scarce) resource is time. And like dollars, time comes in different denominations. A free hour alone on Tuesday afternoon might be worth five dollars; a free hour on Saturday evening when all your friends are available for dinner might be worth 20 dollars. Stalin's mistake was to replace everyone's twenties with fives.

The innovation of weekends increased the value of our leisure hours; smartphones, always-on work culture, and addictive entertainment threaten to reduce their value. Turning off your phone before a family meal; not answering emails in your off-hours; spending Saturdays with people you love—that's putting the power of network effects to work in your own life.

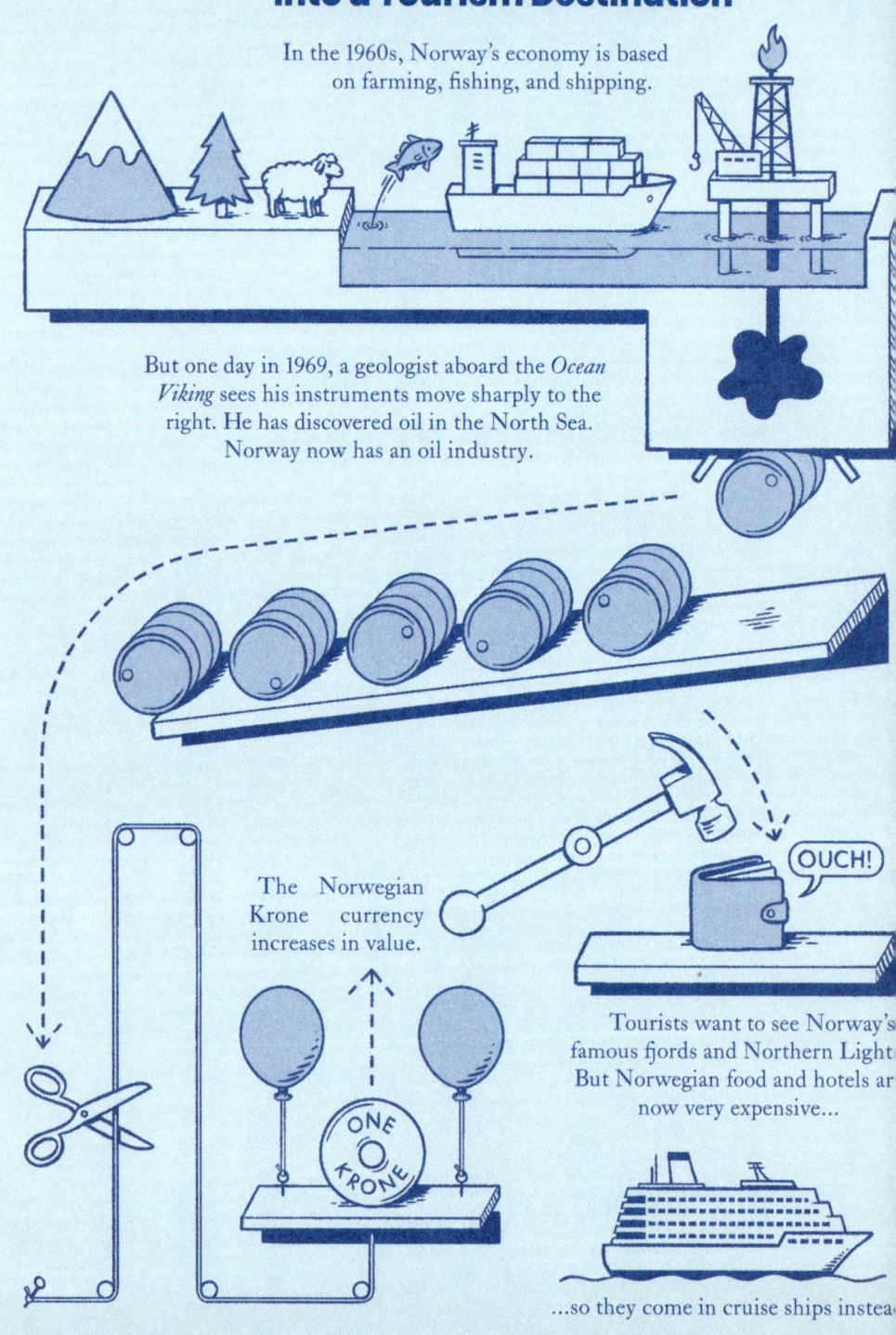

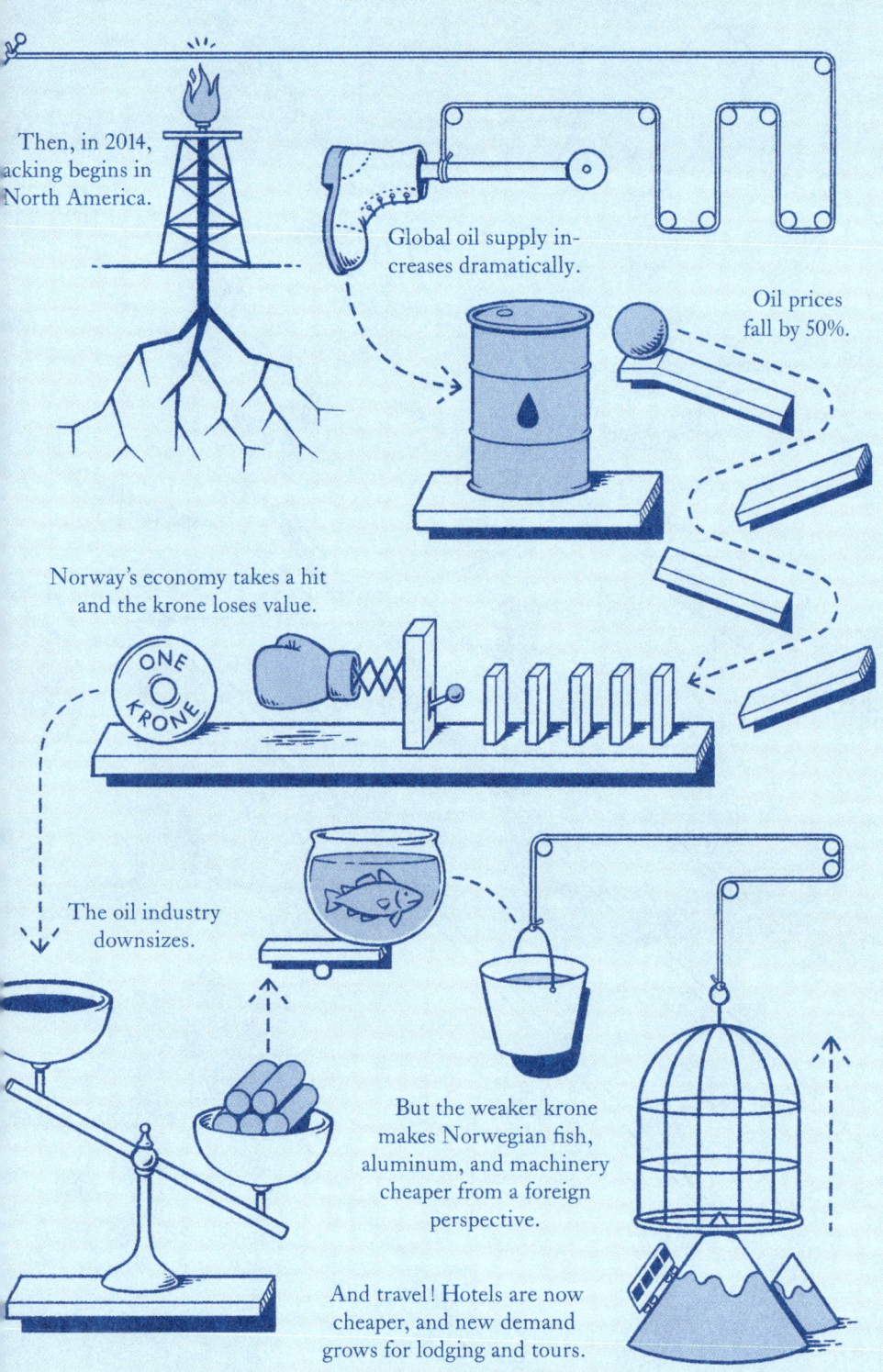

20

What's the Deal with Credit Card Points?

There's no such thing as a free lunch

In 2008, the United States Mint started receiving puzzling reports from banks. Across the country, customers were arriving with boxes of dollar coins and depositing thousands of them each visit.

This was unexpected, odd, because the dollar coins were epically unpopular. A few years earlier, Congress had directed the U.S. Mint to make billions of them, each featuring a different president, starting with George Washington. The idea was to save money: Dollar bills get worn and need to be replaced more frequently than coins.

Unfortunately, evidence literally piled up that Americans preferred dollar bills over pocket-destroying coins. Federal Reserve banks filled rooms the size of soccer fields with rows of unwanted dollar coins shelved in clear plastic bags. So the Mint offered free shipping to anyone who'd order some. Customers later showed up at banks with thousands of dollar coins—all still in the Mint's tidy boxes.

Mint staff solved the mystery quickly: The depositors were travel hackers.

Jane Liaw was one of these travel hackers: people who realize that a credit card is not just a way to pay for stuff, but a magic wand that can conjure up free flights and hotel stays. Liaw and her brethren had realized that the Mint's free-shipping offer enabled an amazing travel hack. She went to the Mint website, ordered several thousand coins, and charged them to a credit card that gave her airline miles for every dollar she spent. Then she settled the credit card bill, thousands of points richer.

"We're thinking of Greece and Istanbul," Liaw explained in 2011, referencing her family's travel plans, ". . . all on miles and points."

Liaw and her husband tried to help the Mint by spending handfuls of coins at farmers markets. But other travel hackers were ordering as many as 600,000–7000,000 coins and then depositing as many as 70,000 at a time, to different banks and using different credit cards. By signing up for a new credit card with a bonus—like getting 75,000 airline miles once they spent $1,000—they could do well from even small orders. A Mint spokesperson said they felt "a little bit violated," and they banned orders via credit card.

The mystery of the dollar coins perfectly represents the strange phenomenon of credit cards. If you visit the websites of Wells Fargo or Chase Bank, they'll show you credit cards and promise you the world: Sign-up bonuses of cash and airline miles. Two dollars back for every $100 you spend. Private airport lounges. Early access to Taylor Swift tickets! Why are these rewards so extravagant? Where is the money coming from?!

A swipe fee is born

THERE IS A SIMPLE ANSWER: the rewards are funded by swipe fees. Every time you pay with a credit card, the store pays a small fee to the bank and to companies like Visa that handle the payment. Also known as the interchange fee, it's usually around 2 percent. You spend $100, the swipe fee is around $2, and you get maybe $1 worth of cash back or points.

But this doesn't explain why there's enough money sloshing around to fund free vacations and why banks feel so generous. That requires tracing the evolution of credit cards, which begins with a wild product launch.

In 1958, a Bank of America loan officer and assistant manager, Kenneth Larkin, walked into a drugstore in Bakersfield, California, to pitch the owner on a new product: the BankAmericard. Larkin's bosses had recently chosen nearby Fresno to pilot what they hoped would be the first universal credit card. Fresno had plenty of stores and customers, but it was sleepy enough that reporters might not notice if the card flopped.

The drugstore owner was familiar with the concept. Some stores distributed charge plates, which were similar to dog tags assigned to soldiers, except given to customers. Each had a unique account number that could be pressed onto receipts. Another product, the Diners Club Card, was essentially a credit card, although in its first year it only worked at 28 Manhattan restaurants and two hotels. Department stores such as Bloomingdale's launched their own cards, too, which only worked in their stores. But at many establishments, including the drugstore, staff used manual Burroughs bookkeeping machines like the Comptometer to process each customers' purchases. The drugstore billed some 4,000 people monthly. Tabs were as little as $4.58.

This was a pain. Every month the owner sweated over unpaid debts. Larkin said the drugstore could stop the stress and accept BankAmericards instead. Larkin has passed away, but in *A Piece of the Action: How the Middle Class Joined the Money Class*, he told author Joe Nocera that the owner "almost knelt down and kissed my feet." Avoiding all this work, and the risk of unpaid bills, was very much worth the 6 percent fee Bank of America would charge.

The secret weapon of Larkin's pitch, though, was the bank's plan for overcoming the chicken-and-egg problem facing any universal credit card. Why would customers sign up for BankAmericards if no stores accepted them? Why would stores bother with the cards if no customers had them? In other words, credit cards were a network good!

The bank had sent families in Fresno a BankAmericard. The bank hadn't asked if they wanted one. They'd just mailed thousands of working cards, all on the same day, a tactic dubbed "the drop."

In September 1958, more than 60,000 Fresno homes had received blue-and-gold BankAmericards. The recipients were puzzled, then started using the cards, occasionally gathering around store counters to watch them in action.

Bank of America executives had planned to soberly study Fresno for a year before expanding the program to places like Bakersfield. Then they learned that another bank was planning to launch a card in San Francisco. The race was on. By 1978, 11,000 American banks issued credit cards, and 52 million Americans had two or more credit cards.

But getting credit cards to work smoothly was a Herculean task. Banks distributed cards so indiscriminately (one family's dachshund received four cards) that 22 percent of bills went unpaid. Cashiers spent precious minutes calling customers' banks to check their balance, and now banks had to send each other thousands of bills each month. It was a mess.

In the late 1960s, banks found a way to stop drowning in bills and get shopkeepers off the phone: Two groups of banks formed competing organizations, Visa (which had had its start in Bank of America's BankAmericard program) and MasterCard (known earlier as the Interbank Card Association and then as Master Charge), to handle each consortium's credit card payments. Visa and MasterCard computerized the process of checking credit card numbers and account balances so that paying with plastic was a prompt process. They signed up more stores, expanded overseas, and funded an advertising marathon to ensure the whole world knew the names Visa and MasterCard.

By the 1980s, credit cards were extremely profitable. Every time a customer paid by credit card, the banks, Visa, and MasterCard got a cut. And every year, credit cards made up a greater share of all transactions.

It was a good deal for stores too. Placing Visa and MasterCard stickers on the door signaled convenience, and the psychological effect of not pulling out cash led people to spend more freely. (Stores that accept credit cards are, today, estimated to see a 25 percent boost in sales.) But the enshittification of Visa and MasterCard was coming.

You bought something? Here's a treat!

BY 1980, banks had gotten credit cards into most eligible Americans' hands. (Plus a few paws.) Their new challenge was convincing customers to use *their* card rather than a competitor's.

This is a unique feature of credit cards as network goods. They have the winner-take-all effect: Measured by cards in circulation, today Visa and Mastercard (rebranded as such in 2016) dominate market share, with 37 percent and 32 percent, respectively. In purchase volume, they are (after China's UnionPay) in second and third place, at 32 percent and 21 percent. Credit card companies have ample moats, but bankers compete intensely to poach each other's customers: Any bank can launch a credit card, as can stores like Sears or REI (often by partnering with small banks or financial institutions and splitting the profits).

For bankers, credit cards in the 1970s had become a commodity. They needed a way to differentiate, and it wasn't clear how to do it. Banks couldn't compete on price—stores were paying the swipe fees, not customers. They couldn't advertise a superior swiping experience, since Visa and MasterCard handled most of that. And while banks could offer lower interest rates, many wealthy customers who created the biggest swipe fees tended to pay on time and ignore interest rates.

Then airline executives showed bankers the way: free stuff! Starting in 1981, American Airlines customers who flew enough miles earned free first-class tickets. United launched their frequent-flier program a week later. Southwest held out, but when sales slipped, they launched a loyalty program too. People loved airline miles. "Every piece of market research that we did then and have done since shows that people like travel bet-

Companies' Secret Side Hustles

A weird outcome of the bountiful profits of swipe fees: The biggest U.S. airlines lose money flying people around. Their profits instead come from miles (they make more from a seat booked with credit card points than from a normal sale), and their share of swipe fees (from the United Explorer card or the various Delta SkyMiles cards).

But airlines are not the only industry where the profits come from an unexpected source:

- Starbucks encourages customers to load money onto the Starbucks app to pay for their Egg Bites and Frappuccinos—and to buy Starbucks gift cards for friends and family. As of 2024, this has filled Starbucks coffers with $1.77 billion in unspent gift card and mobile app money ("breakage"), on which it can earn interest.

- Avis and Hertz profit more from upsells than from renting cars. ("Would you like us to refill the tank for you when you return? Or the additional insurance?") But car sales are another hidden profit center. They buy new cars at a discount by buying in bulk, then profitably sell the cars 20,000 miles later.

- McDonald's is a burger company. But if you squint, it's a real estate company. That's because McDonald's owns their store locations, which are on prime real estate, and rents them out to their franchisees, who make the burgers, fix the McFlurry machines, and pay McDonald's for using the name and logo.

- Mattel makes toys and games like Hot Wheels and Uno. In 2018, they hired a former TV executive as CEO, who announced that Mattel did not manufacture toys but intellectual property, which could be made into movies. The first *Barbie* movie was a hit. (Maybe you heard?) Now movies based on Hot Wheels, Rock'Em Sock'Em Robots, and other toys are in production.

ter than any other award," Bob Crandall, former chief financial officer of American Airlines, explained in an interview.

Bankers craved customer loyalty like this. So, in the mid-1980s, banks created credit cards that rewarded customers with airline miles. Much like how banks entice customers to deposit their money by offering them interest, essentially sharing the profits from the bank's loans, the key to the credit card business was now sharing a portion of swipe fees as perks and rewards.

Swiping enough miles for a free flight, though, was like skiing in Vail—an elite pursuit for families able to afford the cards' high annual fees. In 1985, Sears saw an opportunity to steal banks' middle-class customers. The company invented cash back, introducing their cash-reward, no-annual-fee Discover card in a Super Bowl ad with the vibes of *Top Gun*'s shirtless volleyball scene ("This is the dawn, the dawn of Discover . . . now you have a brighter day in store"). It was a hit: By 1992, Discover had gained in market share, accounting for 6.5 percent of dollars charged in the United States.

Over ensuing decades, competition did its thing, driving bankers to offer customers ever-better deals. The original Discover card offered a maximum of 1 percent cash back; credit cards now regularly offer 2 percent, with ways to earn 5 percent or more. In 2016, Chase Bank unleashed their Sapphire Reserve card, whose generous perks included a sign-up bonus worth $1,500 of airline miles, access to airport lounges, and the ability to drop the card, which was made of metal, on restaurant tables and experience its pleasing "plunk factor." (Nice restaurants use heavy plates for the same reason—heavy stuff feels fancy.) Financial press treated the card's arrival like an iPhone launch: It graced the cover of *Bloomberg Businessweek*, and Chase ran out of metal for the card.

Today, reward cards are a juggernaut. In 2023, Delta's CEO said that people charged so many billions of dollars on Delta's American Express cards that it was almost 1 percent of U.S. GDP. This has made Delta too valuable to fail—too valuable to American Express. Years earlier, in 2004, American Express rescued Delta from bankruptcy by loaning the ailing company $100 million and paying $500 million in advance for more Sky-Miles for AmEx customers.

Beware the Power of Free!

If you consider every possible price—99 cents, $5, $350—there is just something different about zero dollars. A price tag of free can break our brains. In most transactions, we engage in a quick calculation of the costs and benefits. (Is an "organic" peanut butter cup really worth twice the cost of a regular one? What's organic candy, anyway?) But we can't help ourselves from grabbing a freebie. Even when we don't especially want it. Even when the freebie comes with hidden costs, like waiting in line or signing up for a sweepstakes. Companies have harnessed the power of free against us!

FREE SAMPLES

That farmers market peach slice feels free, until you spend five dollars for a single piece of fruit because you feel guilty for taking the sample.

FREMIUM

Whether it's Spotify for music streaming or Mailchimp for sending newsletters, many software companies allow you to use a limited or ad-dominated version of the service for free, and then work on converting you to a paying user.

FREE SHIPPING

You have $20 worth of goods in your online cart. Shipping costs $5. But it's free if you spend $25 or more. Hmm!

FREE BUNDLING

You've scored a sweet deal buying that plane ticket with points. But you find yourself paying real money to check your bag, upgrade your seat, and use the wi-fi.

Why are we still doing this?

ECONOMICS DOESN'T HAVE MANY FABLES, but there is one about a king facing a great depression ("plague of poverty") who demands that his advisers write a "short and simple text" on economics to explain its cause. When his counselors return, a year later, with 600-page volumes, he executes them. Then, a lone survivor tells the king he will "reveal to you all the wisdom that I have distilled through all these years from all the writings of all the economists who once practiced their science in your kingdom."

In eight words, his text is: "There ain't no such thing as free lunch."

The journalist Jamie Lauren Keiles has described the world of rewards and points as "a worldwide hamster tube, connecting Sky Club lounges to Ritz-Carlton lobbies to Wolfgang Puck Expresses to Uber Black cars." Cash back, free flights, airport lounges that literally give out free lunches... Credit card rewards are designed to *feel* free! But they have a cost, and it's paid by stores and merchants. After Bank of America blanketed Fresno with BankAmericards, swipe fees went down from the initial 6 percent. But after banks introduced airline miles and other rewards, that trend reversed. Swipe fees have been going up for decades. This is strange, because in that same period, payment technology has advanced, and moving money is easier and more efficient than ever.

There are two reasons why credit cards have defied markets' price-dropping powers. One is that funding all those rewards is expensive, which

Premium Credit Cards Have Higher Transaction Costs

Type of card	Interchange fee
Basic debit	0.8% + 15¢
Debit business	1.7% + 10¢
Basic credit	1.51% + 10¢
Rewards traditional	1.65% + 10¢
Rewards Signature	1.65% + 10¢
Rewards Signature Preferred	2.1% + 10¢

Select Visa interchange rates for 2025 according to Helcim.

is why premium cards like the Chase Sapphire Reserve require stores to pay higher swipe fees.

Higher swipe fees are why many stores don't accept American Express. But the Chase Sapphire Reserve is powered by Visa, and Visa and Mastercard don't let stores pick and choose which cards to accept. Take all our credit cards, they say, or none at all.

The second reason is network effects. A few behemoths like Walmart and Starbucks have enough leverage to negotiate lower swipe fees. But Visa and Mastercard are so dominant, and so essential to stores' finances, that most merchants have no leverage and simply accept the standard interchange fees.

As a result, many business owners hate credit cards. "This is the economic world we're living in," the owner of my favorite local bookstore told me resignedly. "It's not the best." The bookstore's café has a "Cash is queen" sign encouraging people to pull out bills and coins. Swipe fees are especially costly for businesses that rely on many small transactions. In California in the second half of 2021, transit agencies lost almost 7 percent of their fares to swipe fees, and Visa, Mastercard, and banks often make more profit from a café or deli than the owners.

But it's not just merchants paying these fees. Since stores raise their prices to help cover the cost of swipe fees, all of us pay higher prices. The burden of higher prices isn't shared equally, though. Consultants who have Chase Sapphire Reserve cards get airline miles and other rewards that at least partially offset the increase in prices. But anyone paying in cash or with a basic debit card just pays higher prices and subsidizes everyone else's rewards. In 2023, four economists affiliated with the Federal Reserve, the International Monetary Fund, and other organizations calculated that each year, credit card rewards cause $15 billion to flow "from less to more educated, from poorer to richer, and from high- to low-minority areas," exacerbating income inequality.

This means that, unless you're at a cash-only spot, every purchase involves a tiny redistribution of wealth. And since banks don't give rewards cards to people with poor credit scores, people on the losing end tend to be poor.

It's a "reverse Robin Hood," says Aaron Klein, an economist who previously worked at the Treasury and on Obama-era policy. High-rewards cards are "taking from the poor and giving to the rich."

Wealthy People Earn More Credit Card Rewards

Income	Any Rewards	Cash Back	Airline Miles
Under $20,000	48%	27%	17%
$20,000-$49,999	50%	28%	17%
$50,000-$79,999	62%	35%	26%
$80,000-$99,999	68%	38%	36%
$100,000-$119,999	71%	37%	33%
$120,000-$149,999	82%	44%	39%
Over $150,000	75%	33%	48%

Data from 2007–2008 Consumer Finance Monthly survey conducted by the Ohio State University.

(He notes that many European countries cap swipe fees, or allow stores to charge customers an extra fee for using premium credit cards.)

In other words, credit cards are in their enshittification era. In the 1960s and '70s, they solved technical problems and provided a useful service. Making it possible to use one piece of plastic to book a flight over the phone, pay for a glass of Malbec in Buenos Aires, or pay for bus fare in Manhattan? That was a crazy accomplishment!

But now credit card networks are extracting value. Their fees squeeze small businesses. Their rewards cards raise prices on poor people.

The unfortunate reality, though, is that there's no way to opt out of the world that credit cards built. If you instead pay with cash or basic debit, you'll end up subsidizing wealthy people's purchases and points. There is hope of systemic change: In November 2025, Visa and MasterCard entered into a settlement agreement that (among other things) allows stores and other merchants to charge people an additional or higher fee for using rewards cards. But the settlement may face additional legal challenges, and stores may be too fearful of customer backlash to tack on fees for using their favorite credit card. So how should you think about your own swiping in the meantime?

When you buy a coffee or a sandwich, you probably don't say to yourself, "I need a little loan to pay for this." But that is what a credit card transaction is. If you don't pay your little loans on time, the interest will cost you dearly. But if you can pay your balance on time, in full, every month, then it pays to pay with credit. Compared to cash or debit cards, it's like picking $5 bills off the sidewalk.

Do you spend a lot on flights and gifts each holiday season? If you get a new card with a big sign-up bonus, your holiday spending might earn you a free flight.

Planning to travel overseas? Maybe look for a travel card that has no exchange fees when you use it abroad.

Did you last get a new credit card years ago? Consider researching your options again. You might now qualify for one that offers better rewards and benefits.

Hoping to buy a house one day? Responsibly paying off a credit card bill on time can raise your credit score and help you get a mortgage.

That said, if you qualify for a basic cash back card, and if your goal is to reduce your participation in an unfair system, you could just use that basic card, or alternate between it and a no-rewards debit card. It's as close as you'll get to earning *just enough* rewards to break even and recoup the price increases caused by swipe fees. By avoiding premium cards and constant use, you won't contribute to the reverse Robin Hood of credit card points.

So what does it take to make an entire economic system more fair? Let's go watch a race.

21

Advanced Fairness at the Marathon

Strategies for allocating scarce resources

On September 13, 1970, when around 125 runners assembled in Central Park for the first New York City Marathon, the rest of the city barely noticed. After four hot and humid laps of Central Park, the finishers received recycled soccer and bowling trophies. No one envied the runners. No one was left out.

In the following years, the popularity of marathons rose like heart rates on Boston's Heartbreak Hill. New York Road Runners (NYRR), the nonprofit that organizes the race, worked with the city to redraw the course, which now shuts down dozens of streets as it races through each of New York's five boroughs. But the remapped course still couldn't accommodate everyone who wanted to run. Today NYRR hands race bibs to more than 50,000 racers from around the world, but has to turn away more than 190,000 people.

A spot in the NYC Marathon is a scarce resource: the demand from people who want to run is greater than the number of people who can be accommodated, and NYRR can't manufacture more spots or marathons. Most businesses would respond to this kind of situation by increasing the entry fee. If the price was higher, fewer people would want to run. The goal would be to maximize their profits by reaching the **market-clearing price**, where the number of people who want to pay for a bib would equal the number of runners the race can accommodate.

But New York Road Runners is a nonprofit that relies on the city's goodwill, and they have goals other than maximizing profits. So instead of hiking prices, NYRR developed a portfolio of methods for deciding who gets to run each year.

This is what makes the NYC Marathon so economically interesting. Their system evolved organically, but the result is a master class in fairly allocating a scarce resource. Even though tens of thousands of motivated marathoners are excluded from the race each year, NYRR's multiple methods, each of which achieves a different goal and represents a different ideal of fairness, manages to feel inclusive, like no one is left out.

Why prices again?

IN CHAPTER 1, Feeding America learned that markets did a better job distributing cereal and pickles than a centrally planned system. When headquarters estimated each food bank's need for different items, they often got it wrong. When local food banks instead bid in auctions, they expressed their preference in terms of their **willingness to pay**, and the auction's winner was the food bank with the greatest need for each truckload of peanut butter or pasta.

This is why most economists believe that markets, when working well, maximize social utility (total happiness or satisfaction for all of society).

<aside>The official name for this is the First Fundamental Theorem of Welfare Economics.</aside>

Prices direct companies and individuals to efficiently produce and provide goods and services that people want, which then flow to the people who most need or value them, as measured by willingness to pay.

It's an elegant model and theory with multiple Achilles' heels. We've explored many of them in this book: Markets, especially those with strong network effects, are often dominated by a few monopolistic companies whose self-interest costs the rest of us. Markets underproduce public goods, which is why governments fund worm walls and storm tracking, and the Delawarean nature of corporations spawns externality machines that pollute and warm the globe.

The NYC Marathon is relevant for another weakness of markets: In a world with high inequality, willingness to pay becomes a bad proxy for people's preferences and needs. If a billionaire pays $2 million for a third apartment, that doesn't mean they need it more than local teachers and construction workers. If a poor person isn't "willing" to pay 50 dollars for a doctor's appointment, that doesn't mean they don't want or need health care.

The textbook response to this shortcoming is to let markets efficiently do their thing, and then redistribute income and wealth. The Feeding America auctions regularly redistributed fake money to less wealthy food banks. The free-market advocate Milton Friedman supported a negative income tax that would boost poor people's incomes.

In practice, though, redistribution is hard: Voters and leaders disagree on what's fair, and the wealthy can use their resources and power to block redistribution. Ronald Reagan liked Friedman's ideas about free markets and made him an adviser, but Reagan never proposed a negative income tax and instead reduced redistribution.

The economist Mohammad Akbarpour has made this market failure the heart of his research agenda. "That idea that market equilibrium maximizes the total value, total surplus, or even total welfare comes from the belief that getting . . . one dollar from me, and giving it to Elon Musk, is welfare-neutral. That one dollar has the same value for Elon Musk or Mohammad." He believes that reexamining economic fundamentals, while incorporating real-world inequality, reveals many cases where alternatives to markets, or strategic interventions in them, can improve allocation and boost collective well-being.

Trying to improve on the market outcome, though, can easily go wrong.

Why do scalpers exist?

IN 2013, *Planet Money* spoke to Robert James Ritchie, the Detroit musician better known as Kid Rock. He described how—after releasing "Cowboy," the hit song that vaulted him onto the stage of the Super Bowl halftime show—he started getting approached by "the leeches."

"I've been approached by scalpers in the underground who say, 'We can make you hundreds of thousands of dollars, cash,'" he explained. "'Just give us a few of those front rows for every show.'"

Scalpers are a fact of life, a fixture of the concert ecosystem. But if you think like an economist, their existence is puzzling. Why is it possible to make hundreds of thousands of dollars reselling Kid Rock tickets? And how does it make any sense to offer Kid Rock the service of selling his own tickets? He's Kid Rock! He can sell his tickets for as much as he wants!

But like NYRR, many musicians don't want to raise the cost of their tickets to the market-clearing price. They don't want to alienate true fans who stream their music and buy their merch but can't afford a $150 ticket. They don't want an audience drawn only from those who can afford to be there; they want enthusiastic fans singing along.

"I'm tired of seeing the old rich guy in the front row with the hot girlfriend . . . standing there like he could care less," Kid Rock explained.

Bands recognize that high prices (and willingness to pay) won't get tickets into their fans' hands. But when they respond by setting prices lower than the market-clearing price, their fans don't benefit. The low prices instead summon and enrich an army of scalpers who resell the tickets to bored old rich guys.

Something similar happens in the housing market. Recognizing that some working families can't afford rent, many towns and cities pass rent-control or rent-stabilization laws that require landlords to charge less than the market-clearing price.

The intentions are noble; the policies are usually counterproductive. Researchers have documented how rent control reduces the incentive to build new rental housing, nudges landlords toward selling their apartments as condos, reduces the city's tax revenues, and benefits many wealthy renters who could pay market rates.

The best possible way to disappoint 190,000 marathoners

TO SOLVE THE PROBLEM of allocating their scarce resource, New York Road Runners became accidental market designers. One tool they reached for was a lottery. Aspiring runners mailed in a postcard with their name on it, and NYRR staff picked lucky winners who got to jog 26.2 miles.

This is still one of the four main methods that NYRR uses today—although an online form has replaced the postcards. In 2025, about 200,000 runners entered the drawing (as NYRR calls it) for around 6,000 marathon spots.

The NYC Marathon drawing is what is known as a "uniform lottery." Unlike a raffle, where you can increase your odds of winning by buying more raffle tickets, each person can enter their name just once. It's brute-force fairness: straightforward and perfectly egalitarian. Which is why uniform lotteries are often used to give away undesirable things like jury duty or draft numbers. Sorry you got picked! But everyone had the same odds.

NYRR does not distribute every spot by luck of the draw. If they did, most runners would be slow. There would be no drama at the finish line, and it wouldn't be an elite athletic event. That's why NYRR has, since its earliest days, directly invited elite runners to participate.

This is another fair way to distribute scarce resources: by merit. NYRR extends invitations to marathoners like Olympic silver medalist

Abdi Nageeye, who won the 2024 NYC Marathon, and nonprofessional competitors can earn a bib by running another marathon or half-marathon extremely fast. For example, in 2024, a guy between 35 and 39 years old could have won entry by running a marathon in two hours and 55 minutes or less. (If too many runners match or beat the qualifying times, then the organizers take only the fastest in that age and gender category.)

NYRR does have its own version of high prices, but they are oriented toward benefiting New York City and local charities. If you spend $10,000 a year for a charitable NYRR membership, rather than the standard $60, you're guaranteed a Marathon bib. Or international runners can buy marathon packages that include a bib, flights, and hotel stay. (NYRR gives spots to tour operators to attract more international runners, support the city's economy, and expand the Marathon's TV audience.) Or you can qualify by raising money, usually $3,000 or so, for charities selected by NYRR.

> If you wanted to found a new marathon, you could gain a lot of entrants by designing a gentle, downhill course, so that marathoners can finish with a fast qualifying time for the NYC or Boston marathons.

Another fair approach is to give bibs to people who value them highly, regardless of skill. Instead of giving a spot to someone on the fence about running a marathon, you'd prefer it go to Dawn Papacena, a social worker in New York City who decided in 2016 that she needed a goal or aspiration. All her friends were having babies, buying houses, or making leaps in their career. Even though she describes herself as someone who "doesn't even run [to catch] the bus or train," Papacena decided that her aspiration was to run the Marathon.

Papacena could enter the lottery, but it's hard to get motivated to train if you're not sure you'll get in. Running another marathon fast enough to qualify for a bib wasn't realistic for her. And she couldn't afford $10,000. So runners like Papacena need another option.

Another way to prove you value something is paying with time and effort. So she qualified through NYRR's 9+1 program: She ran nine of NYRR's qualifying local races and volunteered at another. (Entry fees vary, but running the nine races costs a couple of hundred dollars rather than $10,000.) Economists call such hurdles ordeals. (True ordeals are pure deadweight loss—like standing in long lines or filling out unnecessary paperwork. The 9+1 program is much better: It helps runners train and prepare.) The program allowed Papacena to train for the marathon for months, confident she'd get a spot, and the method ensures that actual New Yorkers get to race. Papacena went on to become a marathon buff—she's run the Chicago, Paris, and Berlin marathons, among others.

The NYC Marathon offers a smattering of other ways to earn a spot. But most race bibs are allocated through these methods, which map onto four different kinds of fairness:

Four Forms of Fairness

Type of Fairness	NYC Marathon Version
Luck/Equality	Drawings or lotteries
Merit	Qualifying times
Willingness to pay	Expensive memberships, international tour packages, charitable giving*
Effort/Ordeals	9+1 program

*Fundraising for charity could alternatively be considered effort!

With this framework in mind, you can spot organizations around the world allocating scarce resources using alternatives to high prices. Yosemite National Park, which only allows 300 hikers per day up to the summit of Half Dome, distributes permits via one main lottery (brute-force fairness!) and smaller, daily lotteries (that favor locals). Kid Rock started selling $20 front-row tickets to winners of a lottery drawing and playing multiple shows in the same city, to flood the market with list-price tickets. Many bands offer discounted tickets to their followers during presales. The Sistine Chapel offers tickets for around $35, which sell out during peak tourist season. But they also sell "early access" tickets for around $70, and visitors can book private, after-hours tours for $500 to $5,000.

A good way to appreciate what's special about the NYC Marathon's system, though, is to consider its opposite: getting into Berghain, the legendary techno nightclub in Berlin.

Like NYRR, Berghain's managers face overwhelming demand, and they don't allocate admission by willingness to pay. Getting to the front of the club's ever-present line takes hours, which filters out some less committed partiers. (And people who actually prefer pop or hip-hop.) But for years, Berghain's true allocation mechanism has been a legendary bouncer, Sven Marquardt, who rendered judgment on each group that reached the front of the line.

During Marquardt's 20 or so years guarding Berghain's doors, neither he nor the club have ever explained how he decides who to let in. (Unlike most clubs, Berghain doesn't favor wealthy patrons or young women.) The result is maximum envy. Why did Marquardt let that other group in and not mine? Most informed sources think he judges your commitment to the techno scene and filters out merely curious tourists. But you'll never know for sure, and it feels personal.

With the NYC Marathon, though, the clear criteria and multiple methods result in less envy. Each method has flaws. Each method leaves people out. Taken together, though, they give everyone a shot. If you really want to run, you can.

Scarcity amid abundance

THERE IS ONLY ONE SISTINE CHAPEL. Only one legendary Berghain club. Only one hike that takes you to the epic summit of Half Dome. In an ever-wealthier world connected by highways, cheapish flights, and social media, demand for these **Berghain Goods** will likely increase. We can't mass-produce Sistine Chapels; we can't clone Taylor Swift. The gatekeepers and producers of these famous places and experiences have become de facto market designers, needing to decide, like NYRR, how to allocate their scarce resources.

In more traditional markets, willingness to pay works best when people have very different preferences. Some people value Pokémon cards highly; others barely know what they are. Some people love records; others prefer to stream music. Prices and free markets excel at distributing these goods.

But demand for heart surgery doesn't depend on personal preferences. Someone who isn't "willing" to pay $1,500 a month for rent isn't saying they don't value having a home. In these cases, intervening in markets or engaging in Marathon-esque market design can improve the allocation and make the distribution more fair.

Should we have a market economy for health care, but subsidize poor people's access to it? Or should governments provide free health care, and rely on doctors and health-care professionals to allocate treatment based on medical need? In cities with yearslong wait-lists for public housing, how should we decide who gets in?

Economics can't answer the question "What is fair?" or "Who deserves what?" That's a societal debate, and those are ethical questions. But the tools of economics can help us achieve more fair outcomes.

The story of the economy over the past two centuries is one of increasing prosperity and abundance. Each year, our understanding of how we can increase our collective prosperity grows. That's not the only goal, though. We're learning how to achieve a fairer world too.

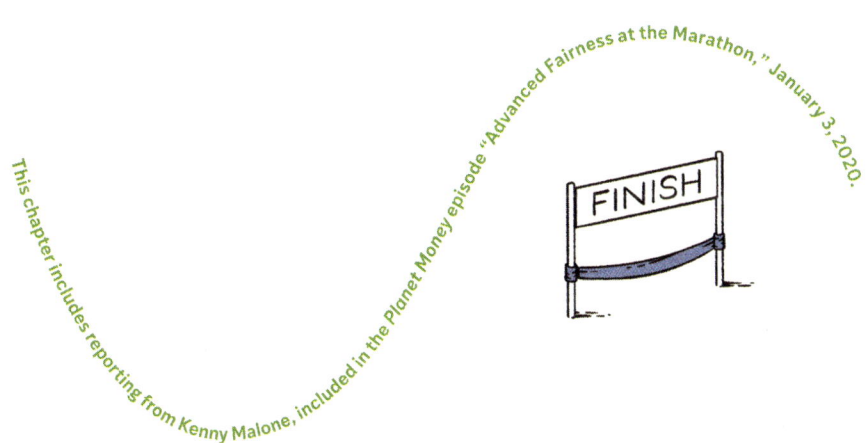

This chapter includes reporting from Kenny Malone, included in the Planet Money episode "Advanced Fairness at the Marathon," January 3, 2020.

Acknowledgments

WRITING A BOOK CAN BE A SOLITARY ENDEAVOR. So it was an absolute gift to collaborate with, interview, and clown around with so many talented and interesting people while working on this one.

Thank you to everyone whose stories and expertise fill the pages of this book. We are incredibly grateful for your time and trust. We spoke to more people than could fit in each chapter, and received generous assistance from additional experts and readers. Among many others, I'm indebted to Jon Hilsenrath, Adriana Robertson, Eric Budish, Greg Sadetsky, Rishon Blumberg, Naz Koont, Renée Suzanne, Laura Jackson, Liz Baldridge, Scott Wiener, Eugy Han, Julie Williamson, Susan Clampet-Lundquist, Penelope Gurstein, Eugene Groysman, Steven Carpenter, Chad Brand, Sara Rathner, Robert Manning, Peter Jones, Costis Daskalakis, Jessica Leigh Hester, Phil Balliet, Mary Clare Peate, and Brendan Greeley.

A huge thank you to my editor, Tom Mayer, who provided strategic affirmation and encouragement; calmly and confidently guided this book through both our journey-of-discovery phase and our race-to-the-finish stage; and set deadlines with a proper appreciation for Parkinson's Law. Few editors would spend so much time indulging my dream of making the cover of the book smell like money.

Thank you as well to the many people at W. W. Norton who literally made this book and got it into readers' hands, especially Nneoma Amadi-obi, Julia Druskin, Rebecca Springer, Steve Attardo, Beth Steidle, Steve Colca, Meredith McGinnis, Rachel Salzman, and Meghan Brophy.

This book would not have been possible without Kristin Hartmann, Laura Hogan, and Anya Grundmann. Mito Habe-Evans, María Jesús Contreras, and Julian Frost are responsible for the amazing illustrations. Laura Nolan, Jane von Mehren, and Howard Yoon provided invaluable guidance. Thanks also to Janet Byrne, Sierra Juarez, and Jane Cavolina, for expert copy editing and more, and to Devin Mellor, who wrangled things that needed wrangling.

Everyone on the *Planet Money* team, past and present, jointly created the DNA that this book shares, and its pages contain reporting, insights, and great turns of phrase from dozens of producers, hosts, and editors. Special thanks to Stacey Vanek Smith, Kenny Malone, Jacob Goldstein, David Kestenbaum, and Robert Smith, who contributed an outsized share of economic storytelling, including gems like cheese caves and the smartphone at the end of the world. And to Jess Jiang, for innumerable behind-the-scenes contributions, and Sonari Glinton, because this book is so much better with Desi Arnaz in it.

Every member of the *Planet Money* and *Indicator* teams provided support: by reviewing chapter pitches and drafts, by collaboratively creating the definitive list of economist power couples, and by talking through ideas at Zoom roulette. It was hard to write about the downsides of remote work when this book came together with the help of such a creative and high-performing team that happens to work remotely. I'm particularly grateful to Darian Woods, Mary Childs, Sam Yellowhorse Kesler, Kenny Malone, and Greg Rosalsky, who provided insightful feedback on multiple chapters—along with last-minute reassurance on key points and passages. I'm similarly grateful to Jeff Guo, for his help on a complex chapter, and to Sarah Gonzalez, for her key contributions to the Love and Family section and for telling me that I was going to do a great job on the book in a tone so confident that I had no choice but to believe her.

And thank you, thank you, thank you to Alex Goldmark for championing this book from start to finish, for trusting me with this project, for making so many lines and chapters better (and suggesting others), and for all the troubleshooting sessions that led to, among other improvements and additions, the money obelisk making it into the book.

A final thank you to my parents for the gift of their steadfast support as I found a career I love.

—Alex Mayyasi, June 2025

Notes

1. The Pickle Problem
This chapter draws multiple facts and details from the following sources: Jacob Goldstein, Stacey Vanek Smith, and Jess Jiang, "The Pickle Problem," *Planet Money*, NPR, November 25, 2015; Susannah Morgan, interview and email with Alex Mayyasi, March 2024; and Canice Prendergast interview with Alex Mayyasi, April 2024.

- 4 **invited the economists:** Canice Prendergast, "The Allocation of Food to Food Banks," *Journal of Political Economy* 130, no. 8 (August 2022): 1993–2017.
- 5 **What is an economic problem?:** See, for example, Roger E. Backhouse and Steven G. Medema, "Retrospectives: On the Definition of Economics," *Journal of Economic Perspectives* 23, no. 1 (Winter 2009): 226; Kenny Malone, Bryant Urstadt, and Darian Woods, "Advanced Fairness at the Marathon," *Planet Money*, NPR, January 3, 2020.
- 6 **9 percent of American households:** "Food Security in the U.S.—Key Statistics & Graphics," U.S. Department of Agriculture, updated January 8, 2025.
- 8 **After three months:** Prendergast, "The Allocation of Food to Food Banks."
- 9 **"a signal wrapped up":** "I, Rose" video, Principles of Economics, Microeconomics online course, Marginal Revolution University, George Mason University.
- 10 **massive champagne factories:** Jessica Gingrich, "How Stalin and the Soviet Union Created a Champagne for the Working Class," *Atlas Obscura*, November 5, 2019; Alex Mayyasi, "To Defy the United States, Fidel Castro Built the World's Greatest Ice Cream Parlor," *Atlas Obscura*, November 8, 2019.
- 10 **"roam[ing] the aisles":** Craig Hlavaty, "When Boris Yeltsin Went Grocery Shopping in Clear Lake," *Houston Chronicle*, updated January 31, 2018.
- 10 **"last vestige":** Marilyn Berger, "Boris Yeltsin, Russia's First Post-Soviet Leader, Is Dead," *New York Times*, April 23, 2007; Leon Aron, *Yeltsin: A Revolutionary Life* (HarperCollins, 2000), 329.

2. Why Delaware?
This chapter draws multiple facts and details from the following sources: Lawrence Hamermesh, interview with Alex Mayyasi, October 2023, and email correspondence, June 2025; Lynn LoPucki, interview with Alex Mayyasi, October 2023; William Magnuson, *For Profit: A History of Corporations* (Basic Books, 2023).

- 14 **pay the association $18 million:** *ATP Tour, Inc. v. Deutscher Tennis Bund et al.*, no. 534 (2013).
- 17 **tap the wallets:** Malmendier represents the joint-stock company interpretation, while Poitras and Willeboordse criticize that position but suggest the recruiting of partners, including some who provided money or acted as financial guarantors (*praedes*).

17 **potentially live forever:** See Geoffrey Poitras and Frederick Willeboordse, "The *Societas Publicanorum* and Corporate Personality in Roman Private Law," *Business History*, September 17, 2019; Ulrike Malmendier, "Roman Shares," in *The Origins of Value: The Financial Innovations That Created Modern Capital Markets*, ed. William N. Goetzmann and K. Geert Rouwenhorst (Oxford University Press, 2005).

17 **not personally responsible:** Magnuson says that the *societates* had shares that limited liability, but notes that the property of the *manceps* (leader) could be seized (37, 26). Malmendier argues that investors who bought shares had limited liability. Poitras and Willeboordse argue against the existence of shares, but instead note how members of the *societates* were not liable for the actions of every member of the organization (18).

18 **Roman state itself was small:** Poitras and Willeboordse, "The *Societas Publicanorum* and Corporate Personality," 2–3.

18 **provided tribute:** Frederic Hicks, "Tetzcoco in the Early 16th Century: The State, the City, and the 'Calpolli,'" *American Ethnologist* 9, no. 2 (May 1982): 230–49; Alex Mayyasi, email correspondence with Manvir Singh, January 2025.

18 **contracts called *commendas*:** Francesca Trivellato, "Renaissance Florence and the Origins of Capitalism: A Business History Perspective," *Business History Review* 94, no. 1 (Spring 2020): 229–51.

19 ***societates publicanorum* were mostly sidelined:** Ulrike Malmendier, "Law and Finance 'at the Origin,'" *Journal of Economic Literature* 47, no. 4 (2009), 1076–1108.

19 **criticized joint-stock corporations:** Adam Smith, *The Wealth of Nations*, ed. Jim Manis (Pennsylvania State University Press, 2005), book V, chapter 1, part 3.

19 **continuing to export grain:** Senjuti Mallik, "The British East India Company and the Great Bengal Famine of 1770: Towards a Corporate Colonial Biopolitics," *Geographical Review* 114, no. 4 (2024)

19 **rare permission:** S. Samuel Arsht, "A History of Delaware Corporation Law," *Delaware Journal of Corporate Law* 1, no. 1 (1976).

20 **"lucrative Wall Street practice":** William L. Cary, "Federalism and Corporate Law: Reflections upon Delaware," *Yale Law Journal* 83, no. 4 (March 1974): 687.

20 **had to accept the offer:** Marty Lipton, interview with Jessica C. Pearlman, *Business Lawyer* 75 (Spring 2020).

21 **Businesses fled across the river:** Cary, "Federalism and Corporate Law," 664–65.

22 **roughly 30 percent of the state budget:** Sarah Petrowich, "Delaware Could Drain Budget Reserves in Two Years and Still Face Deficit, Difficult Decisions Ahead," Delaware Public Media, February 4, 2025.

22 **drafted the language:** "Tenth Modification of the Declaration of a State of Emergency for the State of Delaware Due to a Public Health Threat," Delaware.gov, April 6, 2020.

23 **value sustainability over profits:** Rose Conlon, "Why These Nuns Have Filed More Than 350 Shareholder Resolutions," *All Things Considered*, NPR, October 23, 2024.

23 **Chevron, ExxonMobil, and other oil companies:** See, for instance, *District of Columbia v. Exxon Mobil Corp. et al.*, June 25, 2020; and see Juliana Kim and Michael Copley, "California's Lawsuit Says Oil Giants Downplayed Climate Change. Here's What to Know," *Weekend Edition*, NPR, September 16, 2023.

A World Tour of Spectacular Public Goods

26 **Raining billions of sterile worms:** Jason Bittel, "Why the Government Breeds and Releases Billions of Flies a Year," *National Geographic*, December 11, 2019.

26 **eradicated the parasites:** Sarah Zhang, "America's Never-Ending Battle Against Flesh-Eating Worms," *Atlantic*, May 2020.

27 **economic value far exceeding its price tag:** "The Economic Benefits of the LHC Research Programme," CERN, https://fcc.web.cern.ch/society; Andrea Bastianin and Massimo Florio, "Social Cost Benefit Analysis of HL-LHC," FCC Document Report No. CERN-ACC-2018-0014, May 18, 2018.

27 **data gathered by the government:** Michael Lewis, *The Fifth Risk* (W. W. Norton, 2018), 148; Robert C. Jones, "Hurricane Hunters, the True Storm Chasers," Rosenstiel School News and Events, September 6, 2024.

28 **first GPS:** "A Brief History of GPS," Aerospace Annual Report, 2022; Gideon Grudo, "The Rise of GPS," *Air & Space Forces*, March 30, 2017.

28 **a very special clock:** Mark Esser, "Keeping Time at NIST," National Institute of Standards and Technology (NIST), U.S. Department of Commerce, June 23, 2020; "How Do We Know What Time It Is?," NIST, August 16, 2024, updated October 21, 2024.

29 **crossing was perilous:** "Barbary Wars, 1801–1805 and 1815–1816," Office of the Historian, U.S. Department of State.

29 **assumption that unprotected cargo ships:** Nick Fountain, Alex Mayyasi, Molly K. Messick, and Sam Yellowhorse Kesler, "How the Navy Came to Protect Cargo Ships," *Planet Money*, NPR, February 16, 2024.

3. The Raisin Outlaw

This chapter draws multiple facts and details from the following sources: Zoe Chace, Caitlin Kenney, and Robert Smith, "The Raisin Outlaw," *Planet Money*, NPR, June 24, 2015; Laura Horne, interview with Alex Mayyasi, April 2024; Joe Balagtas, interview with Alex Mayyasi, April 2024.

32 **small number of legal cartels:** See Trevor Burrus, "Rebel Farmers and Government Cartels: How the New Deal Cartelized U.S. Agriculture," Cato Institute, April 24, 2015.

33 **Imagine that you're the head engineer:** This hypothetical is based on the storyline in Jacob Goldstein, Robert Smith, and Phia Bennin, "How Stuff Gets Cheaper," *Planet Money*, NPR, November 28, 2014.

34 **allowing cartels or cooperatives:** Donald A. Frederick, "Antitrust Status of Farmer Cooperatives: The Story of the Capper-Volstead Act," U.S. Department of Agriculture, September 2002.

34 **there are dozens:** For potatoes, see Code of Federal Regulations, Title 7, Subtitle B, Chapter IX, Part 945, "Idaho & Oregon Potatoes," updated March 25, 2025.

35 **not full of sand or mold:** "Natural Condition (Incoming) Raisins Inspection Instructions," U.S. Department of Agriculture, July 2021.

35 **set 10 percent of the crop aside:** Benjamin Z. Rubin, "The Grapes of Wrath Part 2—A Return to Horne," Nossaman LLP, June 16, 2014.

35 **Claymation raisins:** Jonah E. Bromwich, "The Raisin Situation," *New York Times*, April 27, 2019. According to the U.S. Department of Agriculture, "California raisin acreage (essentially accounting for all U.S. raisin acreage) peaked in 2000 at 280,000 acres." Agricultural Marketing Resource Center, USDA, March 2023.

35 **world's leading exporter:** Osman Cakiroglu, "Raisin Annual," USDA Foreign Agricultural Service GAIN Report, Ankara, Turkey, 2009.

35 **ripped out their venerable grapevines:** Robert Rodriguez, "Kerman Raisin Grower Calls It Quits," *Fresno Bee*, November 1, 2014.

35	**"A lot of us, we all jumped up":** David A. Fahrenthold, "One Grower's Grapes of Wrath," *Washington Post*, July 7, 2013.	
36	**the legislation that created the RAC:** U.S. Department of Agriculture, Agricultural Marketing Agreement Act of 1937, Reenacting, Amending, and Supplementing the Agricultural Adjustment Act, as Amended (7 U.S.C. 601, 602, 608a–608e, 610, 612, 614, 624, 627, 671–674).	
36	**found a raisin broker:** Michael Doyle, "Court Rules Against Calif. Raisin Farmer's Complaint with USDA," *Sacramento Bee*, May 16, 2014.	
36	**half a million dollars:** Ilya Shapiro and Randal John Meyer, "Supreme Court Dries Price Controls Like a Raisin in the Sun," Cato Institute, June 23, 2015.	
37	**$90 billion:** "Farm Bill: Reducing Crop Insurance Costs Could Fund Other Priorities," U.S. Government Accountability Office, GAO-23-106228, February 2023.	
37	**"government cheese":** Kenny Malone, Karen Duffin, and Bryant Urstadt, "Big Government Cheese," *Planet Money*, NPR, August 31, 2018.	
37	**drained the lakes:** Hannah Staab, "Wine Lakes Are Nowhere Near as Fun as They Sound," VinePair, February 26, 2024.	
37	**up the food chain:** Wil Chung, "Salmon Sushi Isn't a Japanese Invention," *Medium*, October 23, 2017; Jacob Goldstein, Jess Jiang, and Frances Harlow, "The Salmon Taboo," *Planet Money*, NPR, September 16, 2015.	
38	**Takings Clause:** *Horne v. Department of Agriculture*, 135 S. Ct. 2419 (2015); Brian T. Hodges and Christopher M. Kieser, "Horne v. United States Department of Agriculture: The Takings Clause and the Administrative State," *Federalist Society Review* 16, no. 3 (September 2015).	
38	**previous four years:** Doyle, "Court Rules Against Calif. Raisin Farmer."	
40	**Consider Cuties:** Miriam Jordan, "The Big War over a Small Fruit," *Wall Street Journal*, July 13, 2012; Diemer & Wei, "Partnership That Owns Cuties Brand California Clementine Name Dissolving," n.d.	
41	**SweeTango apple:** Dan Charles, Jacob Goldstein, and Bryant Urstadt, "The Miracle Apple," *Planet Money*, NPR, May 27, 2015.	

4. The Phone at the End of the World

This chapter draws multiple facts and details from the following source: Stacey Vanek Smith, Jacob Goldstein, Bryant Urstadt, Nick Fountain, and Sally Helm, "The Phone at the End of the World," *Planet Money*, NPR, February 18, 2017.

44	**We aren't making things:** "National Trade Estimate Report on Foreign Trade Barriers: Argentina," Office of the United States Trade Representative, 2010.	
44	**open a factory in Tierra del Fuego:** "Keep Out," *Economist*, September 24, 2011.	
45	**"At the time":** Nick Fountain, Jacob Goldstein, and Bryant Urstadt, "13,000 Economists. 1 Question.," *Planet Money*, NPR, January 10, 2020.	
46	**Lyons Community School:** Caitlin Kenney and David Kestenbaum, "Why Economists Hate Gifts," *Planet Money*, NPR, December 23, 2011.	
46	**China's manufacturing exports:** David H. Autor, David Dorn, and Gordon H. Hanson, "The China Shock: Learning from Labor Market Adjustment to Large Changes in Trade," *Annual Review of Economics* 8 (2016): 209 and Figure 2.	
46	**competition from China:** Daron Acemoglu, David Autor, David Horn, Gordon H. Hanson, and Brendan Price, "Import Competition and the Great US Employment Sag of the 2000s," *Journal of Labor Economics* 34 (January 2016), 145; Greg Rosalsky, "How Ameri-	

can Leaders Failed to Help Workers Survive the 'China Shock,'" *Planet Money* newsletter, NPR, November 2, 2021.

49 **Johnson imposed the "chicken tax":** Sonari Glinton, Robert Smith, and Frances Harlow, "The Chicken Tax," *Planet Money*, NPR, June 13, 2015.

50 **tariffs on certain raw materials:** Douglas A. Irwin, "The Aftermath of Hamilton's 'Report on Manufactures,'" NBER Working Paper 9943; Alexander Hamilton, "Report on Manufactures," Philadelphia, December 5, 1791, Founders Online, National Archives.

50 **bounties to Europeans:** Christopher Klein, "The Spies Who Launched America's Industrial Revolution," History.com, March 5, 2025.

51 **expensive and wasteful:** David Sacks and Seaton Huang, "Onshoring Semiconductor Production: National Security Versus Economic Efficiency," Council on Foreign Relations, April 17, 2024.

5. How We All Get Richer, Forever

This chapter draws multiple facts and details from the following sources: Jacob Goldstein, David Kestenbaum, and Jess Jiang, "The Invention of 'The Economy,'" *Planet Money*, NPR, March 5, 2017; Zachary Karabell, *The Leading Indicators: A Short History of the Numbers That Rule Our World* (Simon & Schuster, 2014).

54 **unemployment reached 25 percent:** "Great Depression Facts," FDR Presidential Library and Museum.

54 **directed it to Simon Kuznets:** Moshé Syrquin, "Simon Kuznets and Russia: An Uneasy Relation," Working Paper 2021-13, Duke University Center for the History of Political Economy (CHOPE), 2021.

54 **his first report:** Simon Kuznets, "National Income, 1929–1932," NBER, June 7, 1934.

56 **approaches such as:** Jutta Bolt and Jan Luiten van Zanden, "Maddison-Style Estimates of the Evolution of the World Economy: A New 2023 Update," *Journal of Economic Surveys* 39, no. 2 (April 2024): 631–71.

56 **little to no growth at all:** Paul Bouscasse, Emi Nakamura, and Jón Steinsson, "When Did Growth Begin? New Estimates of Productivity Growth in England from 1250 to 1870," *Quarterly Journal of Economics* 140, no. 2 (May 2025): 835–888.

56 **Robert Solow suggested:** Robert M. Solow, "Technical Change and the Aggregate Production Function," *Review of Economics and Statistics* 39, no. 3 (August 1957): 312–20.

57 **fairy dust:** Tyler Cowen and Alex Tabarrok, "Paul Romer," Marginal Revolution University, video, n.d.

58 **"Gross National Product":** Robert F. Kennedy, "Remarks at the University of Kansas," March 18, 1968, John F. Kennedy Presidential Library and Museum.

6. How Desi Invented TV

This chapter draws multiple facts and details from the following sources: Sonari Glinton, Robert Smith, Bryant Urstadt, and James Sneed, "How Desi Invented Television," *Planet Money*, NPR, January 23, 2021; Coyne Steven Sanders and Tom Gilbert, *Desilu: The Story of Lucille Ball and Desi Arnaz* (Quill/William Morrow, 1993).

64 **life scripted by his family:** Joe Morella and Edward Z. Epstein, *Forever Lucy: The Life of Lucille Ball* (Berkley Books, 1990); Ed Gross, "'I Love Lucy' Star Desi Arnaz Went from 'Prince of Cuba' to King of Hollywood—and Risked It All," *Closer Weekly*, November 5,

2019; Desi Arnaz, *A Book* (Warner Books, 1976); Tom Gjelten, *Bacardi and the Long Fight for Cuba: The Biography of a Cause* (Viking Penguin, 2008).

64 **30 million viewers:** "How Desi Arnaz Defied the Suits and Got Lucille Ball's Pregnancy on TV: 'Don't F--k Around with the Cuban,'" *Vanity Fair*, May 29, 2025.

65 **"B Movie Queen":** Mark Peikert, "How Lucille Ball Went from B-Movie Queen to Comedy Superstar," *Town & Country*, December 21, 2021; Lucille Ball, National Women's Hall of Fame, 2001.

66 **"the studio system":** Olivia B. Waxman, "How Did Marilyn Monroe Get Her Name? This Photo Reveals the Story," *Time*, August 16, 2018; David Low, "Heyday of the Studio Stars," *Wesleyan Magazine*, January 20, 2008.

66 **broke the studios' iron grip:** *United States v. Paramount Pictures, Inc.*, 334 U.S. 131 (1948).

66 **"They would not believe":** "Lucille Ball & Barbara Walters: An Interview of a LifeTime," YouTube, August 12, 2012; Nell Beram, "Being Desi Arnaz: The 'Flawed Genius' That 'Being the Ricardos' Doesn't Show–or See," *Salon*, January 2, 2022.

67 **didn't even have stations:** Trudie Osborne, "TV Gold Rush," *Atlantic*, May 1952.

67 **millionaires did not inherit their wealth:** Thomas J. Stanley and William D. Danko, *The Millionaire Next Door: The Surprising Secrets of America's Wealthy* (Taylor Trade Publishing, 2016); Gigi Zamora, "The 2023 Forbes 400 Self-Made Score: From Silver Spooners to Bootstrappers," *Forbes*, October 3, 2023.

69 **recorded them with a kinescope:** Jon Krampner, "Myths and Mysteries Surround Pioneering of 3-Camera TV," *Los Angeles Times*, July 29, 1991

70 **actors like Bob Gunton:** Russell Adams, "The Shawshank Residuals," *Wall Street Journal*, May 22, 2014.

71 **cooperative, one among:** "2023 Worker Cooperative State of the Sector Report," Democracy at Work Institute, n.d.

71 **graffiti artist David Choe:** Emmie Martin, "How This Graffiti Artist Made $200 Million Overnight," CNBC, September 7, 2017.

71 **Frederick "Flips" Richard:** Wailin Wong, Adrian Ma, Kate Concannon, and Corey Bridges, "The Olympian to Influencer Pipeline," *The Indicator from Planet Money*, NPR, August 29, 2024.

72 **half a million Packers fans:** Jake Piazza, "The Green Bay Packers Are the One NFL Team Owned by Its Fans. Here's How It Works," CNBC, September 6, 2024; Tony Catalina, "Who Owns the Packers? A Closer Look at the Ownership Structure in Green Bay," Pro Football and Sports Network, June 24, 2024.

72 **dominant singers, executives, and writers:** Sherwin Rosen, "The Economics of Superstars," *American Economic Review* 71, no. 5 (December 1981): 845–58.

72 **shows they produced or filmed:** Sarah Bea Milner and Mark Donaldson, "*Star Trek* Happened Thanks to Lucille Ball," Screen Rant, March 11, 2024.

7. The Zoom Boom vs. Happy Hour

This chapter draws multiple facts and details from the following sources: Stacey Vanek Smith, Nick Fountain, and Sally Helm, "Open Office," *Planet Money*, NPR, June 4, 2016; Paul Spencer, interview with Alex Mayyasi, July 2024; Alex Mayyasi, "How Prohibition Tossed a Wet Blanket on America's Inventors," *Atlas Obscura*, September 4, 2019.

76 **corner offices:** David Dix, "Virtual Chiat," *Wired*, July 1, 1994.

76 **Turf battles broke out:** Warren Berger, "Lost in Space," *Wired*, February 1, 1999.

77 **standard office hours:** Jose Maria Barrero, Nicholas Bloom, and Steven J. Davis, "Why

Working from Home Will Stick," WFHResearch.com, and the authors' "SWAA January 2025 Updates of WFH Research," 5, chart.

77 **the main event:** Nikil Saval, *Cubed: A Secret History of the Office* (Doubleday, 2014).

77 **source talented workers:** Emily Wilson, "Meet the Indispensable Bagel Rollers of NYC," *Atlas Obscura*, June 10, 2021.

78 **Economist Prithwiraj Choudhury:** Stephen J. Dubner and Mary Diduch, "Will Work-from-Home Work Forever?," *Freakonomics Radio*, June 2, 2021.

78 **benefits he observed:** Prithwiraj Choudhury, "Our Work-from-Anywhere Future," *Harvard Business Review*, November–December 2020.

79 **working remotely for chunks of time:** Jason Fried and David Heinemeier Hansson, *Remote: Office Not Required* (Crown, 2013); Nicholas Bloom, Jose Maria Barrero, and Steven J. Davis, "The Evolution of Working from Home," *Journal of Economic Perspectives* 37, no. 4 (Fall 2023): 1–28.

79 **Chinese travel agency:** Nicholas Bloom, James Liang, John Roberts, and Zhichun Jenny Ying, "Does Working from Home Work? Evidence from a Chinese Experiment," *Quarterly Journal of Economics* 130, no. 1 (February 2015): 165–218.

79 **no one was certain:** Bloom, Barrero, and Davis, "The Evolution of Working from Home," 2.

79 **35 percent of American workdays:** Barrero, Bloom, and Davis, "Why Working from Home Will Stick," and the authors' "SWAA January 2025 Updates of WFH Research," 5, chart.

79 **responses to Brazilian job postings:** Emanuele Colonnelli et. al, "Polarizing Corporations: Does Talent Flow to 'Good' Firms?," NBER Working Paper 31913, November 2023.

79 **share of WFH days began to fall:** Barrero, Bloom, and Davis, chart.

79 **put beds in the office:** James Clayton and Ben Derico, "Elon Musk Turns Twitter into 'Hotel' for Staff," BBC, December 7, 2022; Victor Ordonez and Stephanie Wash, "Meeting Audio Reveals Musk Told Twitter Staff Either Return to Office or 'Resignation Accepted,'" ABC News, November 10, 2022.

80 **so they couldn't shirk:** Dominice Rushe, "Elon Musk Tells Employees to Return to Office or 'Pretend to Work' Elsewhere," *Guardian*, June 1, 2022.

80 **"The young generation is being damaged":** Rebecca Ungarino, "Leaked Audio: Here's What JPMorgan CEO Dimon Said About Hiring and Remote Work," *Barron's*, February 13, 2025.

80 **showed up in pay raises:** Natalia Emanuel, Emma Harrington, and Amanda Pallais, "The Power of Proximity to Coworkers: Training for Tomorrow or Productivity Today," NBER Working Paper 31880, November 2023.

80 **"Mentorship of junior engineers":** Jerusalem Demsas, "Who Really Benefits from the Great Remote-Work Experiment?," *Atlantic*, June 4, 2024.

82 **grasped this trade-off:** Emanuel, Harrington, and Pallais, "The Power of Proximity to Coworkers"; U.S. Census Bureau, "Household Pulse Survey: Measuring Emergent Social and Economic Matters Facing US Households," December 19, 2024.

82 **"Collaborating and inventing":** Andy Jassy, "Update from Andy Jassy on Return to Office Plans," Amazon, February 17, 2023.

83 **during the Great Depression:** Stacey Vanek Smith and Alex Mayyasi, "An Economist Walks into a Bar," *The Indicator from Planet Money*, NPR, October 13, 2020; Michael Andrews, "Bar Talk Informal Social Networks, Alcohol Prohibition, and Invention," Research Briefs in Economic Policy 343, August 2, 2023.

84 **patent bumps:** Michael Andrews and Chelsea Lensing, "Cup of Joe and Knowledge Flow: Coffee Shops and Invention," August 7, 2024. Available at SSRN.

84 **"If bumping into people":** Mike Andrews, interview with Alex Mayyasi, July 2024.

84 **28 percent of all workdays:** Barrero, Bloom, and Davis, "Why Working from Home Will Stick," and the authors' "SWAA January 2025 Updates of WFH Research," 5, chart; Statistisches Bundesamt, "Employed Persons Working from Home," 2025; Statistic Canada, "Share of Workers Usually Working from Home, Canada, 2016 to 2023," Infographic 1.

86 **"This study offers powerful evidence":** Nicholas Bloom, Ruobing Han, and James Liang, "Hybrid Working from Home Improves Retention Without Damaging Performance," *Nature*, June 12, 2024, 920–25; Kaya Ginsky, "'Win-Win-Win': Three-Day Hybrid Work Week Is a Success, Largest Study to Date Published in *Nature* Says," CNBC, June 14, 2024.

8. A Tale of Two Gig Workers

This chapter draws multiple facts and details from the following sources: Gustavo Ajché, interview with Alex Mayyasi, September 2024, and email correspondence, March 2025; Rishon Blumberg, interview with Alex Mayyasi, September 2024; Preethi Vaidyanathan, interview with Alex Mayyasi, September 2024; Erica L. Groshen, interview with Alex Mayyasi, September 2024; David Weil, *The Fissured Workplace: Why Work Became So Bad for So Many and What Can Be Done to Improve It* (Harvard University Press, 2014); Maria Figueroa et al., "Essential but Unprotected: App-Based Food Couriers in New York City," School of Industrial and Labor Relations (ILR), The Worker Institute, Cornell University, 2023.

90 **36 percent of Americans:** André Dua et al., "What Is the Gig Economy?," American Opportunity Survey, McKinsey & Company, August 23, 2022.

91 **every company is similarly inefficient:** R. H. Coase, "The Nature of the Firm," *Economica* 4, no. 16 (November 1937): 386–405.

92 **If you walk into a Marriott hotel:** "Union Square Hospitality Group Awarded Marriott Marquis Hotel Food and Beverage Contract," *IX Legal* blog, September 13, 2021.

93 **"got into accidents":** Orlando Mayorquin, "Food Delivery Workers, Overlooked in Life, Are Honored in Death," *New York Times*, January 11, 2024. "A Minimum Pay Rate for App-Based Restaurant Delivery Workers in NYC," New York City Department of Consumer and Worker Protection, 2022, table 12.

93 **a broader sense of fairness:** M. Todd Henderson, "Everything Old Is New Again: Lessons from Dodge v. Ford Motor Company," John M. Olin Program in Law and Economics Working Paper No. 373, 2007.

94 **technology and automation:** David Autor and Anna Salomons, "Is Automation Labor-Displacing? Productivity Growth, Employment, and the Labor Share," Brookings Institution, March 8, 2018; Anna M. Stansbury and Lawrence H. Summers, "Productivity and Pay: Is the Link Broken?," NBER Working Paper 24165, December 2017.

95 **hire some back as contractors:** "NYC's Marriott Marquis Set to Outsource $50 million+ Food & Beverage Operation," Total Food Service, March 17, 2021; Lauren Rosenblatt, "Laid Off by Big Tech, Then Recruited for Contract Work—at the Same Place," *Seattle Times*, April 16, 2023.

96 **a different playbook:** Adrian Ma, Wailin Wong, Kate Concannon, and Viet Le, "A Super-Sized Labor Experiment," *The Indicator from Planet Money*, NPR, September 14, 2022; Peter Romeo, "California's Fast Food Council Wonders What the Heck It's Doing," Restaurant Business, September 12, 2024.

96 **sectoral bargaining:** Jack Corbett, Alex Goldmark, and Mito Habe-Evans, "It's Illegal to Retaliate Against Union Organizing. Does It Still Happen? Yup," *Planet Money* Tik-

Tok, October 19, 2022; "Industrial Relations in France: Background Summary," European Trade Union Institute, April 2, 2016:

97 **said the laws would be disastrous:** Claudia Irizarry Aponte and Sujin Shin, "Food Delivery Workers Veer into Warfare over Breakthrough Wage Proposal," *The City*, April 5, 2023.

97 **sued to prevent:** Joanna Fantozzi, "New York City's Minimum Wage Law for Delivery Workers Upheld by the Courts," *Nation's Restaurant News*, December 1, 2023.

97 **beat the apps' legal challenge:** "Delivery Workers Win a Dignified Pay Rate: Court Allows Minimum Pay Rate for App-Based Restaurant Delivery Workers to Take Effect," NYC Department of Consumer and Worker Protection, September 28, 2023.

97 **If Netflix instead paid Amazon:** James Bourne, "Netflix 'Testing Waters' with Google Illustrates How It's a Mad, Mad, Multi-Cloud World," CloudTech, April 23, 2018; Steve Henn, "Hard Work Is Irrelevant," *Planet Money*, NPR, August 29, 2015.

97 **core competencies:** "Netflix: What Happens When You Press Play?," High Scalability, December 11, 2017.

100 **like John Mayer and Vanessa Carlton:** Lizzie Widdicombe, "The Programmer's Price," *New Yorker*, November 17, 2014.

101 **backlash is less likely:** Hannah Riley Bowles, "How Women Can Negotiate for the Academic Career They Truly Want," Harvard Business Publishing/Education, March 7, 2023; Hannah Riley Bowles, Bobbi Thomason, and Julia B. Bear, "Reconceptualizing What and How Women Negotiate for Career Advancement," *Academy of Management Journal* 62, no. 6 (December 2019).

102 **just as good, if not better:** Greg Sadetsky, interview with Alex Mayyasi, September 2024.

The Laws of the Office

This chapter draws multiple facts and details from the following source: Kenny Malone, Sarah Gonzalez, Alexi Horowitz-Ghazi, and Alex Goldmark, "The Laws of the Office," *Planet Money*, NPR, November 21, 2018.

9. The Hopeful Tale of the ATM and the Bank Teller

This chapter draws multiple facts and details from the following sources: Angie Douglas, interview with Alex Mayyasi, December 2024; James Bessen, interview with Alex Mayyasi, November 2024; James Bessen, *Learning by Doing: The Real Connection Between Innovation, Wages, and Wealth* (Yale University Press, 2015).

108 **"excitement" and "awe":** "Credit Unions in the '80s: A Trip Down Memory Lane," *CUSO Magazine*, October 24, 2019.

108 **traces our modern "automation anxiety":** David H. Autor, "Why Are There Still So Many Jobs? The History and Future of Workplace Automation," *Journal of Economic Perspectives* 29, no. 3 (Summer 2015): 3–30.

110 **cut the rope:** Natasha Frost, "What Was the Point of Elevator Music?," *Atlas Obscura*, May 31, 2018; John C. Abell, "March 23, 1857: Mr. Otis Gives You a Lift," *Wired*, March 23, 2010.

110 **Tillie the All-Time Teller:** Wayne King, "The Automatic Bank Tellers Are Here," *The Dispatch*, May 15, 1976; Marianne Babal, "Dispensing Money Like Magic," Wells Fargo site, "History," n.d.

110 **put ATMs in vans:** Mark J. Price, "Local History: Futuristic Bank Machines Offered 24-Hour Service in 1970s," *Akron Beacon Journal*, November 29, 2021; Ellen Florian, Doris Burke, and Jenny Mero, "The Money Machines," *Fortune*, July 26, 2004.

110 **an accountant named Alan Snyder:** Jacob Goldstein, David Kestenbaum, and Jess Jiang, "Spreadsheets!," *Planet Money*, NPR, February 26, 2015.

111 **a consistently unprofitable decade:** Colby Hopkins, "The History of Amazon and Its Rise to Success," *Michigan Journal of Economics*, May 1, 2023; Jacqueline Doherty, "Amazon.bomb," *Barron's*, May 31, 1999.

112 **"I trust that no one":** Maria Gloria Cobas, Larry R. Mote, and James A. Wilcox, "A History of the Future of Banking: Predictions and Outcomes," in *The Future of Banking*, ed. Benton E. Gup (Quorum Books, 2003), 53, 55.

113 **lump of labor fallacy:** Markus Furendal and Karim Jebari, "The Future of Work: Augmentation or Stunting?," *Philosophy & Technology* 36 (May 2023).

113 **more tellers overall:** Autor, "Why Are There Still So Many Jobs?," 6.

114 **would actually *increase* coal consumption:** W[illiam] Stanley Jevons, *The Coal Question: An Inquiry Concerning the Progress of the Nation, and the Probable Exhaustion of Our Coal-Mines* (London: Macmillan and Co., 1865).

114 **"that six electronic digital computers":** John Kopplin, *An Illustrated History of Computers*, Part 3, Kent State University website.

115 **demand for financial managers and analysts:** Greg Ip, "We Survived Spreadsheets, and We'll Survive AI," *Wall Street Journal*, August 2, 2017.

115 **more hirings than firings:** Greg Rosalsky, "Why the AI World Is Suddenly Obsessed with a 160-Year-Old Economics Paradox," *Planet Money* newsletter, February 4, 2025.

115 **replaced the women who operated switchboards:** James Feigenbaum and Daniel Gross, "Answering the Call of Automation: How the Labor Market Adjusted to Mechanizing Telephone Operation," NBER Working Paper 28061, November 2022, revised February 2024.

116 **multidecade career:** "Dorothy Vaughan," National Advisory Committee for Aeronautics (NACA)/National Aeronautics and Space Administration (NASA) biography, November 2016; "Hidden Figures and Human Computers," National Air and Space Museum, Smithsonian Institution, January 26, 2017; "Hidden Figures and Katherine Johnson," National Air and Space Museum, Smithsonian Institution, July 12, 2018.

117 **Ada Lovelace:** "Ada Lovelace and the First Computer Programme in the World," Max. Planck-Gesellschaft, https://www.mpg.de/female-pioneers-of-science/Ada-Lovelace.

117 **many women took the lead:** "The Gendered History of Human Computers," Clive Thompson, Smithsonian Magazine, June 2019.

117 **35 percent of tech jobs:** "Diversity and STEM: Women, Minorities, Persons with Disabilities 2023," U.S. National Science Foundation, January 2023

117 **equally interested:** Steve Henn, Caitlin Kenney, and Phia Bennin, "When Women Stopped Coding," *Planet Money*, NPR, October 17, 2014.

117 **faced sexism and misogyny:** See "Barriers to Equality in Academia: Women in Computer Science at M.I.T.," Prepared by female graduate students and research staff in the Laboratory for Computer Science and the Artificial Intelligence Laboratory at M.I.T., February 1983.

117 **discrimination can hold back:** See for example Lisa Cook's work covered in Mary Childs, Karen Duffin, and Bryant Urstadt, "Patent Racism," *Planet Money*, NPR, June 12, 2020.

119 **"prompt engineers":** Adrian Ma, Darian Woods, Kate Concannon, and Cooper Katz McKim: "One of the Hottest Jobs in AI Right Now: 'Types-Question Guy,'" *The Indicator from Planet Money*, NPR, July 5, 2024.

120 **faster translation done by computers has increased demand:** U.S. Bureau of Labor Statistics, "Interpreters and Translators," *Occupational Outlook Handbook*, 2025; Greg Rosalsky, "If AI Is So Good, Why Are There Still So Many Jobs for Translators?" *Planet Money* newsletter, June 18, 2024.

10. The Labor of Finding Love

This chapter draws multiple facts and details from the following sources: Alex Mayyasi, Sarah Gonzalez, Bryant Urstadt, James Sneed, and Maria Paz Gutierrez, "The Marriage Pact," *Planet Money*, NPR, March 6, 2021; Liam McGregor, interview with Alex Mayyasi, August 2024; Paul Milgrom, interview with Alex Mayyasi and Sarah Gonzalez, February 2021.

128 **America's radio spectrum:** Joshua Gans, "Paul Milgrom, Price Discoverer and Nobel Laureate," VoxEU, Centre for Economic Policy Research, November 15, 2020.

128 **amateurs using the same frequencies:** Ben Christopher, "The Spectrum Auction: How Economists Saved the Day," Priceonomics, August 19, 2016.

128 **"I'm just an economic theorist!":** Christopher, "The Spectrum Auction."

128 **bull preserved in formaldehyde:** Arifa Akbar, "A Formaldehyde Frenzy as Buyers Snap Up Hirst Works," *Independent*, September 16, 2008.

128 **the right value for the spectrum:** Paul Milgrom, *Discovering Prices: Auction Design in Markets with Complex Constraints* (Columbia University Press, 2021), chap. 1; Eric Budish, interview with Alex Mayyasi, August 2024.

128 **might take decades:** Milgrom writes about the Georgia land lottery and how it took 100 years to unwind its inefficiencies (*Discovering Prices*, chap. 1).

129 **their value depended on:** Christopher, "The Spectrum Auction."

129 **Milgrom added rules:** Gans, "Paul Milgrom, Price Discoverer and Nobel Laureate."

129 **brought his models to the FCC:** Evan Kwerel, Thomas M. Lenard, Scott Wallsten, and Sarah Oh Lam, "Evan Kwerel on the Origins of Spectrum Auctions," *Two Think Minimum*, Technology Policy Institute, April 28, 2022; Christopher, "The Spectrum Auction."

130 **"We've all just sort of decided":** Tayfun Sönmez and M. Utku Ünver, "Market Design for Living-Donor Organ Exchanges: An Economic Policy Perspective," *Oxford Review of Economic Policy* 33, no. 4 (2017): 676–704; Ian Rose, "How an Economist Helped Thousands Get a New Kidney," BBC, December 16, 2019.

130 **outcome is always stable:** Alvin E. Roth, "The Economist as Engineer: Game Theory, Experimentation, and Computation as Tools for Design Economics," *Econometrica* 70, no. 4 (July 2002).

131 **got into one of their top-choice schools:** Atila Abdulkadiroğlu, Parag A. Pathak, and Alvin E. Roth, "The New York City High School Match," *American Economic Review* 95, no. 2 (2005): 364–67.

131 **punch-card questionnaires:** T. JAY Mathews, "Operation Match," *Harvard Crimson*, November 3, 1965; Lawrence J. Krakauer, "Data-Mate," ljkrakauer.com, March 13, 2014.

132 **inflate their height:** "The Big Lies People Tell in Online Dating," OkCupid Dating Blog, Medium, July 7, 2010; Sydney Lake, "Women Are Using ChatGPT to Catch Men in Lies About Their Height on Dating Apps," *Fortune*, August 16, 2024.

132 **"Listen. Finding a life partner":** Marriage Pact flyer provided by McGregor.

133 **must avoid congestion:** Alvin E. Roth, "The Art of Designing Markets," *Harvard Business Review*, October 2007.

134 **said yes to the investors:** Matthew Turk, "Marriage Pact Secures $5 million in Seed Funding," *Stanford Daily*, September 28, 2022.

134 **heads of dating apps:** Darian Woods, Wailin Wong, Kate Concannon, and Julia Ritchey, "Trying to Fix the Dating App Backlash," *The Indicator from Planet Money*, NPR, October 24, 2024.

134 **case *against* better matchmaking:** Ali Cudby, *Keep Your Customers: How to Stop Customer Turnover, Improve Retention and Get Lucrative, Long-Term Loyalty* (Morgan James Publishing, 2020), 4.

135   **researchers interviewed speed daters:** Paul W. Eastwick and Eli J. Finkel, "Sex Differences in Mate Preferences Revisited: Do People Know What They Initially Desire in a Romantic Partner?," *Journal of Personality and Social Psychology* 94, no. 2 (2008): 245–64.

135   **did not predict whom they requested to date:** Richard E. Nisbett and Timothy D. Wilson, "The Halo Effect: Evidence for Unconscious Alteration of Judgments," *Journal of Personality and Social Psychology* 35, no. 4 (1977): 250–56; Eric W. Dolan, "The Reality of Romantic Preferences: Large-Scale Study Reveals Surprising Truths," PsyPost, August 17, 2024.

135   **twice as likely to find:** Anna Brown, "Lesbian, Gay and Bisexual Online Daters Report Positive Experiences—but Also Harassment," Pew Research Center, April 9, 2020.

135   **find matches more efficiently:** Claus Wedekind, Thomas Seebeck, Florence Bettens, and Alexander J. Paepke, "MHC-Dependent Mate Preferences," *Biological Sciences* 260, no. 1359 (June 22, 1995): 245–49; Giovanni Frazzetto, "The Science of Online Dating: Can the Application of Science to Unravel the Biological Basis of Love Complement the Traditional, Romantic Ideal of Finding a Soul Mate?," *EMBO Reports* 11, no. 1 (2009): 25–27.

136   **more intentional design:** Monika Brown, "A Blueprint for a Better Stock Exchange," *Chicago Booth Review*, November 21, 2023.

136   **"For markets to work freely":** Paul Donovan, "Alvin E. Roth, Nobel 2012, Kidney Exchange Market Design: Can Economics Save Lives?," UBS Nobel Perspectives; Roth, "Art of Designing Markets."

11. The Opportunity Atlas

This chapter draws multiple facts and details from the following sources: Karen Duffin, Bryant Urstadt, Jessica Weisberg, and Aviva DeKornfeld, "Moving to Opportunity?," *Planet Money*, NPR, August 30, 2019; Sean Saldana, Amanda Aronczyk, and Alex Goldmark, "Moving to the American Dream? (update)," *Planet Money*, NPR, November 6, 2024; Lydia Grayson-Cross, interview with Alex Mayyasi, October 2024; Xavier de Souza Briggs, interview with Alex Mayyasi, September 2024; Xavier de Souza Briggs, Susan J. Popkin, and John Goering, *Moving to Opportunity: The Story of an American Experiment to Fight Ghetto Poverty* (Oxford University Press, 2010); Greg Rosalsky, "Why the American Dream Is More Attainable in Some Cities Than Others," *Planet Money* newsletter, August 1, 2022; Jon E. Hilsenrath and Rafael Gerena-Morales, "How Much Does a Neighborhood Affect the Poor?," *Wall Street Journal*, December 28, 2006.

140   **one of 4,608 families:** Larry Orr et al., "Moving to Opportunity for Fair Housing Demonstration Program: Interim Impacts Evaluation," U.S. Department of Housing and Urban Development (HUD), September 2003.

142   **didn't kill jobs:** David Card and Alan B. Krueger, "Minimum Wages and Employment: A Case Study of the Fast Food Industry in New Jersey and Pennsylvania," NBER Working Paper 4509, October 1993.

142   **eventually earned Nobel honors:** Card, Joshua D. Angrist, and Guido W. Imbens won in 2021. Esther Duflo, Abhijit Banerjee, and Michael Kremer won in 2019 for experiments and randomized controlled trials designed to find answers to global poverty.

142   **free distribution worked way better:** "Free Bednets to Fight Malaria," J-PAL (Abdul Latif Jameel Poverty Action Lab), July 2022.

143   **saw their children graduate:** James E. Rosenbaum and Julie E. Kaufman, "The Education and Employment of Low-Income Black Youth in White Suburbs," *Educational Evaluation and Policy Analysis* 14, no. 3 (1992): 229–40.

143   **based on fake data:** Nick Fountain, Jeff Guo, Keith Romer, Emma Peaslee, and Willa

Rubin, "Fabricated Data in Research About Honesty. You Can't Make This Stuff Up. Or, Can You?," *Planet Money*, NPR, July 28, 2023.

144 **mental and physical health improved:** Orr et al., "Moving to Opportunity," ix, x.

145 **stayed in public housing:** Hilsenrath and Gerena-Morales, "How Much Does a Neighborhood Affect the Poor?"; Lisa Sanbonmatsu et al., "Moving to Opportunity for Fair Housing Demonstration Program Final Impacts Evaluation," U.S. Department of Housing and Urban Development, November 2011.

146 **Families with upward economic mobility:** Raj Chetty et al., "The Fading American Dream: Trends in Absolute Income Mobility Since 1940," NBER Working Paper 22910; Raj Chetty, interview with Douglas Clement for the Federal Reserve Bank of Minneapolis, December 10, 2014.

146 **increased their lifetime income:** Raj Chetty, Nathaniel Hendren, and Lawrence F. Katz, "The Effects of Exposure to Better Neighborhoods on Children: New Evidence from the Moving to Opportunity Experiment," Harvard University and NBER, August 2015.

146 **older sons have both struggled:** Jon Hilsenrath and Kate King, "New York Starts Mapping Out the Road Back from Coronavirus—and It's Long," *Wall Street Journal*, May 27, 2020.

147 **communities in rural Iowa and North Dakota:** "Raj Chetty on Economic Mobility," *EconTalk* podcast, August 22, 2022.

147 **high-mobility neighborhoods:** Peter Bergman et al., "Creating Moves to Opportunity: Experimental Evidence on Barriers to Neighborhood Choice," NBER Working Paper 26164, August 2019, rev. January 2023.

147 **Yesler Terrace:** Levi Pulkkinen, "As America's First Racially Integrated Housing Project Is Rebuilt, Ripples of Displacement Follow," *Next City*, January 14, 2019.

148 **their biggest finding:** Raj Chetty et al., "Social Capital I: Measurement and Associations with Economic Mobility," *Nature* 608 (2022a): 108–21; Chetty et al., "Social Capital II: Determinants of Economic Connectedness," *Nature* 608 (2022b), 122–34.

148 **alive and well:** Chetty et al., "Social Capital I."

148 **class-stratified workplaces:** Roberts, "Raj Chetty on Economic Mobility."

149 **desegregated due to court orders:** Linda Gorman, "Long-Term Effects of School Desegregation and School Quality," NBER's *The Digest*, May 1, 2011, summary of Rucker C. Johnson, "Long-Run Impacts of School Desegregation and School Quality on Adult Attainments," NBER Working Paper 16664, January 2011, rev. September 2015.

149 **expanded their social networks:** Stefanie DeLuca, Susan Clampet-Lundquist, and Kathryn Edin, *Coming of Age in the Other America* (Russell Sage Foundation, 2016).

150 **next door to a doctor or lawyer:** Michael J. Andrews, Ryan R. Hill, Joseph Price, and Riley Wilson, "Like a Good Neighbor: The Role of Neighbors in Career Choice," provisional, shared with Alex Mayyasi; an earlier version is posted in Economics of Mobility, Fall 2024, NBER, September 27, 2024.

12. The Rent Is Too Damn High

This chapter draws multiple facts and details from the following sources: Sxwíxwtn Wilson Williams, interview with Alex Mayyasi, December 2024; Paítsmuḵ (David Jacobs) and Chief Gibby Jacob, interview with Alex Mayyasi, December 2024; Douglas C. Harris, "Property and Sovereignty: An Indian Reserve and a Canadian City," *University of British Columbia Law Review* 50, no. 2 (2017); Daryl Fairweather, interview with Alex Mayyasi, December 2024.

154 **"the place inside the head":** Another translation is "'inside the head of the bay,' at False Creek" (Squamish Nation, *Tina'7 Cht Ti Temíxw—We Come from This Land: A Walk Through the History of the Squamish People* (Page Two/Macmillan, 2024), 20.

154 **original Sen̓áḵw village:** Angela Sterritt, "The Little-Known History of Squamish Nation Land in Vancouver," CBC News, April 21, 2019.

154 **height and density of new buildings:** See, for instance, see John Infranca, "Single-Family Zoning and the Police Power: Early Debates in Boston and Seattle," *Cityscape: A Journal of Policy Development and Research* 25, no. 3 (2023): 11–42, and "Mapping the Zoning of First Nations in Metro Vancouver," Balanced Supply of Housing, March 7, 2025.

154 **third most expensive:** Wendell Cox, "Demographia International Housing Affordability Report Highlights Global Housing Affordability Crisis," *Chapman News*, June 14, 2024.

154 **Trudeau attended Sen̓áḵw's groundbreaking:** Darryl Greer, "B.C. Court Rejects Challenge to Huge Squamish Nation Housing Project in Vancouver," *Canadian Press*, October 3, 2023.

154 **"We need to work together":** "Canada Provides $1.4 Billion for 3,000 Rental Homes in Deal with Vancouver-Area First Nation," Canadian Press/CBC, September 6, 2022.

155 **Paítsmuḵ, a Squamish Nation Elder:** Correspondence with Squamish Nation public relations representative, March 2025. Paítsmuḵ wrote the foreword to Squamish Nation, *Tina'7 Cht Ti Temíxw*, viii–xi.

155 **"cultural genocide" and "evil":** Nadine Yousif, "Pope Francis: Pontiff Says He Is 'Deeply Sorry' to Canadian Residential School Survivors," BBC, July 25, 2022.

155 **who had watched Sen̓áḵw burn:** "Jack, August," Squamish History Archives, https://squamishlibrary.digitalcollections.ca/chief-august-jack.

155 **bounties of duck:** "History of the Sen̓áḵw Lands," http://senakw.com/history.

155 **transcontinental railroad arrived:** "1886—The First Transcontinental Train Arrives in Vancouver," Legislative Assembly of British Columbia.

156 **"honor of the Crown":** Alexandra Flynn, interview with Alex Mayyasi, December 2024.

157 **a series of legal claims:** Canada (Attorney General) v. Canadian Pacific Ltd., [2000] B.C.T.C. 397 (SC).

158 **locals derailed:** Kim Mai-Cutler, "How Burrowing Owls Lead to Vomiting Anarchists (or SF's Housing Crisis Explained)," *TechCrunch*, April 14, 2014.

158 **rent seeking:** See Smith, *The Wealth of Nations*, ed. Manis, book I, chap. 11.

158 **Beginning in the 1960s:** Gordon Tullock, "The Welfare Costs of Tariffs, Monopolies, and Theft," *Western Economic Journal* 5, no. 3 (1967): 224–32; Anne O. Krueger, "The Political Economy of the Rent-Seeking Society," *American Economic Review* 64, no. 3 (1974): 291–303.

160 **"recognize[d] and affirm[ed]":** Government of Canada, "INAN—Section 35 of the Constitution Act 1982—Background," Canada.ca, January 28, 2021.

160 **"a good mug of beer":** "Squamish Settlement," CBC News, June 9, 2000; "Squamish Nation Trust," n.d., squamish.net/partnerships-entities/entities/squamish-nation-trust/.

161 **neighborhoods outlined in red:** Lawrence T. Brown, "Pair HOLC Maps with FHA Maps to Tell a More Complete Story," *Metropole* (blog), n.d.; Jonathan Rose, "Revisiting How Two Federal Housing Agencies Propagated Redlining in the 1930s," Federal Reserve Bank of Chicago, April 2022.

161 **"state-sponsored segregation":** Richard Rothstein, *The Color of Law: A Forgotten History of How Our Government Segregated America* (Liveright, 2017), 224.

161 **With few exceptions:** Terry Gross, "A 'Forgotten History' of How the U.S. Government Segregated America," *Fresh Air*, NPR, May 3, 2017.

161 **updating their maps:** Brown, "Pair HOLC Maps with FHA Maps."

162 **effectively excluded most minorities:** Rothstein, *The Color of Law*, 78–79; Federal Reserve, "Redlining," June 2, 2023.

162 **standard application of law:** Linda J. Bilmes and Cornell William Brooks, "Normalizing Reparations: U.S. Precedent, Norms, and Models for Compensating Harms and Implications for Reparations to Black Americans," *Russell Sage Foundation Journal of the Social Sciences* 10, no. 2 (June 2024): 30–68.

162 **Indigenous saying:** Oren Lyons, *Exiled in the Land of the Free: Democracy, Indian Nations, and the U.S. Constitution* (Clear Light Publishers, 1992), 32–33.

162 **$1.4 billion low-interest loan:** Dan Fumano, "Feds Announce $1.4 Billion Loan for Squamish Nation's Senákw Project," *Vancouver Sun*, September 6, 2022.

163 **judge rejected their challenge:** Darryl Greer, "B.C. Supreme Court Rejects Challenge to Huge Squamish Nation Housing Project Near Downtown Vancouver," CBC, October 3, 2023; Michelle Cyca, "Vancouver's New Mega-Development Is Big, Ambitious and Undeniably Indigenous," *Maclean's*, March 11, 2024.

163 **15 percent Squamish representation:** "Nch'ḵay Quarterly Update to the Squamish People," nchkay.com, Spring 2024.

163 **forecast as upward of $10 billion:** "Senákw Lands Presentation," November 2019, http://perma.cc/6VPP-CNCL; Irene Serrano, "Can Indigenous Urbanism Counter Vancouver's Pressing Lack of Housing?," *El País*, October 26, 2024.

163 **projected to more than double:** "2023 Housing Progress Update," City of Vancouver/Housing Vancouver, Vancouver.ca; "City of Vancouver - Housing Target Progress and Interim Housing Needs Reports," November 2024.

164 **housing in 12 American cities:** Evan Mast, "The Effect of New Market-Rate Housing Construction on the Low-Income Housing Market," *Journal of Urban Economics* 133 (January 2023).

164 **2.5 percent lower:** Stuart S. Rosenthal, "Are Private Markets and Filtering a Viable Source of Low-Income Housing? Estimates from a 'Repeat Income' Model," *American Economic Review* 104, no.2 (2014): 687–706.

165 **in the direction of balance:** Alex Mayyasi, email correspondence with a representative of the city of Vancouver, March 2025: "In 2009, the city began permitting secondary suites and laneway homes (also known as granny suites). By 2018, secondary suites and duplexes were allowed, and in 2023, multiplexes with up to 8 units were legalized."

13. The Global Conspiracy to Make Childcare More Expensive

This chapter draws multiple facts and details from the following sources: Sarah Gonzalez, Jeff Guo; Keith Romer, and Sam Yellowhorse Kesler, "Baby's First Market Failure," *Planet Money*, NPR, February 3, 2023; Jacob Goldstein, David Kestenbaum, Robert Smith, Cailin Kenney, and Damiano Marchetti, "The History of Light," *Planet Money*, NPR, November 30, 2016; Alex Mayyasi, email correspondence with Bill Nordhaus, January 2025.

170 **wick inside an oily seabird:** Alexander L. Bond, Jógvan Hammer, and Sjúrður Hammer, "Historic Evidence of the Use of Storm-Petrels *Hydrobates* sp. as Candles," *Seabird* 35 (February 2023).

171 **Economists adjust for inflation:** Tim Harford, "Why the Falling Cost of Light Matters," BBC, February 6, 2017.

171 **overestimating inflation-driven:** This was the hypothesis of the Boskin Commission Report ("Final Report to the Senate Finance Committee from the Advisory Commission to Study the Consumer Price Index"), December 4, 1996

172 **"I would just measure":** William D. Nordhaus, "Do Real-Output and Real-Wage Measures Capture Reality? The History of Lighting Suggests Not," in *The Economics of New Goods*, ed. Timothy F. Bresnahan and Robert J. Gordon (University of Chicago Press, 1996), 27–70.

173 **Abraham Gesner:** Daniel Yergin, *The Prize: The Epic Quest for Oil, Money & Power* (Free Press, 2009), 7.

174 **don't have to pay up front:** Jacob Goldstein, David Kestenbaum, and Nadia Wilson, "How Solar Got Cheap," *Planet Money*, NPR, April 10, 2015.

174 **Baumol's most famous theory:** William J. Baumol and William G. Bowen, *Performing Arts: The Economic Dilemma* (Twentieth Century Fund, 1966); W. J. Baumol and W. G. Bowen, "On the Performing Arts: The Anatomy of Their Economic Problems," *American Economic Review* 55, nos. 1/2 (1965): 500.

176 **1,000 American parents:** "The Tooth Fairy Is on a Budget," Delta Dental, February 25, 2025.

177 **$11,000 per child per year:** "Child Care at a Standstill: Price and Landscape Analysis," Child Care Aware, 2023.

177 **more than $300,000:** Morgan Welch and Isabel Sawhill, "Future Estimated Annual Expenditures of Raising a Child, Assuming a Higher Inflation Rate of 4 percent After 2020," Brookings Institution, August 2022.

177 **subsidizing services:** William J. Baumol et al., *The Cost Disease: Why Computers Get Cheaper and Health Care Doesn't* (Yale University Press, 2012).

178 **delay having children:** "Women in 30s Now Having More Babies Than Younger Moms in US," Associated Press and CNBC, May 17, 2017; Brady E. Hamilton, Joyce A. Martin, and Michelle J. K. Osterman, "Births: Provisional Data for 2023," National Vital Statistics System, Report No. 35, April 2024. Note that fertility rates were slightly higher for women in their twenties.

14. Bobby Bonilla Day

This chapter draws multiple facts and details from the following sources: Kenny Malone, James Sneed, Amanda Aronczyk, Brittany Cronin, and Alex Goldmark, "Bobby Bonilla Day," *Planet Money*, NPR, June 25, 2021.

184 **"July 1st is probably the worst":** Dashiell Bennett, "The Worst Contract in Sports History Begins Today," *Business Insider*, July 1, 2011.

185 **didn't want to pay:** Darren Rovell, "Bobby Bonilla Day Exclusive: Bonilla Interview on Mets Contract, Sports History's Most Famous Deal," Action Network, July 1, 2022, YouTube.

187 **is worth $185 million:** These numbers come from a simplified calculation of $6 million earning 10 percent returns every year, with the interest (the 10 percent return) being re-invested annually. Many loans pay interest every month, and the stock market goes up and down rather than growing at a consistent rate. Still, this demonstrates the power of compound interest!

189 **took every dollar:** David Waldstein, "Madoff Nearly Ruined the Mets. The Team Has Moved On," *New York Times*, April 14, 2021.

189 **Steven Cohen, a finance guy:** "I hope everybody is enjoying my favorite day of the year, Bobby Bonilla Day," @StevenACohen2, Twitter (X) post, July 1, 2022.

15. How We All Fell for a Confidence Trick

This chapter draws multiple facts and details from the following sources: Farley Grubb, interview with Alex Mayyasi, June 2024; Katie Moore, interview with Alex Mayyasi, June 2024; Don

Hayner, interview with Alex Mayyasi, June 2024; Farley Grubb, "Colonial Monetary Systems," in *Handbook of Cliometrics*, ed. Claude Diebolt and Michael Haupert (Springer Nature, 2024), 1719–48; Katie A. Moore, "America's First Economic Stimulus Package: Paper Money and the Body Politic in Colonial Pennsylvania, 1715–1730," *Pennsylvania History: A Journal of Mid-Atlantic Studies* 83, no. 4 (Autumn 2016): 536; Don Hayner, *Binga: The Rise and Fall of Chicago's First Black Banker* (Northwestern University Press, 2019); Joe Nocera, *A Piece of the Action: How the Middle Class Joined the Money Class* (Simon & Schuster, 2013); Matt Levine, "Money Stuff," *Bloomberg*.

192 **30,000 in 1717:** Peter B. Kotowski, "The Best Poor Man's Country? William Penn, Quakers, and Unfree Labor in Atlantic Pennsylvania" (PhD diss., Loyola University Chicago, August 2016), 171–72.

192 **"Wee are full of Goods":** Katie A. Moore, "America's First Economic Stimulus Package: Paper Money and the Body Politic in Colonial Pennsylvania, 1715–1730," *Pennsylvania History* 83, no. 4 (Autumn 2016): 536.

192 **had a liquidity problem:** Mica McCarthy, "What Was Happening in 1628 in the Caribbean Islands," 1628 Across the Continent, Thirteen PBS; Brenda Milkofsky, "Connecticut and the West Indies: Sugar Spurs Trans-Atlantic Trade," ConnecticutHistory.org, January 7, 2021; Johnson, "'What Must Poor People Do?'"

193 **"had lived well":** Richard A. Lester, "Currency Issues to Overcome Depressions in Pennsylvania, 1723 and 1729," *Journal of Political Economy* 46, no. 3 (June 1938): 330, 331.

193 **throughout the Mediterranean:** William N. Goetzmann, *Money Changes Everything: How Finance Made Civilization Possible* (Princeton University Press, 2016).

193 **When Marco Polo arrived in China:** John Lanchester, "The Invention of Money," *The New Yorker*, July 29, 2019.

193 **no society managed:** Jacob Goldstein, Mary Childs, Robert Smith, and Darian Woods, "The Murderer, the Boy King, and the Invention of Modern Finance," *Planet Money*, NPR, September 4, 2020; Liz Covart, "Why Colonial America Suffered from a Currency Shortage," LizCovart.com (blog), March 8, 2013.

194 **bills of credit:** Katie A. Moore, *Promise to Pay: The Politics and Power of Money in Early America* (University of Chicago Press, 2024).

195 **credited the transformation:** Farley Grubb, "Benjamin Franklin and the Birth of a Paper Money Economy," Federal Reserve Bank of Philadelphia, 4.

195 **throw bricks at the home:** Johnson, "'What Must Poor People Do?,'" 126; Theodore Thayer, "The Land-Bank System in the American Colonies," *Journal of Economic History* 13, no. 2 (Spring 1953): 145–59.

195 **experimenting with paper banknotes:** "John Law," *Britannica Money*, updated March 17, 2025; "Early Banknotes," Bank of England Museum, updated January 31, 2023.

195 **running on paper money:** Farley Grubb, "The Paper Money of Colonial America," in *The Elgar Companion to Modern Money Theory*, ed. Yeva Nersisyan and L. Randall Wray (Edward Elgar Publishing Company, 2024).

195 **colonists' beloved paper money:** For a summary of the Currency Act, see Mark Dziak, "Currency Act (Paper Bills of Credit Act)," EBSCO, 2023.

195 **the nation's own mints:** Stephanie Meredith, "The History of U.S. Circulating Coins," U.S. Mint, April 2019, updated March 25, 2025.

196 **more than 300 banks:** Warren E. Weber, "Early State Banks in the United States: How Many Were There and Where Did They Exist?," *Quarterly Review* 3012 (September 1, 2006), Federal Reserve Bank of Minneapolis (Weber notes that his methodology shows fewer banks than other estimates).

196	**Jesse Binga arrived:** Rachel Kranz, *African-American Business Leaders and Entrepreneurs* (Facts on File, 2004), 19–21.
196	**refused to rent:** Zachary Leiter, "Chicago's 250 Year History of Segregation," *Chicago Reporter*, August 30, 2023.
197	**a kind of "street banker":** "Jesse Binga: The Making of the First Black-Owned Bank on the South Side of Chicago," *Chicago Southsider*, February 17, 2023.
198	**"behind the prison bars":** Christopher W. Shaw, "The Man in the Street Is for It: The Road to the FDIC," *Journal of Policy History* 27, no. 1 (January 2015): 40.
198	**"confidence trick":** Nick Rowe, "Finance as Magic," *Worthwhile Canadian Initiative* (blog), January 13, 2010.
198	**star shortstop:** Shaw, "The Man in the Street," 39.
199	**Eudora Johnson:** Carl R. Osthaus, "The Rise and Fall of Jesse Binga, a Black Chicago Financial Wizard," *Journal of Negro History* 58, no. 1 (January 1973): 46–47.
199	**"Black Wall Streets":** Crystal Moten, "How Maggie Lena Walker Became the First Black Woman to Run a Bank in the Segregated South," *Smithsonian*, February 17, 2021; Dell Gines and Chad Wilkerson, "The Past, Present and Future of Black Wall Street," Federal Reserve Bank of Kansas City, May 6, 2021.
199	**reductions in poverty:** Meghana Ayyagari, Thorsten Beck, and Mohammad Hoseini, "Finance and Poverty: Evidence from India," Centre for Economic Research Discussion Paper No. DP9497, June 6, 2013.
200	**fewer mortgages:** Ozgur Emre Ergungor, "Bank Branch Presence and Access to Credit in Low- to Moderate-Income Neighborhoods," *Journal of Money, Credit and Banking* 42, no. 7 (October 2010): 1321–49.
201	**interest rate on savings accounts:** FDIC, "History, 1930–1939, FDIC.gov, June 27, 2023; "Requiem for Regulation Q: What It Did and Why It Passed Away," Federal Reserve Bank of St. Louis, February 1986.
201	**crested over 10 percent:** Alan S. Blinder, "The Anatomy of Double-Digit Inflation in the 1970s," in *Inflation: Causes and Effects*, ed. Robert E. Hall (University of Chicago Press, 1982), 264–65.
201	**shadow bank emerged:** Stephen Miller, "Co-Inventor of Money-Market Account Helped Serve Small Investors' Interest," *Wall Street Journal*, August 16, 2008.
202	**even after charging a fee:** Naz Koont, interview with Alex Mayyasi, June 2024.
202	**trillions of dollars:** Linus Wilson, "Broken Bucks: Money Funds That Took Taxpayer Guarantees in 2008," *Journal of Asset Management* 21, no. 5 (August 2020): 375, 377.
202	**higher yield:** "Reserve Primary Fund Distributes Assets to Investors," SEC press release, January 29, 2010.
203	**$785 million:** "Reserve Primary Fund Distributes Assets to Investors"; Tami Luhby, "SEC Charges Money Market Fund with Fraud," CNN, May 5, 2009; David Callaway, "Lehman and the Day the Buck Broke," *USA Today*, September 11, 2013, updated September 12, 2013.
203	**guaranteed money in MMFs:** "Treasury Announces Temporary Guarantee Program for Money Market Funds," U.S. Department of the Treasury, press release, September 29, 2008.
203	**bought troubled loans:** "Commercial Paper Funding Facility," Federal Reserve Bank of New York, July 8, 2021.
203	**allowed the firms that ran MMFs:** "Asset-Backed Commercial Paper Money Market Mutual Fund Liquidity Facility," Board of Governors of the Federal Reserve System, updated March 18, 2020; Financial Crisis Inquiry Commission, *The Financial Crisis*

Inquiry Report: Final Report of the National Commission on the Causes of the Financial and Economic Crisis in the United States, January 2011.

203 **return more than 98 percent:** "Reserve Primary Fund Distributes Assets to Investors."

203 **flowing to shadow banks:** Amit Seru, "Regulation of the Mortgage Market Must Consider Shadow Banks," Stanford Institute for Economic Policy Research (SIEPR), December 2018.

16. Weighing a Cow and Picking Stocks

This chapter draws multiple facts and details from the following sources: David Kestenbaum, Jacob Goldstein, and Nadia Wilson, "How Much Does This Cow Weigh?," *Planet Money*, NPR, August 7, 2015; Anthony Mitchell, interview with Alex Mayyasi, June 2024.

208 **he wanted in:** Daniel B. Klein, "Ken Kam and Market Efficiency," *Econ Journal Watch* 1, no. 1 (April 2004): 185–91.

208 **invest just as well as:** Matthew Schifrin, *The Warren Buffetts Next Door: The World's Greatest Investors You've Never Heard Of and What You Can Learn from Them* (John Wiley & Sons, 2010), 167.

208 **"impressed" by their burritos:** Peter Lynch with John Rothchild, *One Up on Wall Street: How to Use What You Already Know to Make Money in the Market,* 2nd ed. (Simon & Schuster, 2000), 36.

210 **conducted by Francis Galton:** Steven A. Farber, "U.S. Scientists' Role in the Eugenics Movement (1907–1939): A Contemporary Biologist's Perspective," *Zebrafish* 5, no. 4 (2008): 243–45.

210 **average of all the guesses:** James Surowiecki, *The Wisdom of Crowds* (Anchor Books, 2005), xii.

210 **off by 83 pounds:** Quoctrung Bui, "17,205 People Guessed the Weight of a Cow. Here's How They Did," *Planet Money*, NPR, August 7, 2015.

211 **measly five dollars:** Stacey Vanek Smith, Cardiff Garcia, Paddy Hirsch, Leena Sanzgiri, and Darius Rafieyan, "We Buy a Junk Bond," *The Indicator from Planet Money*, September 9, 2020.

212 **Internal Revenue Code:** "Sec. 165 Losses," *Tax Notes,* n.d., https://www.taxnotes.com/research/federal/usc26/165.

215 **a beauty contest:** John Maynard Keynes, *The General Theory of Employment, Interest and Money* (Harcourt, Brace and Company, 1936), 156.

215 **"meme stock" GameStop:** Ortenca Aliaj, Michael Mackenzie, and Laurence Fletcher, "Melvin Capital, GameStop and the Road to Disaster," *Financial Times*, February 6, 2021; Jamie Powell, "GameStop Can't Stop Going UP," *Financial Times*, January 25, 2021; Stephen Gandel, "GameStop Shares Fall More Than 40% as Prominent Booster Draws Inquiry," CBS News, February 5, 2021.

216 **working on an MBA:** Maggie McGrath, "Scoring a 28% Annual Return with Peter Lynch–Style Stockpicking," *Forbes*, December 10, 2014.

217 **ending the contest:** Matt Schifrin, "Senior Contributor Ken Kam: Wisdom in the Crowd," *Forbes*, October 11, 2019.

217 **"talent discovery approach":** Kara Swisher, "Presto Chango: KaChing Becomes Wealthfront," *AllThingsD*, October 19, 2010.

217 **only seven out of their 450,000 gamers:** Sarah Milstein and Andy Rachleff, "Case Study: kaChing, Anatomy of a Pivot," Eric Ries's *Startup Lessons Learned* (blog), July 28, 2010.

17. The Biggest Bet of Your Life

This chapter draws multiple facts and details from the following source: Jacob Goldstein, David Kestenbaum, and Nick Fountain, "Brilliant vs. Boring," *Planet Money*, NPR, March 4, 2016.

220   **underperform the market:** Paul A. Samuelson, "Challenge to Judgment," *Journal of Portfolio Management* 1, no. 1 (Fall 1974): 17–19.
220   **annual return of 10 percent:** J. B. Maverick, "S&P 500 Average Returns and Historical Performance," Investopedia, updated December 26, 2024.
221   **Why not me?:** Matthew Boyle, "'Be Prepared for a Lot of Bumps,'" *Fortune*, December 17, 2007.
221   **"Who wants to be operated on":** Eric Balchunas, *The Bogle Effect: How John Bogle and Vanguard Turned Wall Street Inside Out and Saved Investors Trillions* (Matt Holt Books, 2022), 153–54.
221   **famous finance book:** Fred Schwed Jr., *Where Are the Customers' Yachts?: or A Good Hard Look at Wall Street* (Simon & Schuster, 1940).
221   **priest outfit to match his evangelizing:** Robin Wigglesworth, *Trillions: How a Band of Wall Street Renegades Invented the Index Fund and Changed Finance Forever* (Portfolio, 2021), 127.
222   **"the only free lunch":** As often as the quote is attributed to him, there is no evidence for his having said or written this. He did write about diversification, however, in Harry Markowitz, "Portfolio Selection," *Journal of Finance* 7, no. 1 (March 1952): 77–91.
222   **"winning strategy for investing in stocks":** John C. Bogle, *The Little Book of Common Sense Investing: The Only Way to Guarantee Your Fair Share of Stock Market Returns* (John Wiley & Sons, 2007), xv.
222   **more than 50 million customers:** "Vanguard in a Nutshell," 2025.
222   **more in index funds:** Allan Sloan, "The Democratization of Investing': Index Funds Officially Overtake Active Managers," Yahoo! Finance, May 22, 2022.
222   **10,000 investor accounts:** Terrance Odean, "Do Investors Trade Too Much?," *American Economic Review* 89, no. 5 (December 1999): 1279–98.
223   **investment gains of $57.6 billion:** "David Swensen's Coda," *YaleNews*, October 22, 2021.
223   **diversified into real estate:** Chis Arnold, "David Swensen, the Greatest Investor You Maybe Never Heard of, Leaves Powerful Legacy," NPR, May 8, 2021; Geraldine Fabrikant, "David Swensen, Who Revolutionized Endowment Investing, Dies at 67," *New York Times*, May 6, 2021.
224   **every penny in index funds:** Timoty W. Martin, "What Does Nevada's $35 Billion Fund Manager Do All Day? Nothing," *Wall Street Journal*, October 19, 2016.
224   **"illusion of skill":** Daniel Kahneman, "The Illusion of Stock-Picking Skill," *Wealthfront* (blog), March 19, 2015; Daniel Kahneman, *Thinking, Fast and Slow* (Farrar, Straus and Giroux, 2011), 206–20.
224   **charity in Omaha:** "My Bet with Warren Buffett"—Ted Seides CEO Capital Allocators," interview with Simon Brewer, *Money Maze* (podcast), May 13, 2021.
224   **if you'd invested $10,000:** Jennifer Saibil, "You Won't Believe How Much More Warren Buffett Has Made Than the Market Since 1965," *Motley Fool*, March 14, 2023.
225   **wooing talented traders:** Alex Morrell, "The Rise of the Hedge-Fund Talent Whisperers," *Business Insider*, May 3, 2024; Matt Levine, "Here, Have Some Extra Carbon Credits," Bloomberg, May 6, 2024.

18. Why Is My Money Worth Less Every Year?

This chapter draws multiple facts and details from the following sources: Chana Joffe-Walt and Jacob Goldstein, "How Four Drinking Buddies Saved Brazil," *Planet Money*, NPR, October 1, 2010; David Kestenbaum, Jacob Goldstein, and Nick Fountain, "The Great Inflation," *Planet Money*, NPR, November 20, 2015, updated July 17, 2021; Jeff Guo, Nick Fountain, Keith Romer, and Dave Blanchard, "The Quest to Save Macroeconomics from Itself," *Planet Money*, NPR, July 7, 2023; André Lara, interview with Alex Mayyasi, August 2024; Emi Nakamura, interview with Alex Mayyasi, July 2024.

232 **"all the staff came out":** Willa Rubin, Nick Fountain, Molly K. Messick, and Sam Yellowhorse Kesler, "How the Phillips Curve Shaped Macroeconomics," *Planet Money*, NPR, September 8, 2023.

233 **prevent, or at least moderate:** Robert Smith and Adam Davidson, "Keynes vs. Hayek," *Planet Money*, NPR, October 28, 2011. For an overview of Keynes's thoughts on government intervention, see Sarwat Jahan, Ahmed Saber Mahmud, and Chris Papageorgiou, "What Is Keynesian Economics?," *Finance & Development* 51, no. 3 (September 2014).

236 **didn't believe the Phillips Curve:** Bill Dupor, "The Volcker Tightening Cycle: Explaining the 1982 Course Reversal," Federal Reserve Bank of St. Louis, January 16, 2025; David E. Lindsey, Athanasios Orphanides, and Robert H. Rasche, "The Reform of October 1979: How It Happened and Why," Board of Governors of the Federal Reserve System, January 2005.

236 **care what the actual rate is:** Marvin Goodfriend and Robert G. King, "The Incredible Volcker Disinflation," *Journal of Monetary Economics* 52 (2005): 1007.

236 **Volcker increased rates radically:** Federal Reserve Bank of St. Louis, Federal Funds Effective Rate, https://fred.stlouisfed.org/series/FEDFUNDS.

236 **tried to abduct members of the Fed:** "Suspect Is Seized in Capital in Threat at Federal Reserve," United Press International/*New York Times*, December 8, 1981; "Museum Shooter's Fed Fixation," *Forbes*, June 10, 2009.

237 **would exceed 2,000 percent:** Julia P. Araujo and Mauro Rodrigues Jr., "Price Setting in Brazil from 1989 to 2007: Evidence on Hyperinflation and Stable Prices," Banco Central do Brasil, October 2018.

238 **inflation targeting:** Sarah Gonzalez, Karen Duffin, Alexi Horowitz-Ghazi, and Bryant Urstadt, "The Secret Target," *Planet Money*, NPR, November 30, 2018; Matthew Wells, "The Origins of the 2 Percent Inflation Target," Federal Reserve Bank of Richmond, First/Second Quarter 2024.

239 **Monthly inflation fell:** Jérôme Sgard, "Hyperinflation and the Reconstruction of a National Money: Argentina and Brazil, 1990–2002," Centre d'Études Prospectives et d'Informations Internationales (CEPII) Working Paper No 2003-01, 20.

239 **worth more than a dollar:** "Brazil Exchange Rate Against USD, 1986–2023," CEIC Data.

240 **Academy of Letters:** "A Brazilian Inflation Fighter Becomes Immortal," *Economist*, April 12, 2017.

241 **items that Americans buy:** Stacey Vanek Smith, Darian Woods, Kate Concannon, and Julia Ritchey, "How Do You Measure Inflation?," *The Indicator from Planet Money*, NPR, July 13, 2021; Caitlin Kenney and Adam Davidson, "The Price of Lettuce in Brooklyn," *Planet Money*, NPR, January 7, 2015.

241 **America's missing disinflation:** Jonathon Hazell, Juan Herreño, Emi Nakamura, and Jón Steinsson, "The Slope of the Phillips Curve: Evidence from U.S. States," NBER Working Paper 28005. The authors cite, among other sources, Peter Hooper, Frederic S. Mishkin,

and Amit Sufi, "Prospects for Inflation in a High Pressure Economy: Is the Phillips Curve Dead or is It Just Hibernating?" NBER Working Paper No. 25792, 2019.
242   **various fixes to the curve:** See, for example, Mathias Trabandt and Jesper Lindé, "Resolving the Missing Deflation and Inflation Puzzles," VoxEU, Centre for Economic Policy Research, November 12, 2019.
242   **"Americans' memory of inflation":** Pedro Pou, "Argentina's Structural Reforms of the 1990s," *Finance & Development* 37, no. 1 (March 2000); World Bank Group, "Inflation, GDP Deflator (Annual %)—Argentina," World Bank National Accounts Data and OECD National Accounts data files, World Bank Open Data.

19. Why Weekends Are Like Subways and Uber

248   **bourgeois and inefficient:** Judith Shulevitz, "Why You Never See Your Friends Anymore," *Atlantic*, November 2019; Tony Wood, "Labor Days: Reinventing the Workweek in the Soviet Union," *Cabinet Magazine*, Spring–Summer 2016; Solomon M. Schwarz, "The Continuous Working Week in Soviet Russia," *International Labour Review* 23 (1931): 157–80.
248   **"What are we to do at home":** Schwarz, "The Continuous Working Week in Soviet Russia," 175.
249   **famous axiom of innovation:** "Quote Origin: If You Build a Better Mousetrap the World Will Beat a Path to Your Door," Quote Investigator, March 24, 2015.
249   **long bundle of wire:** "Senate Stories," "'What Hath God Wrought': Morse's Telegraph in the Capitol," Senate Historical Office, U.S. Senate, May 7, 2024; Tom Standage, *The Victorian Internet: The Remarkable Story of the Telegraph and the Nineteenth-Century's On-Line Pioneers* (Walker & Company, 1998), 42.
249   **even across oceans:** "Flying Cloud," Vessel History: "Her 1854 passage from New York to San Francisco was a record-holding 89 days and 8 hours," Navesink Maritime Heritage Association, n.d.; Standage, *The Victorian Internet*, 38–40.
249   **"den[ied] myself all pleasures":** J[ohn] Munro, *Heroes of the Telegraph* (London: The Religious Tract Society, 1891), 63.
250   **from "starving artist":** David Levine, "Looking Back at Samuel Morse and the Telegraph in the Hudson Valley," *Hudson Valley Magazine*, April 18, 2022.
251   **networks and platforms degrading:** Cory Doctorow, "TikTok's Enshittification," *Pluralistic*, January 21, 2023.
252   **thanks to network effects:** James Currier, "70 Percent of Value in Tech is Driven by Network Effects," NFX, July 2019 ; Geoffrey G. Parker, Marshall W. Van Alstyne, and Sangeet Paul Choudary, *Platform Revolution: How Networked Markets Are Transforming the Economy and How to Make Them Work for You* (W. W. Norton, 2016).
253   **nurse a hangover:** "How We Divide Time," Royal Museums Greenwich, London; Witold Rybczynski, "Waiting for the Weekend," *Atlantic*, August 1991, and see his book of the same name (Viking, 1991); "Who Invented the Weekend?," BBC Bitesize, July 2019; David Montgomery, *The Fall of the House of Labor: The Workplace, the State, and American Labor Activism, 1865–1925* (Cambridge University Press, 1987).
253   **In 1938, the United States':** Fair Labor Standards Act (29 U.S.C. 201), 1938; Jonathan Grossman, "Fair Labor Standards Act of 1938: Maximum Struggle for a Minimum Wage," U.S. Department of Labor, n.d.
253   **cathedral in time:** Abraham Joshua Heschel, *The Sabbath: Its Meaning for Modern Man* (Farrar, Straus and Giroux, 1951).
253   **popularity of leisure activities:** Rybczynski, *Waiting for the Weekend*.

254   **a handful dominate:** Alex Mayyasi, "The Man Who's Saving America's Forgotten Grapes," *Smithsonian*, December 2023.
254   **"marquee strategy":** Parker et al., *Platform Revolution*.
255   **"essential characteristic of the weekend":** Cristobal Young and Chaeyoon Lim, "Time as a Network Good: Evidence from Unemployment and the Standard Workweek," *Sociological Science* 1 (February 2014): 11.
255   **leisure time over the last century:** Valerie A. Ramey and Neville Francis, " A Century of Work and Leisure," *American Economic Journal: Macroeconomics* 1, no. 2 (2009): 189–224.
255   **some 3,500 expected:** John Noble Wilford, "World's Languages Dying Off Rapidly," *New York Times*, September 18, 2007.

20. What's the Deal with Credit Card Points?

This chapter draws multiple facts and details from the following source: Aaron Klein, interview with Alex Mayyasi, March 2024.

262   **"a little bit violated":** Scott McCartney, "Miles for Nothing: How the Government Helped Frequent Fliers Make a Mint," *Wall Street Journal*, December 7, 2009; David Kestenbaum and Robert Smith, "Dollar Coins in the Wild," *Planet Money*, NPR, July 22, 2011; Robert Benincasa and David Kestenbaum, "$1 Billion That Nobody Wants," *Morning Edition*, NPR, June 28, 2011.
264   **52 million Americans:** Kaz Nejatian, *A Payment History of the United States* (Magna Carta, 2017), 849, Kindle; Lewis Mandell, *The Credit Card Industry: A History* (Twayne Publishers, 1990), xiv; "The Story Behind the Card," Diners Club International, n.d., https://www.dinersclubus.com/home/about/dinersclub/story.
264   **one family's dachshund:** Matty Simmons, *The Credit Card Catastrophe: The 20th Century Phenomenon That Changed the World* (Barricade Books, 1995), 118.
264   **22 percent of bills went unpaid:** Nocera, *A Piece of the Action*; Alex Mayyasi, "How Credit Cards Tax America," Priceonomics, January 8, 2016.
264   **competing organizations:** M. Mitchell Waldrop, "The Trillion-Dollar Vision of Dee Hock," *Fast Company*, October 31, 1996.
265   **not pulling out cash:** Sachin Banker, Derek Dunfield, Alex Huang, and Drazen Prelec, "Neural Mechanisms of Credit Card Spending," *Scientific Reports* 11, no. 1 (February 2021): 4070.
265   **25 percent boost:** Lulu Wang, "Regulating Competing Payment Networks," Kellogg School of Management, March 21, 2025; Alex Mayyasi, email correspondence with Lulu Wang, June 2025.
265   **cards in circulation:** Jack Caporal, "Credit and Debit Card Market Share by Network and Issuer," Motley Fool, February 14, 2025.
265   **Starting in 1981:** Jamie Lauren Keiles, "The Man Who Turned Credit Card Points into an Empire," *New York Times*, January 5, 2021, updated June 15, 2023.
265   **"Every piece of market research":** Adam Davidson and John Hodgman, "Frequent Flyer Miles," *Surprisingly Awesome* (podcast), March 8, 2016.
266   **The biggest U.S. airlines:** Aaron Rennie, "The Big Airlines Lost Money Flying Passengers Last Year. So How Did They All Turn Profits?," Investopedia, January 30, 2025; Ganesh Sitaraman, *Why Flying Is Miserable: And How to Fix It* (Columbia Global Reports/Columbia University Press, 2023).
266   **Starbucks app:** Steve Goldstein, "The Bank of Starbucks: Coffee Retailer Has $1.77 Billion in Unredeemed Gift Cards," MarketWatch, July 31, 2024, updated August 1, 2024;

Wailin Wong, Darian Woods, Kate Concannon, and Brittany Cronin: "Is This a Bank?," *The Indicator from Planet Money*, NPR, August 10, 2023.

266 **unspent gift card :** Starbucks: Banking & Serving Coffee," Fintech Talents, July 19, 2022; Neil Patel, "How Starbucks Quietly Benefits from Its Most Passionate Customers," Motley Fool, June 17, 2020.

266 **hidden profit center:** Mitchell Hartman, "How Do Rental Car Companies Make Money?," *Marketplace*, February 10, 2014.

266 **but intellectual property:** Natalie Kitroeff, "Can Barbie Be Rebranded as a Feminist Icon?," *The Daily* (podcast), *New York Times*, July 21, 2023, updated August 2, 2023.

266 **are in production:** Ayomikun Adekaiyero, "Mattel Is Planning 19 Movies Based on Its Famous Toys and Brands After the Success of 'Barbie'—Here They All Are," *Business Insider*, February 26, 2025.

267 **"dawn of Discover":** "Dawn of Discover," *Ad Age*, 2016; TPG Staff, Danyal Ahmed, and Katie Genter, "The Complete History of Credit Cards, from Antiquity to Today," The Points Guy, December 5, 2024.

267 **It was a hit: By 1992:** Saul Hansell, "The Man Who Charged Up Mastercard," *New York Times*, March 7, 1993.

267 **1 percent cash back:** Simmons, *The Credit Card Catastrophe*, 177.

267 **like an iPhone launch:** Sam Grobart, "How Chase Made the Perfect High for Credit Card Junkies," *Bloomberg Businessweek*, September 22, 2016.

267 **almost 1 percent of U.S. GDP:** Sean Cudahy, "How Much Do We Charge to Our Delta Air-American Express Cards?" *Fast Company*, August 9, 2023.

267 **rescued Delta from bankruptcy:** John Helyar, "AmEx to Delta: We'll Bail You Out!," CNN, November 15, 2004.

269 **"There ain't no such thing":** "Quote Origin: There Ain't No Such Thing as a Free Lunch—TANSTAAFL," Quote Investigator, August 27, 2016.

269 **"worldwide hamster tube":** Keiles, "The Man Who Turned Credit-Card Points."

270 **fares to swipe fees:** Aaron Klein, interview with Alex Mayyasi, March 2024; Aaron Klein, "How Better Payment Systems Can Improve Public Transportation," Brookings Institution, Center on Regulation and Markets, January 2023.

270 **more profit from a café:** Aaron Harris, *Startup School Radio*, "Alexis Ohanian and Kaz Nejatian," July 2015; John Biggs, "Kash Now Offers Faster and Cheaper Alternative to Old Payment Networks," *TechCrunch*, September 2, 2015.

270 **cause $15 billion to flow:** Sumit Agarwal, Andrea Presbitero, André F. Silva, and Carlo Wix, "Who Pays for Your Rewards? Redistribution in the Credit Card Market," Finance and Economics Discussion Series, January 2023.

271 **many European countries cap:** Klein interview, March 2024.

271 **entered into a settlement agreement:** Imani Moise, "Using Your Credit Card at the Checkout Is Set to Get a Lot More Complicated," *Wall Street Journal*, November 11, 2025.

21. Advanced Fairness at the Marathon

This chapter draws multiple facts and details from the following sources: Kenny Malone, Bryant Urstadt, and Darian Woods, "Advanced Fairness at the Marathon," *Planet Money*, NPR, January 3, 2020; Robert Smith, Caitlin Kenney, Alex Blumberg, and Jess Jiang, "Kid Rock vs. the Scalpers," *Planet Money*, NPR, April 20, 2016.

276 **more than 190,000:** Maria Aldrich, "Thousands Apply for Iconic New York City Marathon—Few Selected," *Sports Illustrated*, March 6, 2025; Theo Kahler, "Only 4% of

Those Who Applied for the New York City Marathon Were Accepted," *Runner's World*, March 28, 2024.

278 **"That idea that market equilibrium":** Kevin Cool "Is Money Really the Best Measure of Value?," *If/Then: Business, Leadership, Society* (podcast), April 3, 2024; Dylan Walsh, "Mohammad Akbarpour," Faculty Voices, Stanford Graduate School of Business, February 8, 2019.

279 **reduces the incentive to build:** Rebecca Diamond, "What Does Economic Evidence Tell Us About the Effects of Rent Control?," Brookings Institution, October 18, 2018; "Rent Control Literature Review," D.C. Policy Center, April 1, 2020; Roger Valdez, "How Rent Control Makes Housing Less Affordable," Foundation for Research on Equal Opportunity (FREEOP), May 22, 2020.

279 **200,000 runners entered:** Claire Murashima and Majd Al-Waheidi, "Running in the New York City Marathon? It's Hard to Get into but Here's How Some Do It," NPR, March 6, 2025.

280 **could have won entry:** New York City Marathon, "Marathon Time Qualifiers," https://www.nyrr.org/tcsnycmarathon/runners/marathon-time-qualifiers.

280 **spend $10,000 a year:** "What Benefits Will I Receive by Becoming a Member?," NYRR Membership, NYRR.com, 2025.

280 **qualify by raising money:** See New York City Marathon, "Entry Methods." and "Run with a Charity."

280 **"doesn't even run":** Dawn Papacena, interview with Kenny Malone.

282 **explained how he decides:** PJ Vogt, "Why Didn't Chris and Dan Get into Berghain?," parts 1 and 2, *Search Engine*, June 21 and 26, 2024; Finn Cohen, Jelka von Langen, and Roman Goebel, "Audience Report: At Berghain, They've Been Waiting in Line for 20 Years," *New York Times*, December 13, 2024.

Index

active investing, 221, 223
agents, 101
agglomeration, 77–79, 83
AI. *See* artificial intelligence
Aiken, Howard, 114
Ajché, Gustavo, 90–97
Akbarpour, Mohammad, 278
alpha (edge over market), 210
Amazon, 79, 94, 95, 97–98, 111, 135, 252
American Airlines, 265, 267
American Dream, 139–50
American Express, 267, 269–70
Andrews, Mike, 83–84, 150
Anthropic, 119
antitrust laws, 57
Apple, 14, 21, 44, 72, 76, 208–9
Apple app store, 253
apple varieties, 41
Argentina, 44, 45, 47–50, 242–43
Arida, Pérsio, 230, 240
Arnaz y de Acha, Desiderio "Desi" Alberto, III, 64–70, 72, 73
Arnold, John, 6–9
artificial intelligence (AI), 108, 114, 115, 119–20
Association of Tennis Professionals (ATP), 14
Athens, ancient, 193
ATMs. *See* automated teller machines
atomic clock, 28
ATP (Association of Tennis Professionals), 14
AT&T, 79, 115, 116, 118
auctions
    with food bank fake money, 7–9, 11
    of radio spectrum licenses, 129, 135
automated teller machines (ATMs), 108–10, 113, 118
automation, 107–20

"Automation Jobless, The," 108
automobile manufacturing, 49
Autor, David, 108
Avis, 266
Aztecs, 18

Bacha, Edmar Lisboa, 230–32, 237–40
Balagtas, Joe, 34, 38
Ball, Lucille, 64–70, 72, 73
BankAmericard, 263–64
banks and banking, 191–203
    ATMs, 108–10, 113, 118
    bank runs, 198, 200–202
    central banks, 234, 235, 238–43
    credit cards, 263–65
    fractional reserve, 196
    innovations in, 118–20
    land banks, 194
bargaining power, 93–97
BATNA (Best Alternative to a Negotiated Agreement), 101
Baumol, William, 174–77
Baumol's cost disease, 174–78
Bay, Michael, 35
B Corps, 24
beating the market, 207–17, 220
Bedford, David, 41
Berghain, 281–82
Berghain Goods, 282
Berkshire Hathaway, 72, 224–25
Bessen, James, 110–12, 115, 116, 118–19
Best Alternative to a Negotiated Agreement (BATNA), 101
bills of credit, 194–95
Binga, Jesse, 196–200
Binga Bank, 197, 198
Binga State Bank, 199, 200
BlackBerry, 44, 45, 47–48, 50
"Black Wall Streets," 198–99

Bloom, Nicholas, 79, 86
Bogle, John, 220–22, 225
bond funds, 211
bonds, 201, 211
Bonifacini, Hugo, 45, 47–48, 50, 51
Bonilla, Bobby, 184–89, 198
Bowen, William, 174
Bowles, Riley, 101
Bowling Alone (Putnam), 148
Brazil, 230–32, 237–40
Britain, 105, 156, 192–95, 232, 234
Buffett, Warren, 222, 224, 225
Bureau of Labor Statistics, 241
business cycle, 233
ByteDance, 51

CAC (customer acquisition cost), 134
California Milk Processor Board, 35
California Raisins, 35
Canada, 86, 155–57, 159–60
capital expenditures, 56
Card, David, 142
Cardoso, Fernando Henrique, 240
careers. *See* work and career
Carson, Johnny, 66
cartels, 32–41
CBS, 65–67, 69, 72
central banks, 234, 235, 238–43
central planning, 5–6
champagne, 41
Chase Sapphire Reserve, 267
Chetty, Raj, 145–50
Chevron, 14, 23–24
Chiat, Jay, 76
Chiat\Day, 76
Chicago Black Belt, 196–99
"chicken tax," 49
childcare, 169–70, 174–78
China, 46, 50–51, 55, 56, 193
Choe, David, 71
Choudhury, Prithwiraj, 78–79
clocks, standardization, 28
CLV (customer lifetime value), 134
Coal Question, The (Jevons), 114
Coase, Ronald, 91–92
Cohen, Steven, 189
coinage, 193
collaborative filtering, 135
collective bargaining, 93–97
college endowments, 222

Color of Law, The (Rothstein), 161
commodity trap, 31–41
comparative advantage, 45–46
compensation, 94–97, 99–102, 142, 184–89
competition, 32–33, 57, 267
compound interest, 184–89, 198, 208
computer science work, 117, 118
confidence trick, banking and finance as, 198–200, 202
contractors, 90; *See also* gig work
Copy.ai, 119
core competencies, 97–98
Corning Glass, 105
corporate law, 13–25
Corporation Law Council, 15–16, 21, 22, 24, 25
corporations, 16–17, 19, 23–24
"cost disease," xi, 174–78
cost of living, 171
Court of Chancery (Delaware), 21–22
COVID-19, 22, 51, 58, 77, 242
Cowen, Tyler, 9
Crandall, Bob, 267
credibility revolution, 142, 143
credit, 194, 198–99, 202
credit cards, 261–72
Crestline Hotels & Resorts, 92
Crocs, 71
cross-class relationships, 148–50
customer acquisition cost (CAC), 134
customer lifetime value (CLV), 134
Cuties, 40

dairy farmers, 37
Danko, William, 67
dating apps, 126, 131, 134–36, 167
decoy offers, 167
deferred-acceptance algorithm, 130–33
deflation, 238
Deggans, Eric, 69
Delaware corporate law, 16, 20–25
delivery apps, 90, 95–97
Delta, 267
Desilu, 66, 67, 69, 72
de-skilling, 111–12
diminishing returns, 56–58
Diners Club Card, 263
Discover card, 267
discrimination, 117

Disney, 70
diversification, 198, 211, 222, 223
Doctorow, Cory, 251
DoorDash, 90, 95, 97
dot-com bubble, 209, 214
Douglas, Angie, 108–10, 113, 118, 119
Dow, Charles, 209
Dow Jones index, 209
DreamWorks, 79

East India Company, 19
economic growth, 55–58, 175
economic indicators, 53–59
economic mobility, 141, 146–48, 157
economics, x–xi
   credibility revolution in, 142, 143
   defined, 5
   research in, 142, 143
economy(-ies), ix–x
   centrally planned, 5–6
   of colonial America, 192–96
   commodity trap, 31–41
   corporate law, 13–25
   created concept of, 54
   economic indicators, 53–59
   financial anxiety in, 200–201
   free trade, 43–51
   global, xi, 11, 174, 177
   power of prices, 3–11
   public goods, 26–29
   sectors of, 174–75
edge over market, 210
Edison, Thomas, 173
efficiency, 46, 91, 92, 129
efficient markets hypothesis, 213–14
Emanuel, Natalia, 80
Emerson, Ralph Waldo, 249
employee retention, 78
employment
   and housing lottery, 144, 145
   and inflation, 234–36
Energizer Bunny, 76
England, 19, 54, 114, 195, 196, 253
environmental governance, 29
equity
   forms of, 71–72
   private, 209
   in profits, 64–73
Etsy, 22
European Union, 37

expected value, 68
externalities, 24–26, 204
ExxonMobil, 23–24

Facebook, 71, 148, 149, 251
Fair Labor Standards Act, 253
fairness
   in contracting work, 100, 102
   in gig work, 93–94
   in market design, 11
   in resource allocation, 275–83
Fairweather, Daryl, 157–59, 164, 165, 167
family. *See* love and family
Fast and the Furious, The (film), 173
FCC (Federal Communications Commission), 128, 129
FDIC (Federal Deposit Insurance Corporation), 200
Federal Communications Commission (FCC), 128, 129
Federal Deposit Insurance Corporation (FDIC), 200
Federal Housing Association (FHA), 161
Federal Reserve, 236, 237, 243
Federal Reserve Board, 201
Feeding America, 4–9, 11, 277
Feeld, 127
Feigenbaum, James, 115, 116, 118
Fernandez, Jose, 186, 187
FHA (Federal Housing Association), 161
fiat currency, 235
filtering, 164
financial time travel, 188
First Fundamental Theorem of Welfare Economics, 277
First Nations, 155–57, 159–62
fiscal policy, 234, 235
Flynn, Alexandra, 159
Food Bank of Alaska, 4–8
food banks, 4–9, 11
Ford, 93
Ford, Henry, 93, 253
For Profit (Magnuson), 18
fractional reserve banking, 196
France, 96–97, 195
franchises, x
Franklin, Benjamin, 195

free, power of, 268
Freedom of the Seas policy, 29
freelancers, 90; *See also* gig work
free markets, 6–9, 32–33, 136
free-rider problem, 26
free trade, 43–51, 57
Friedman, Milton, 277, 278

Gale-Shapley algorithm, 130, 167
Galton, Francis, 210
GameStop, 215–16
GDP. *See* Gross Domestic Product
GE, 93
General Mills, 4, 8
Germany, 49, 86
Gesner, Abraham, 173
gig work, 89–102
GitHub, 99
global business, 13–25
global economy, 11, 174, 177
globalization, 44, 51
global trade, 45–47
GM, 72
Goldblum, Jeff, 240
gold standard, 234–35
Goodhart's Law, 105
goods
    costs of, 170–75, 177
    network, 249–51, 264
Google, 22, 98, 157, 158, 249, 251, 252
Gourdlets, 99
GPS, 28
Grayson-Cross, Lydia, 140, 141, 144–47, 149, 150
Great Depression, 54, 161, 200, 253
greater fool theory, 216
Great Inflation, 236
Great Moderation, 242
Great Recession, 241–42
Great Resignation, 242–43
Green Bay Packers, 72
grocery stores, 10–11, 40–41
Groshen, Erica, 118
Gross, Daniel, 115, 116, 118
Gross Domestic Product (GDP), 55–56, 58
groupthink, 214, 215
Grubb, Farley, 195
Grubhub, 97
Gunton, Bob, 70

Hamermesh, Lawrence, 14–16, 20–22, 24–25
Hamilton, Alexander, 50
Hampton, Mike, 188
Harford, Tim, 167
Harrington, Emma, 80
Hayner, Don, 196, 197, 199
health care, 282–83
Heckscher, August, 174
hedge funds, 222, 224
Hendren, Nathan, 145–50
Hertz, 266
Heschel, Abraham Joshua, 253
Hidden Figures (Shetterly), 116, 118
Hills v. Gautreaux, 143
Hinge, 127
HOLC (Home Owners' Loan Corporation), 161
Holland, 18
Hollywood studio system, 66
Home Owners' Loan Corporation (HOLC), 161
Horne, Laura, 32, 33, 35–36, 38–39
Horne, Marvin, 32, 33, 35, 36, 38–39
hostile takeovers, 20
housing
    for African Americans, 196–99
    and economic mobility, 141, 146–50
    housing crisis, 153–65
    housing lottery, 140–41, 143–45
    redlining and racial covenants, 161–62
    rent control/stabilization in, 279
HUD. *See* U.S. Department of Housing and Urban Development
human capital, 148
hurricane hunters, 27
hybrid work, 86
hyperinflation, 230–32, 237–39, 243
Hyundai, 50

"identity projects," 149
illiquidity, 222
illusion of skill, 224
I Love Lucy (TV show), 64, 67, 69–70, 72, 73
incentives
    behavior driven by, 117
    corporate, 22, 24, 25

for dating apps, 135
for efficient outcomes, 129
to increase innovation, 57
price signals as, 9, 155
to provide public goods, 26
in raisin market, 33
independent workers, 90; *See also* gig work
index funds, 219–26
Industrial Revolution, 20, 21, 56, 57, 110, 173, 253
inflation, 229–43
   quantifying, 171
   and shadow banks, 201–2
   and time value of money, 185
   tooth fairy, 176
inflation targeting, 238
information asymmetry, 100
initial public offerings (IPOs), 209
innovation(s), 249; *See also* technological change
   and economic growth, 56–58
   growing pains for, 119
   in offices, 82–84
   uptake of, 110–11
innovation cycle, 120
Instagram, 252
insurance, 200, 202–5
Intel, 51
intellectual property, x, 33–34, 57, 83–84
interest and interest rates
   on bank deposits, 202
   compound interest, 184–89, 198, 208
   Federal Reserve rates, 236, 237
   for loans and bank accounts, 198
   on savings accounts, 201
   from shadow banks, 201–2
   simple interest, 186
internet, 250, 252
investing. *See* saving and investing
invisible hand, 11, 127
iPhones, 44
IPOs (initial public offerings), 209
Italy, Renaissance, 18

Jacob, Gilbert "Gibby," 159
Jacobs, David, 155
Japan, 37, 55
Jassy, Andy, 82
Jevons, William Stanley, 114
Jevons paradox, 114, 115, 119–20
Jobs, Steve, 84, 105, 209
Joe's Place, 83
Johnson, Eudora, 199
Johnson, Lyndon, 49
Johnson, Rucker, 149
Jones, Edward, 209
junk bonds, 211

kaChing, 217
Kahneman, Daniel, 224
Kam, Ken, 217
Keiles, Jamie Lauren, 269
Kennedy, Robert F., Sr., 58–59
Keynes, John Maynard, 215, 216, 233
Khahtsahlano, August Jack, 155
Khan, Kublai, 193
Kia, 50
Kirchner, Cristina Fernández de, 44, 45, 47, 48
Kitsilano Indian Reserve No. 6, 155, 156
Klarity, 119
Klein, Aaron, 270
Krueger, Alan, 142
Kuznets, Simon, 54–56, 58

labor force; *See also* work and career
   bargaining power of, 93–97
   in GDP, 56–57
   wage labor, 67
labor law, 93
land banks, 194–95
languages, 244
Lara Resende, André, 230–32, 237–40
Large Hadron Collider, 27
large language models, 115
Larkin, Kenneth, 263–64
Laws of the Office, 105
Learning by Doing (Bessen), 112
Lehman Brothers, 203
leisure
   credit card points, 261–72
   fairness in resource allocation, 275–83
   Norway's tourist industry, 258–59
   weekends and network effects, 247–56

Liaw, Jane, 262
light sources, cost of, 170–74
Lim, Chaeyoon, 255
limited liability, 17, 23–24
Lipsey, Richard, 232
liquidity problem, 192–93
loans
   by banks, 195–200, 238
   to banks, 202–3
   bonds as, 201, 211
   credit cards as, 271
   interest rates on, 198
   land banks, 194
   private credit, 202
local knowledge problem, 6
LoPucki, Lynn, 21–23
Los Deliveristas Unidos, 96, 99
lotteries, 279, 281
love and family
   the American Dream, 139–50
   costs of child rearing/childcare, 169–78
   economists' advice on, 166–67
   housing crisis, 153–65
   market design for finding love, 125–36
Love Island (TV show), 130, 131
Lovelace, Ada, 117
Luddites, 115
lump of labor fallacy, 112–13, 115, 116, 120
Lynch, Peter, 208
Lyons Community School, 46

Madoff, Bernie, 189
Magnuson, William, 18
manufacturing, 45–46, 49
Margolis, Jane, 117
market(s); *See also* stock market
   beating the, 207–17
   efficiency of, 213–14
   flawed, 26
   governments' role in, 127
   matching, 126–27
   power of, 11
   traditional, 126
   weaknesses of, 277–78
market-clearing price, 276, 278–79
market design, 11, 125–36
market economy, 6, 9, 10, 32
market failure, 24
Marketocracy, 208–10, 213–17
Markowitz, Harry, 222
Marquardt, Sven, 282
Marriage Pact, 126, 127, 132–35
Marriott, 71, 92, 94, 98
Massachusetts textile mills, 110, 111
Mast, Evan, 164
MasterCard/Mastercard, 264, 265, 270
Matchbox, 136
matching markets, 126–27
Mattel, 266
maximizing shareholder value, 23
McDonald's, 266
McGregor, Liam, 127, 129–36
Medici family, 18
Meta, 80, 249
Mexico, precolonial, 18
Meyer, Danny, 92
Microsoft, 68, 94, 95
Milgrom, Paul, 127–29, 131–34, 166
Millionaire Next Door, The (Stanley and Danko), 67
minimum wage, 94, 96, 97, 142
Mitchell, Tony, 208–10, 213–17
monetary policy, 235
money
   creation by banks, 192–96
   fake, for food banks, 6–9, 11
   fiat currency, 235
   gold standard, 234–35
   paper, 193–95
   printing, 231
   putting a price on, 198
   supply, 231, 236–40
   time value of, 185–86
money managers, 220, 221, 225
money market funds (MMFs), 201–3, 211
Monroe, Marilyn, 66
Moore, Katie, 194
Morgan, Susannah, 4–8
Morris, Nichols, Arsht & Tunnell, 20
Morse, Samuel, 249–50
Motley Fool, 224
Moving to Opportunity (MTO), 143–49
mRNA vaccine technology, 58
Musk, Elon, 22, 79–80
My Favorite Husband, 65, 66

Nageeye, Abdi, 280
Nakamura, Emi, 143, 240–43
NASA, 116–18, 120
National Bureau of Economic Research, 54
National Income, 1929-1932, 54–55
National Institute of Standards and Technology, 28
national security, 51
"Nature of the Firm, The" (Coase), 91
NBC, 66
negative externalities, 24–25
negotiating compensation, 94, 96, 99–102
Netflix, 97–98, 135
network effects, 247–56, 270
network goods, 249–51, 264
networking, professional, 254
Nevada public employees' pension fund, 224
New Jersey corporate law, 21
New Year's Eve parties, 254
New York City Marathon, 276, 277, 279–82
New York Mets, 184–89
New York Road Runners (NYRR), 276, 279–82
New Zealand, 238
Nicol, Wes, 47
Nocera, Joe, 263–64
Nordhaus, Bill, 171–74
Norway, 37, 258–59
NVIDIA, 72, 221

Odean, Terrance, 221, 223
offices
 designs of, 76–77
 as idea factories, 82–84
 open, 76–77
 post-pandemic return to, 79–80
 purpose of, 77–79, 82
Ohtani, Shohei, 189
oil industry, x, 23–24, 34
OkCupid, 131
One Up on Wall Street (Lynch), 208
OPEC (Organization of the Petroleum Exporting Countries), 34
Operation Match (Harvard), 131
Opportunity Atlas, 147
opportunity costs, 80–82, 84, 185

Opportunity Insights, 147–48
O'Rafferty, Alden, 126, 133–34
ordeals, 280–81
Organization of the Petroleum Exporting Countries (OPEC), 34
organ market, 129–30, 135
Oster, Emily, 45
Otis, Elisha, 110
outsourcing, 92, 98
ownership
 of companies, 14, 17, 18, 71
 equity in TV profits, 64–73
 forms of, 71–72
 stock as, 209

Paítsmuk, 155–57, 159, 160
Pallais, Amanda, 80
"panics," 232, 233
Papacena, Dawn, 280–81
Paramount, 66
Pareto improvements, 167
Parker, Sean, 71
Parkinson, C. Northcote, 105
Parkinson's Law, 105
parks, 29
particle accelerators, 27
passive investing, 221, 225, 226
Pennsylvania colony, 192, 194, 195
P/E (price-to-earnings) ratio, 214
performing arts, 174, 175
Peter, Laurence Johnston, 105
Peter Principle, 105
Pets.com, 214
Petty, Sir William, 54
Philadelphia, colonial, 192–93, 195
Philip Morris, 67
Phillips, Bill, 232, 234, 235
Phillips Curve, 234–37, 242
Piece of the Action, A (Nocera), 263–64
Pipkin, Rocky, 32, 36
pirates, 29
Pixar, 84
Planet Money, ix–xi
positive externalities, 26
poverty
 and banks or credit, 199–200
 climbing out of, 145–47
 and cross-class relationships, 148–50
 and housing, 140–41, 143–45
poverty trap, 141, 145

Prendergast, Canice, 5–9
present value, 214
price(s)
   of borrowing money, 198
   and commodity trap, 33–41
   function of, 8–9
   of housing, 155
   inflation-driven, 171
   market-clearing, 276, 278–79
   in market competition, 32
   markets without, 129–30
   power of, 3–11
   for radio spectrum licenses, 129
   of raising a child, 177
   stock, 221
   wage-price spiral, 234
   willingness to pay, 277, 282
price controls, 32–37
Priceline, 214
price-to-earnings (P/E) ratio, 214
private credit, 202
private equity, 209, 222
productivity, 79, 80, 94
profits
   and commodity trap, 33
   equity in, 64–73
   maximizing, 23
Prohibition, 83, 84
protected designations of origin, 41
protectionism, 48–51
public goods, 26–29
public housing, 140, 147
Putnam, Robert, 148

RAC. *See* Raisin Administrative Committee
Race for the Double Helix, The (film), 240
racism, 196, 198–99
radio spectrum sales, 128–29, 135
Raisin Administrative Committee (RAC), 32–33, 35–36, 38–39
Randall's grocery store, 10
randomized controlled trials, 142
Rawle, Francis, 192–95
Reagan, Ronald, 278
redlining, 161–62
remote work, 75–86
rent seeking, 158–59
Reserve Fund, 201–3, 211

reshoring, 51
resource allocation
   fairness in, 275–83
   housing lottery, 140–41, 143–45
   radio spectrum, 128–29
resource consumption, 114, 115
retirement planning, 183–89
return on investment
   for banks, 200–203
   risk-reward spectrum, 68, 69, 72
   in S&P 500, 220
Richard, Frederick "Flips," 71
right-to-work laws, 94
risk
   with bonds vs. stocks, 211
   and diversification, 222
   insurance for, 204–5
   systemic, 200–201
risk-reward spectrum, 68, 69, 72
Ritchie, Robert James "Kid Rock," 278, 281
RKO, 72
Robinhood, 215
Rockefeller, John D., 173
Rockefeller, John D., III, 174
Roman Republic, 16–19
Romer, Paul, 57–58
Roosevelt, Franklin D., 54–55, 200
Rosen, Sherwin, 72
Roth, Alvin, 133, 136
Rothstein, Richard, 161
Rowe, Nick, 198
Rybczynski, Witold, 252–53

Sahel region, Africa, 29
salmon sushi, 37
Samuelson, Paul, 220, 221, 234
San Francisco, 157, 158
saving and investing
   banking, 191–203
   beating the market, 207–17
   index funds, 219–26
   inflation, 229–43
   retirement planning, 183–89
savings accounts, 201
scalpers, 278–79
Schrödinger, Erwin, 255, 256
Schrödinger Saturdays, 256
search costs, 166
search for yield, 201

Sears, 267
Seattle Housing Authority, 147
sectoral bargaining, 96–97
Securities and Exchange Commission (SEC), 20
Seides, Ted, 224
Sen'áḵw, 154–57, 159–60, 162–64
shadow banks, 201–2
shareholder value, maximizing, 23
Shawshank Redemption, The, 70
"shedding" jobs, 94
Shetterly, Margot Lee, 116, 118
Shroder, Mark, 141, 143, 144
signals
   costly, 166
   price, 9, 155
Silicon Valley, 99
simple interest, 186
Sistine Chapel, 281
Slack, 82
smartphones, 44, 45, 47–48, 50, 51
Smith, Adam, 11, 19, 142
Snyder, Alan, 110
social capital, 148–49
societates publicanorum, 17–19
Solow, Robert, 56–58, 234
Solow residual, 57, 58
songs, popular, 244
Soros, George, 222
South Korea, 50
Southwest Airline, 265
Soviet Union, 5–6, 10, 248
S&P 500, 209–10, 220, 221, 225
SpaceX, 98
Spain, 193
Spencer, Paul, 76
S&P 500 index funds, 221, 222, 224
sports contracts, 184–89
Squamish Nation, 154–60, 162, 163
stable-marriage problem, 130, 131, 167
stagflation, 236, 237
Stalin, Joseph, 10, 248, 256
Standard Oil, 21, 173
Stanford University, 131, 132
Stanley, Thomas, 67
Starbucks, 84, 266, 270
start-ups, 68, 79
status quo bias, 69, 101
Sterling, Sophia, 131–34
stock market
   beating the market, 207–17, 220
   1929 crash, 200
   equity in, 72
   first, in Holland, 18
   index funds, 219–26
stock market crashes, 232
stock options, 71
stock picking, 207–17
streaming services, x, 97–98
subsidies, childcare, 177–78
sunk cost fallacy, 166
Superstar Effect, 72
Supreme Court rulings
   on corporate law, 14
   on Hollywood studio system, 66
   on public housing desegregation, 141, 143
   on raisin cartel, 38
Swensen, David, 223
systemic risk, 200–201

Tabarrok, Alex, 9
Taiwan, 51
Taiwan Semiconductor Manufacturing Company, 51
tariffs, 45, 46, 49–51
taxes
   in controlling inflation, 234
   and cost disease, 178
   on imported goods, 44, 49
   tax-loss harvesting, 212–13
technological change
   automation life cycle, 107–20
   and cost of goods, 173, 174
   and economic growth, 56–58
   for gig work, 92
technology
   internet, 250, 252
   for remote work, 78, 82
   in salary/payout distributions, 70, 72
   for streaming services, 97–98
   telegraph, 249–50
   women working in, 117
Teigen, Kyra Dorado, 126, 133–34
telegraph, 249–50
television (TV)
   equity in profits from shows, 64–73
   network licenses, 129
10x Management, 100, 102
Tesla, 68, 214–16

Thaler, Richard, 166
Theory of the Firm, 92
TikTok, 51, 251
time, as resource, 256
time value of money, 185–86
Tinder, 127
tooth fairy inflation, 176
trade barriers, 45, 46, 49–51
trademarked cultivars, 41
transaction costs, 91, 92, 193
transferable shares, 17
travel hackers, 262
treasury bonds, 201
tree-planting initiatives, 29
trickle-down housing, 164
Trillions (Wigglesworth), 221
Tropical Trip, 66
Trudeau, Justin, 154–55
TV. *See* television
Twitter, 22, 79–80

Uber, 90, 94, 97, 251
UberEats, 90, 95
UK (United Kingdom), 55
unemployment, 234, 236
uniform lottery, 279
unintended consequences, law of, 105
unions, 94–96, 253
Union Square Hospitality Group, 92
unique goods, 128–29
United Airlines, 265
United Kingdom (UK), 55
United States
    bank oversight in, 203
    calculating inflation rate in, 241–42
    dollar coins in, 262
    economic growth in, 57
    forming corporations in, 19–20
    GDP of, 55
    Great Inflation in, 236
    history of money and banks in, 192–96
    independent workers in, 90
    inflation targeting in, 238
    moneylending by banks in, 196
    remote work rates in, 84
    support to parents in, 178
    tariffs in, 50, 51
    workweek hours in, 253
units of real value (URVs), 239

up-skilling, 111, 118–19
U.S. Department of Housing and Urban Development (HUD), 141, 143, 145, 146
U.S. Patent and Trademark Office (USPTO), 78–79, 83

Vaidyanathan, Preethi, 91, 98–100, 102
Vancouver, Canada, 154–56, 159, 162–65
Vanguard, 221
Vanguard 500 Index Fund, 221, 222, 224
Vaughan, Dorothy, 116, 118
virtual currency, 239
Visa, 264, 265, 270
Volcker, Paul, 236, 237, 240–42
Volkswagen Beetles, 49

W. W. Norton, 71
Wade, Giovonni, 170
Wade, Wesley, 170, 177
wage fairness, 93
wage labor, 67
wage-price spiral, 234
Waiting for the Weekend (Rybczynski), 252–53
Wall Street Journal, The, 145, 224
Walmart, 270
Walters, Barbara, 66
Warner Bros., 66
wealth
    in colonial America, 192–93
    and compound interest, 184
    equity vs. salaries for, 67
    real estate as, 194
    redistribution of, 277–78
Wealth of Nations, The (Smith), 19
weather forecasts, 27
WeChat, 51
weekends, 247–56
Weil, David, 94
Western Europe, 55
Wigglesworth, Robin, 221
Williams, Wilson, 160, 162, 163
willingness to pay, 277, 282
Wilpon, Fred, 184–85
Wilson, Woodrow, 21
wine lakes, 37
wisdom of crowds, 210, 212–14

women in computer science, 117, 118
work and career
   equity in profits, 64–73
   gig work, 89–102
   remote work, 75–86
   technology and automation, 107–20
Worker's Justice Project, 95, 96
World Trade Organization, 45, 46, 50
"worm wall," 26
Wozniak, Steve, 209

Yale, 223
Yeltsin, Boris, 10
Yeyati, Eduardo Levy, 48, 50
yield, 201, 202
Yirga, Paul, 10
Yosemite National Park, 281
Young, Cristobal, 255

Zillow, 21
Zoom, 82, 99

Copyright © 2026 by National Public Radio, Inc.

All rights reserved
Printed in the United States of America
First Edition

For information about permission to reproduce selections
from this book, write to Permissions, W. W. Norton &
Company, Inc., 500 Fifth Avenue, New York, NY 10110

For information about special discounts for bulk purchases, please contact
W. W. Norton Special Sales at specialsales@wwnorton.com or 800-233-4830

Manufacturing by Lakeside Book Company
Book design by Beth Steidle
Production manager: Julia Druskin

Library of Congress Cataloging-in-Publication Data is available.

ISBN 978-1-324-07877-7

W. W. Norton & Company, Inc., 500 Fifth Avenue, New York, NY 10110
www.wwnorton.com

W. W. Norton & Company Ltd., 15 Carlisle Street, London W1D 3BS

Authorized EU representative: EAS, Mustamäe tee 50, 10621 Tallinn, Estonia

10 9 8 7 6 5 4 3 2 1